Reading from
the Heart

READING

from the

HEART

WOMEN, LITERATURE, AND THE
SEARCH FOR TRUE LOVE

Suzanne Juhasz

VIKING

VIKING
Published by the Penguin Group
Penguin Books USA Inc., 375 Hudson Street, New York, New York 10014, U.S.A.
Penguin Books Ltd, 27 Wrights Lane, London W8 5TZ, England
Penguin Books Australia Ltd, Ringwood, Victoria, Australia
Penguin Books Canada Ltd, 10 Alcorn Avenue, Toronto, Ontario, Canada M4V 3B2
Penguin Books (N.Z.) Ltd, 182-190 Wairau Road, Auckland 10, New Zealand

Penguin Books Ltd, Registered Offices:
Harmondsworth, Middlesex, England

First published in 1994 by Viking Penguin,
a division of Penguin Books USA Inc.

1 3 5 7 9 10 8 6 4 2

Grateful acknowledgment is made for permission
to reprint excerpts from the following copyrighted works:
Tryst by Elswyth Thane. Copyright Elswyth Thane, 1939. Copyright renewed
Elswyth Thane, 1967. Used by permission of Dutton Signet,
a division of Penguin Books USA Inc.
Mama Day by Gloria Naylor. Copyright © 1988 by Gloria Naylor.
Reprinted by permission of Ticknor & Fields/Houghton Mifflin Co. All rights reserved.
Patience and Sarah by Isabel Miller. Copyright © 1969 by Isabel Miller.
Reprinted by permission of The Charlotte Sheedy Agency.
Prism by Valerie Taylor, Naiad Press, 1991.
Reprinted with the permission of the author and publisher.

LIBRARY OF CONGRESS CATALOGING IN PUBLICATION DATA
Juhasz, Suzanne
Reading from the heart : women, literature, and the search for true love / Suzanne Juhasz.
p. cm.
Includes bibliographical references (p.) and index.
ISBN 0-670-84401-2
1. Love stories, English—History and criticism. 2. American fiction—Women authors—
History and criticism. 3. English fiction—Women authors—History and criticism.
4. Women—Books and reading—History—20th century. 5. Love stories, American—
History and criticism. 6. Women and literature—History—20th century. 7. Love stories—
Appreciation. 8. Women—Psychology. 9. Love. I. Title.
PR830.L69J85 1994
823'.08509—dc20 94–723

Printed in the United States of America
Set in Adobe Garamond
Designed by Ann Gold

FOR MY DAUGHTERS,

ALEXANDRA, JENNIFER, AND ANTONIA,

ALWAYS

AUTHOR'S NOTE

Reading from the Heart is my first book written specifically for a general readership, for "real people," as I tend to put it. I am an academic, a professor, and I have written for many years for an audience of other academics. However, this book is about the passion for reading which has been mine since I was a child, and which remains central to my personal and private life. I know that I share this passion with other people, many of whom are not professional scholars of literature. In writing about reading, especially about the love of reading love stories, I wanted to engage with those who share this experience with me. I wanted not so much to *study* the reading life as to bring it alive in the world of my book. This enterprise has been both challenging and thoroughly exciting. I want to thank my editor, Dawn Ann Drzal, who has been my guide and my companion throughout the process. Her astuteness, wisdom, understanding, humor, and skill have provided a sounding board and a source of inspiration for all the years it took to make this book a reality. She is, in Emily Dickinson's words, a "rare Ear."

Contents

Reading from the Heart

Reading from
the Heart

Prologue

THE PASSIONATE WOMAN READER
AND THE STORY OF TRUE LOVE

When I was a girl, I read in a square green upholstered chair. I curled my legs up under me or hung them over the chair's broad arms. Beside me on the end table was a pile of crackers, and I nibbled on them slowly as I read. The living room was shadowy, its soft carpets and long curtains in half-light whatever the season. And quiet, because the family traffic went the other way, through the "den," with its linoleum floor and TV set. The living room was reserved for company, but I persistently disobeyed that household rule. There I could be found, most afternoons, with, as my mother put it, my nose in a book.

I read my way through childhood and adolescence. Certainly, I was busy in the outside world, at school and Girl Scouts, then later on the yearbook staff and in community theater, and with, at last, those long-anticipated dates with boys. Some would call all that my real world, but I don't know. At the time, I thought of it primarily as preparation—for college, for a career, for true love, for everything that adulthood was going to bring me. As for those books, accumulated during my weekly treks to the Providence Public Library, piles of novels taken home with the most eager anticipation, books rapidly ingested with a pleasure, an intensity that could be found nowhere else, books replaced soon afterwards by more, always more—there in those books, I found not preparation but something already real.

I've never given up the reading habit. In fact, it has become more persistent over the years, perhaps because I now acknowledge its absolute necessity. Even though I've had plenty of real life by now—three children, two marriages, and a career as a university professor—I not only cherish my life in books, I require it.

The books I prefer are novels. A certain kind of novel. Written by a woman, about a woman's life. Best, I like a love story. It can be contemporary fiction, historical fiction, mystery fiction; it can be a "classic" like *Pride and Prejudice* or a best-seller like *The Shell Seekers*. In whatever incarnation, no matter what problems and concerns are raised, there needs to be love; and I confess, I prefer a happy ending. I like comedy best—warmth and wit—but I read my share of tragedy, and everything in between, just as long as the book is intelligent, caring, and illuminating.

This book is about the passion, and the need, that inspire reading such fiction. In my experience, these two energies cannot really be divorced from one another. For even as I engage with the novels with an excitement and a delight that make me feel vitally alive, both stirred and safe within the book, so the lack of this kind of reading for any length of time makes me feel empty, incomplete, and lonely. Whatever else is happening in my life, I need to be reading a novel. I need to know it is there, waiting at home by my bed, with its shiny new cover or its worn familiar one, ready for me to go to when I want it. I may not pick it up until nighttime, if the pressures of work and living have their way, but no day will go by in which I have not entered its world, if only for a little while.

On other days I get to spend real time there. I give myself the pleasure, now. I declare an evening just for reading; sometimes, although rarely, an afternoon! I take a bath (the book comes too). Then, cozy in robe and slippers, I curl up on the couch and get down to it. I read, then I think, then I read some more. The cocoon of comfort is important: the soft pillows, the hot coffee, the crisp crackers. So much the better if the rain patters or the winds howl. The warmth and safety contrast with what is happening in my mind. Because that surpasses comfort: it's excitement, it's intense exertion. It's like when I'm doing big jumps—tour jetés and fouetté turns—across the floor in ballet class. It takes all my energy and concentration, forcing my emotions and thoughts to coalesce. I feel totally alive.

The rest of the time, when I am going about my life outside the book, I continue to carry the book with me, in my head. Especially when what I am doing feels strange to me or unreal—as when, at a meeting or in a conversation or at a party, people don't respond as I expect them to, don't seem to see me as I see myself, and I get frustrated, confused, angry, or anxious. It is then that I find myself thinking about the novel: about what is happening to the characters at the place where I have stopped reading, about the issues being raised in their lives and what it all means. Why is David, Hannah's first lover since her divorce, just calmly picking up and leaving her? What is this going to do to her? She loves him! Does she love him? Is that really love, with the first man you care about after your husband has left you? Is it important for her newly formed independence that he should leave? Thus I call up the world of the novel. It matters to me that I have this other life, for of course, I am a part of the book. I'm Hannah, naturally, but I'm also more than Hannah. I'm in cahoots with the author, Anabel Donald, in our shared concern for the heroine in *Hannah at Thirty-Five*. And I'm me, adventuring in this world of Hannah and Anabel. Going there, I start to feel real again.

I share the heroine's experiences with her, and even beyond that, I listen to the author as she writes the heroine's thoughts or describes the room the heroine is entering or examines the implications of what the heroine is doing, and I say to her, "Oh yes, that's just right. Hannah should be afraid of shifting their relationship into a sexual one," or "Are you sure? Are you sure she should tell him no, that she really needs to be alone on the night of her divorce, when we all know she's in love with him? Maybe he won't come back! Is he the kind of man who will come back? Did you create him that way?" When I am engaged like this, with the characters and with the author herself, I know who I am, and I like that person.

And I have wondered why. Why the passion, why the need? I am aware that I am not alone in this predilection. Sometimes I meet up with other reading women, and as soon as we realize that we share the habit, a glow lights our faces, and we step closer to one another, turning away from the group in which we may have found ourselves, to start right in. "Have you read—?" "Did you like—?" "What did you think about the part where—?" "Has she written anything else?" There is nothing more gratifying than the opportunity to talk about novels, when mostly we keep the pleasures of this solitary passion to ourselves.

Writing this book, I imagine myself to be having one of these conversations with other reading women, women like me. My experiences, after all, cannot be unique. I want to describe my reading life, in all of its complexity, so as to reveal and hopefully to understand something about the passion and the need that many of us feel. To do this, I need to look at my personal world, the world of my feelings. But I also need to talk about the how and why of the books I discuss in these pages. I am a reading girl who grew up to be a scholar, translating my love for books into an intellectual pursuit. In this book I call on all of my reading skills, so that I move continually between personal response and a more analytic appraisal.

To this end I work with psychology as well as literature, because it has helped me to think about my own engagement with romance fiction as well as the more general question which this book raises: why do so many women read (and write) love stories? Because I find myself concerned with basic issues of interpersonal relationship—especially, with the most primary relationship of all, that between infant and mother—the British and American school of object-relations has been particularly illuminating for me. Feminist psychology, too, which raises questions about gender identity, has added to my knowledge. I use some of these ideas to help me talk about reading.

Talking about books with other people is a delight, which may be one reason why I made it my profession. It complements those many hours spent alone with a book. And yet, reading isn't exactly solitary, either. I'm alone in the room when I read, but not in my mind. And maybe that's the key, because the society of the book—its world that I can enter, as well as the deeply intimate and always developing relationship with the author as the book incarnates her—keeps me from being lonely. I am lonelier in the real world situation I've just described—when no one seems to understand *who I am*—than by myself reading, when I feel that the book *recognizes* me, and I recognize myself because of the book.

What does that mean—to be recognized by the book? To recognize myself because of the book? And why is this recognition so centrally important? Looking back to that girl reader, I see how this need was always with me. Reading then, in that green upholstered chair, I was following some kind of trail, one that I devised as I went along. Then, I read anything and everything. Horse stories, ballet stories, ghost stories, love stories; murder mysteries, historical novels, family sagas. Looking for something in those pages. Finding it sometimes; looking further for both more of the same and what might come next. Recently my cousin, a woman two years older than I am, told me that while she was always out of the house as a girl ("I tried to solve my problems with other people"), she remembers me as being at home: "You know, reading," she said. On one level, this can't be true. I was a Curved Bar Girl Scout, the star of every school play, the literary editor of the high school yearbook. I couldn't have been at home *that* much. The truths in my cousin's remark are of a different sort. For one thing, my preoccupation with reading must have stood out, because it marked me as different—back then in the fifties in a middle-class Jewish suburb of a small eastern city. I didn't look weird—thick glasses or funny hair—but of course I was: smart and "bookish," no matter how I tried to pass with my charcoal-gray Bermudas and argyle knee socks. Just as important, though, is how she understood that reading was my way of "solving problems." Problems I couldn't have told you I had, problems, I can see now, associated with the need to feel recognized and loved.

Looking back, I think that the more I tried to be the success my mother wanted me to be, the more I sought to find the person I was without the prizes, and to be loved anyway. My mother had invented that child star, after all. She had given me the will to aspire, but she gave me as well the script to follow, laying out the path for what I could do that she would approve of—no, *notice:* what I could give her that she would like. She knew I could do it, that I had the talent, the brains, and yes, the charm. She cultivated them in me, so that I could stand up there and shine. I could bring home the A's, the awards, the blue ribbons—for my paintings and my poetry and my performances. Bring them home and hand them to her.

Was I anybody else? I had to be, because up there on that stage, I knew I was pretending like mad. But how could I find

6

out? Reflected in her eyes I saw only the girl she wanted me to be. I didn't see any other me; nor did I see her. She was forever hiding, it seemed to me—showing only the woman *she* wanted to be: the other half of the shining girl. For I was a piece of her, I knew—an agent for carrying out her desires in the world. I must have been terribly confused, and terribly lonely. Even if I could find my secret self, she could never come out. Except when I was reading. The reading girl is not out producing something, being successful. Reading was the opposite of the life my mother told me to lead. Reading was not for an audience; it was for me. It differed from my performances in the world, because when I was reading, no one could tell what was happening to me. Consequently, reading met both halves of my need: to find out who I might be; to come into existence.

I needed to discover what other people, real people, were like. How did they think? How did they behave? What happened when they interacted with one another? What was possible? What was not? I did not have this knowledge. But the books could tell me, especially when I could live inside a character— become her, experience her story right along with her. I've never enjoyed, or profited from, standing outside, looking on—reading the way I learned to do for school. No: I need to feel it, to try a life on, to recognize myself in it if I can. Consequently, I'm never comfortable with fiction that either won't let me in (consider "experimental" fiction, where the writing itself is so emphasized that it becomes impossible to treat the characters or the story as lifelike, real) or deals with people too different from me for me to get a foothold—a difference not so much cultural or historical as cognitive and emotional. Reading such fiction surely serves some purposes, but not mine. And mine are powerful, deep, and longstanding. As a professional reader and critic, I can put my desires on hold, now, if I have to—but they remain, always, and they demand food.

Food? Yes. Nourishment. Words to grow on. And this is where the author is so important. They are her words, after all—it's her voice I hear, telling me the story I know I am reading, even as I *imagine* the world of the book and its people. As much as I am living along with the character, I am in the presence (the lap, maybe) of the storyteller. Like a mother, she guides me, comforts me, encourages me, provokes me, *notices* me. Me: the reading girl. That means the girl who is reading because she is lost and lonely and scared and smart and sensitive and eager and full of feelings and energies that do not know where to go. In the presence of the author when she is like a mother, I feel recognized; I feel loved.

It is no wonder that the characters with whom I most identified when I was a girl were precisely those heroines who were different and unloved because they were smart and bookish—reading girls, just like me. Girls like Anne Shirley and Jo March, with unfashionable red hair and inky hands. Nor is it any wonder that smart and bookish girls grew up to write novels about heroines who were smart and bookish, but I didn't know that then, as I read the complete works of Louisa May Alcott or every one of the *Anne of Green Gables* stories. The joy of all those novels was that the heroines didn't remain outcasts. Oh no, they ended up with love, and in the process, they (usually) grew strong and capable (although not all became writers, like the women who created them, women themselves often unmarried). All those orphan girls—from Mary Lennox in *The Secret Garden* to Jerusha Abott in *Daddy Long Legs* to Anne Shirley in *Anne of Green Gables,* and on to Catherine Earnshaw in *Wuthering Heights* and to Jane Eyre—all those not pretty but oh so intelligent girls whose lives amplified mine. To these novels I came as my own kind of orphan, to find an alternative place in which to live and to grow.

Today I read about the same girls, only they're older. Now they're middle-aged women (I also try to find novels about older women, so as to prepare). But no matter what the heroine's chronological age, she is that same kind of orphan when the novel begins. Badly mothered or with no mother at all: never having properly grown. Her story will be about how she grows up and how she finds love. The two plots always, in the novels I like best, go together. This is what I believe to be the crux of the female fantasy of true love. And I live in books like this—inhabiting worlds that are not so much alternatives to my own as appendages to it.

My description of reading indicates that to find the secret self—the true self—a person cannot go it alone. Someone from outside has to be there, to notice, to say, "Oh, it's you!"—for the self to know she is there. And, in a complementary manner, she needs to recognize the presence of another, to know that there is a world in which to exist. Recognition bolstered by love. All else in the way of development follows. A book is not a living person, true; but a relationship is created in the interaction between the reading mind and the words that are read. When there is no active nurture in the child's life, reading may well approximate that process to provide an environment for coming alive that is at once safe and challenging, supportive and guiding. Something to curl up into; something to push against. A "facilitating environment," in the words of the psychologist D. W. Winnicott. Facilitating self-discovery, growth, and maturation.

To a certain extent. But for all the ways in which the book is like another person, there are many ways in which it is not. No flesh; no blood. You *are* alone when you read, despite the feeling that you are not. You are not actually engaged with the outside world. That is both the beauty of the experience and its frustration, because reading enhances the loneliness as much as it reduces it. After all, engaged, stimulated, *active* as you may be, all of this exertion is taking place inside one person, one solitary mind.

This may well be why reading is addictive. No one book ever

gets the reader all the way there. She must find another, and another, to repeat the wonderful process that is finally but a taste, or a template, of the real thing: love and recognition with a person, a mother or someone who can love as a mother should.

I like to read love stories best. Romance fiction: Girl meets boy, girl loses boy, girl gets boy. Or girl meets girl, girl loses girl, girl gets girl. I am deeply, consistently, and avidly interested in true love. Yet I look for a certain kind of love story, the kind that women often write. A story in which love and identity go together, in which the heroine experiences self-development in the context of learning how to love. This is the happy ending that satisfies my readerly longing. Although it has traditionally been understood as marriage, I can be content, in a contemporary novel, with the promise of the lovers being together always. True love, after all, is forever. And whatever else "forever" connotes, it means not wanting to live without the feeling of this kind of love; it means wanting to have it always. Despite the inclusion in modern novels of meaningful work as an important theme, with the conflict between love and work as a major plot complication, the happy ending still focuses on this love. Romances continue to end with a kiss, not a promotion.

My predilection for this particular plot, this version of true love, seems to me to have everything to do with my reading needs, because the female fantasy of true love as I understand it is a version of mother love. It is an idea of recognition, of unconditional and nourishing care that is projected out of that earliest experience into the adult future. It is a story about finally finding such a love, or finding it again, and never having to be without it, that satisfies me so deeply because this is the longing that motivates my life.

The story of true love that I am describing should be familiar to romance readers. It begins with a heroine who is lively and intelligent, not conventionally pretty but—this is important—possessing wonderful eyes. In the traditional version of this novel she is eighteen, but in more contemporary renditions she may be any age; she may even be married or divorced. What is required is that she be, as the novel starts, in some profound way unformed, immature, her "life" not having really begun. The novel is going to be about that life and how she comes to be able to live it. It is going to be about her journey toward selfhood.

Our heroine is essentially unmothered. Her own mother is usually either dead or seriously inadequate in some way. (There is a range of inadequacy that extends all the way from absence to severe deprivation to simply not *enough*.) In the classic romance, like *Pride and Prejudice* or *Jane Eyre,* the heroine's unmothered condition will be immediately apparent. In more contemporary fiction, when she is often already an adult, this information will be conveyed more obliquely, but it will nonetheless come to light.

In such a novel, two stories overlap. The first is the love story. Soon after the opening chapters, if this is a heterosexual romance, the heroine will meet the hero. Usually we won't know that he is the one. *She* certainly won't know it. In fact, they hate each other; she definitely hates him! Their mutual antagonism isn't the only way to establish difficulties, but it's a favorite one. Difficulties there must be. If they met, fell in love, and married, there wouldn't be a story. Why not? Because the *story* is as much about the heroine's growth toward maturity as it is about when and how he kisses her for the first time. It is in the course of the complications, whatever they may be (this is where the plot comes in: family problems, work problems, perhaps a murder), that self-development occurs. Because the complications derive from the heroine's association with the man she will ultimately marry (in the heterosexual version), their relationship stimulates her development. The hero, of course, changes as well throughout and because of their relationship.

The end of the novel is the discovery and affirmation of true love, which goes hand in hand with arriving at a mature identity. The two go together because true love turns out to be responsible, mutual, unconditional, and everlasting. Only a mature person, a person with genuine self-identity and the ability to use it in the world, can love properly. And love is necessary for a person to achieve this kind of selfhood. Consequently, love and identity are not two warring plots but aspects of the same story.

The way in which love and identity go together in this story alerts me to the core of the fantasy being enacted here. So, too, does the *feeling* that this kind of book produces in me. The columnist Anna Quindlen writes in an essay called "Feeling at Home in a Favorite Book" that *Pride and Prejudice* is the kind of book that "take[s] me in its arms and make[s] me part of it." Reviews of Rosamund Pilcher describe her kind of romance as a novel that "exudes comfort as it entertains"; "a perfect book to snuggle up with on a winter night." "I don't know where Rosamund Pilcher has been all my life," writes a *New York Times* reviewer, "but now that I've found her, I'm not going to let her go." Love and identity come together, or should, in the first moments of our lives, and it is from there that this need—and this fantasy—springs.

Many women readers have found themselves unnurtured, denied both the love and the opportunity for self-development that a good mother provides. Sometimes the mother-infant bond was all too short-lived. Sometimes it did not function as it should have. Historically, it has proved difficult for mothers, themselves socialized in a culture that withholds authenticity and agency from women, to give their daughters these primary requisites for selfhood. Sometimes daughters then turn to the father, seeing all the power he possesses and hoping he will share it with them.

Yet the deep desire for the mother persists, especially when the father's response does not provide the kind of love and care that fosters the growth of identity. Some daughters go to books to find it, for true love is at heart a story of mother love.

Yet sometimes in life there is a good (or good enough) mother. Such relationships are the minority, the exception that proves the rule. But why is it that even then the well-mothered daughter has the same fantasy of true love? Why would a well-mothered daughter read romance fiction? Isn't one experience of good mothering *enough?*

I think that in such instances good mothering becomes a template, standing for love at its best. The well-mothered daughter then seeks to replicate the experience in her other loves, because the first love is what feels right. And while the original mother-daughter bond is source and model, it is not all-sufficient. It sets in motion a process for development that is not static but ongoing, especially because between adult lovers sexuality must have a place in the transaction. Ultimately, the well-mothered daughter requires the opportunity to act as a mother herself, to extend home and nurture into the society and into the future.

⁂

I have developed these ideas about the relationship between reading, true love, and the earliest mother-daughter bond from reading the literature of psychology. I wanted to understand my passion for romance fiction, and because I am an academic, the habit of doing research is well ingrained in me. I like to follow the threads and the clues, one author suggesting another, one essay leading me on to the next. Looking in contemporary psychoanalytic and feminist psychology, I discovered a plot that was as exciting to me as a novel. I read a story about the first relationship between mother and infant that both challenged the ideas on which I had been raised about what it means to grow up and, even more important, rang true for me. Reading about mothers and infants—about the wonderful moment when the mother looks into the baby's eyes and recognizes that person (and feels that person recognizing *her*)—brought a thrill of understanding, a throb of yearning. Reading about how that process of empathetic interaction goes awry, when the subtle attunement between the two partners breaks down so that the search for recognition becomes a power struggle, was intensely painful. Again and again I found myself weeping over my psychology text. I knew that I was reading descriptions of my own life, even if I could never remember it; my formative desires, frustrations, griefs, called up before me in the words of what we label in the academy "theory." Reading the psychologists who wrote these stories—D. W. Winnicott, Daniel Stern, Nancy Chodorow, Judith Jordan, Jessica Benjamin—I felt myself in the presence of a new set of mothers: people who understood me—what I needed then and why I continue to need it now. As I read their pages, I felt the maternal recognition that is the springboard of self-development as they describe it.

I have appended a chapter about their work at the end of this book, presenting there in more detail the concepts upon which I have based my own ideas. Here I will tell you the story that I have gleaned from reading these psychologists, because I think it is the basis of the fantasy about true love that women often write, a fantasy very different from other myths that our culture prizes. In the very way that romance fiction itself is derided even as it is misunderstood, so this story of self-development through the interaction of mother and daughter in a period much earlier than the so-called Oedipal crisis that Freud found to be the basis of identity formation has been typically misinterpreted and belittled.

Freud's familiar narrative has become a part of our culture, even when people have no idea of its source. It tells us that the path to maturity is a struggle toward separation, independence, autonomy. Distances between people must be established, so that the adult will be strong—and solitary. This process is first and crucially effected through the Oedipal crisis, the point in a young child's growth in which he ceases to identify with his mother and models himself on his father. In this way he avoids the possibility of incest (too close an attachment to the mother would surely lead to sex with her) and gains access to the powers (symbolized by the wonderful penis) that the father is seen to possess—over the mother, over the child, over the world at large. The maternal body and all its sticky closeness is rejected, and the father, although he becomes a model, is a distant god. This kind of identification is conceptual, not physical. It fosters independence, is suspicious of connection. Leaving home, not finding it, is the path to adulthood. Self-sufficiency means power; intimacy is fearful and demanding. In this story, love and identity do not go together.

My use of the male pronoun is deliberate. This tale is a description of boys. When the pattern is applied to girls, it doesn't work as well, as even Freud noticed. He thought that the girl would want to transfer her love for her mother into anger at her for not having given her daughter "the only proper genital organ" and into desire not to be her father but to have his child (getting the penis on loan, as it were). Since she cannot (should not) perform this act with her own father, Freud reasoned, her desire becomes heterosexuality, and she is ready to be the woman that a man will love. But why should the girl want to disconnect from her mother in the first place? The power of the magic penis, some have suggested, is an idea that only a man would have. Freud himself noted that women frequently have trouble making the transition, maintain their attachment to their mothers, and so end up in a misty place that he saw as unrealized female identity.

Freud's paradigm all but ignores the infant's early relationship with the mother. The story he tells really begins when the father becomes a dominant presence in the child's life and consciousness. But what if it is the mother, in the preoedipal period, who initiates the beginnings of identity? What if dependence is necessary for a self to form—security in the continued presence and loving care of the mother? What if empathy is the process through which infant and mother establish their dynamic of attachment and discrimination? If this is so, then absolute autonomy becomes a myth, or a psychological disorder. The idea of self-in-relation modifies the goal of self-reliance. The boy's trajectory toward masculinity is prescribed by the culture, but it seems to be a tale of damage as much as achievement. And the culture's prescriptions for femininity, based in its ideal of masculinity, based in the dominance of the father, look off base altogether.

The body of psychological literature called object-relations theory presents a different picture of self-development from the one I have just outlined, because it views human development as interpersonal; selfhood as implicated in relationship with others. It focuses on the bond between infant and mother in the preoedipal period, because this is usually the first primary relationship in a person's life. It tells us of the necessary interaction between a self and an "object"—that is, another person who is the object of the self's attention and love. From the beginning there is a self and there is an other; it is through the constant dynamic of their interaction that growth occurs. In the "facilitating environment" of the mother-infant relation, the baby is recognized. The mother's empathy permits her to see who that other person is: "Oh, it's you!" And the baby's empathy permits her to see who her mother is. They are one and one; they are two; they are together in an interchange of gesture and response, a dance of to and fro, give-and-take. This interaction is called "attunement," in which feeling states are shared and reinforced between mother and child by behavior that is matching but not the same. This is the operation of mutual recognition: the baby's "I am, I do" confirmed by the response "You are, you have done." And vice versa.

Recognition and loving support—what Winnicott calls "holding"—form the basis of the facilitating environment. In that space of safety and energy, a sense of self develops. Not all at once, of course—and different writers identify different stages in this development, although all are quick to point out that what we are talking about is not so much a linear process as an incremental one, each layer forming, like the silk of a cocoon, around the other.

In Winnicott's work I saw a pattern that seems particularly helpful, so I have adopted a simplified version of his ideas as a way to talk about the development of a romance heroine. First, the establishment of the facilitating or holding environment. Next, a transitional time in which the tricky relationship between inner and outer, subjective and objective, can be explored. A transitional object, for Winnicott, is something that is created by the self and also belongs to the outside world. Think of the baby's little piece of blanket, or stuffed bear, that holds enormous personal importance for the child but is at the same time not imaginary. The mother's breast, or the mother herself, can be used in this way. Relating to such an object requires the baby to come to some kind of terms between her own sense of omnipotence—"I made this!"—and the fact of a world outside the self: "I cannot destroy this thing at will. It exists, despite my desire, my anger, my fear." This kind of transitional object relating, taking place in the space of safety that is the facilitating environment, prepares the child to engage with the outside world. Ideally, the reciprocity that informs the ongoing association between child and mother will continue in wider and wider circles as the "environment" itself expands.

What does it mean, then, to achieve an identity, to be grown up or mature? First, we see that a great deal of the process of self-development occurs within the mother-child relationship, in the preoedipal period. Language, for example, one marker for socialization, is traditionally taught to the child by the mother, a process that occurs well before the older child's Oedipal crisis. Freudian psychology sees the preoedipal period as a time of symbiotic merger, when the baby cannot distinguish between self and other. The Oedipal moment, and the father, are needed to escape this scary state of undifferentiation. Stern's work in particular invalidates this supposition. Stern shows how both differentiation and connection are always there, from the very beginning. They are not mutually exclusive situations; and relationship is at the heart of any sort of development. Judith Jordan and other feminist psychologists from the Stone Center for Developmental Services and Studies point out how change occurs within relationship, not by severing it. Consequently, the mature woman is a person who operates in relationship authentically and with agency—that is, she is distinct (has viable self-boundaries) and connected (functions in healthy relationship—to individuals and society at large).

This may be an ideal state; but after all, romances are fantasy, not actuality. Their job is to give a form to the need and desire that persist in the teeth of the hard facts of societal conditions. There are many other novels by women that tell the tale of how a woman never finds that identity. Think of George Eliot's *The Mill on the Floss* or Kate Chopin's *The Awakening*. I read them, too, despite the lack of a happy ending. I need to *know*. But romance fiction equates true love and identity, following the path of a heroine whose relationship with her lover has all the elements of the preoedipal mother-child relationship, a plot that grants her, at the end, the kind of maturity I have just described. Now she is able to love: love the hero, or the other heroine, who,

18

having experienced a process similar to her own, is able to love in return. On such a basis the ideal adult and sexual relationship is formed.

In real life many factors militate against the achievement of this kind of identity, factors which, while they may stem from cultural institutions and attitudes, influence the most intimate of interpersonal arrangements. The process of holding and attuning between mother and infant that I have described does not always work so felicitously. The mother may be bored or depressed or too controlling; the baby may be unresponsive or afraid or too compliant. Then the search for recognition can become a power struggle. Independence and connection, ideally aspects of the same dynamic, can split into opposite positions, opposite paradigms. Domination or submission become alternative possibilities—for roles in a relationship, for models of self-identity. For women, the ideal of the autonomous self may seem both distasteful and impossible; they may go too far in the other direction, seeking connection at all costs. Submission to another's will is the price they will pay, which can cost integrity or worse.

This is where, I think, the father comes into the picture. I haven't been talking much about fathers. One of the reasons why I am so drawn to object-relations psychology is that, unlike Freudian theory, it isn't particularly interested in fathers. In its focus on the mother-infant relationship, its description of development in the preoedipal period, it makes fathers peripheral. The Oedipal crisis, if mentioned at all, is a kind of postscript to the main event. I appreciate that idea because I am deeply and abidingly interested in mothers.

My own father was gentle and self-effacing, the object of my mother's derision and rage—or so I remember him. I remember as well constantly imposing my body and my will between them: thinking someone had to defend him, when maybe he was doing a fine job of defending himself by not responding. My involvement with more typically fatherlike men came afterwards, from my first husband on. I sought out men who were animated, energetic, vigorous, and strong: people like me—and like my mother—but who, because they possessed a penis and all the perks that go with it in our culture, were in charge. They had power. I wanted them to recognize me, those boyfriends and department chairmen, as like them. I wanted their love as proof. I wanted to belong to them so that I could participate in their power. And I wanted the world to see that I did belong—me, the smart, bookish girl who was therefore "different." Surely one reason why I believe my intelligent and gifted mother made me her agent in the world was that her path had been twice thwarted: first in being a woman; second in having married my father, who could not or would not achieve power for her. But I didn't want that role, and I tried to escape it by finding a man to be *my* source of power. My first husband was a dynamic, effective man—who was also a lot like my mother. I thought he would recognize me, but he didn't. He set out to create me as the one who, having a sufficient amount of his own qualities, could recognize him. For years afterwards, both in the marriage and after I had left it, I followed the same pattern. Notice me; recognize me; love me: I am just like you. I was always surprised when the father of choice saw me not as a soul mate but as a threat. I never got it, but I finally learned to avoid it wherever I found it: in real life; in novels. Danger!

Reading Jessica Benjamin, whose work extends object-relations theory to discuss problems of domination and submission, helped me to understand why the daughter might be fascinated with the father and what the nature of his seduction might be. Her work also helps to explain why this turn in the plot appears in many romance novels. Disappointment with the mother may arise in several ways. If the delicate interplay of attunement goes awry, the distortion that is dominance and submission may ensue. Seeking to escape the power of the mother, the daughter may look for another source of recognition—and discover the father. Or, conversely, if the mother's powerlessness is revealed as the daughter comes to observe her position vis-à-vis the father or the world at large, the daughter may likewise turn to the father. In either case, the mother's inability to provide the necessary recognition that is the fount of a sense of identity may well stimulate a further search.

The father can look very attractive. Both his power in the world at large and his distance from the bond between mother and daughter make him a likely candidate. The daughter wants him to recognize her as like him. When he doesn't (she is, after all, not like him at all: she is a girl, and he has been taught to keep his distance from mothers and their ilk), she tries another tack, what Benjamin terms "ideal love," in which submission proves a vicarious substitute for a sense of one's own agency. Accepting another's will and desires as one's own seems a way to gain a reflected identity; to ward off separation and abandonment through identifying with and surrendering to the other's will. Benjamin calls this a "perversion of identification," and I think she is right. There is much danger in this scenario. The masochism that derives from seeking self-definition through the father or his representatives can permit terrible violation—of the body and of the soul. And yet the story is so compelling to many women that it is a powerful plot in both real life and fiction. The idea and also the person who incarnates it are seductive. It is a false promise for selfhood that disguises something altogether different: bondage and degradation.

The tension between desire for the mother and desire for the father fuels many of the romance plots that women write. Although my own preference is emphatically for the story where the mother's love triumphs over paternal authority, there is another, darker plot where the mother is disavowed on behalf of the father's protective power. There are other variations on the story of true love as well: the one in which a good mother, a woman who mothers the heroine, competes with a heterosexual lover; and the one where the possibility of recapitulating mother love does not demand turning a man into a mother, because the lover is already a woman. The rule of the father cannot be ignored, but women's fantasies for true love create variations on the possibility that the maternal mode might triumph in some fashion.

In this book about romance fiction, I am going to be the reader reading. I am going to describe my experience in the contexts of many different romances: novels that I have loved since girlhood, and novels that I have read for the first time only recently. I want to enter the world of the book and show what happens when I am in the presence of an author-mother; what it means to feel her care and love, her reliability, as she both supports and challenges me. I want to explore true love, to see what it means for the heroines, their authors, and me, the dedicated romance reader.

But of course, all writers do not mother their readers in this fashion. Even as there are bad mothers in life, so there are bad author-mothers. It is called "narcissistic projection" when a mother uses the child as an extension of herself, a creation of what she wants to be, and does not recognize the other's independent existence. In some novels by women, as in many best-selling romances about beautiful, wealthy, successful heroines and handsome, wealthy, successful heroes, the heroine functions as the author's wish-fulfilling fantasy. No development or growth is necessary for her, because she is already perfect. Nor is there any differentiation between the character and the author. The author is using her text as a narcissistically disturbed mother uses her child. The reader is being used in this way too. Like that badly mothered daughter, she is required to participate in the mother's fantasy, reflecting back only what the mother wants to see. I will not be writing about novels like these here, however much they crowd the best-seller lists. I don't read them. What for?

Some authors are, in fact, not mothers at all. There are daughter-authors, too. Charlotte Brontë writes as a daughter in *Jane Eyre,* and Louisa May Alcott writes as a daughter in *Little Women.* The daughter-author is writing *to* a mother or to a father, attempting to be recognized and thus to come into identity through the words she writes. Brontë, seeking the love of her father, presents her text as proof that she is just like him—clever, talented, and accomplished. The story she tells is a paradigm of what she wants, in which a heroine is appreciated and passionately desired by a father-lover, who literally capitulates to her in the end. Bent on bringing herself into existence, she hasn't the energy or interest to attend to anyone else. She isn't mothering her heroine: she *is* her heroine. She certainly isn't mothering her reader. Instead, she is asking the reader to applaud, to encourage, to gratify her intentions, either by identifying with her and her heroine (daughters all) or perhaps by taking a parental role—i.e., mothering *her.*

Alcott's daughterly designs are a little different. She is writing a story of mother love, but she is nonetheless trying to establish her own identity by means of her writing. Desiring the mother and the mother's recognition, she writes a tale with the perfect love of the mother at its center. Her story is meant to be a model, a guide for any mother who might read it. Alcott's Marmee can mother all daughters, both within the text and without it. The author is one of those daughters; so is the reader. Thus the author aligns the reader as a kind of sister or perhaps a second self, whose participation in the magic circle that is maternal love and nurture validates the author's own enterprise. There are reasons aplenty why a woman might write as a daughter and not as a mother. Reading the daughter-author has its own kind of pleasures, although for me, they are not the choicest ones.

Passion and need: the story of true love, both in the first relationship and in other romances that follow. Having it, wanting it, searching for it, finding it. The story happens in books and in real life, too. Often, they intertwine. *Reading from the Heart* tells that story by following my own reading life. The life of a passionate reader: an eager young girl, an ardent woman. Imagine me, then, in the green chair (in the house where I live now, it is blue), nibbling on crackers, sipping coffee or soda. The house is humming, or it is quiet. It surrounds me, while I go into my book. I am reading. I am happy.

1

Becoming a Romance Reader

JANE AUSTEN'S *PRIDE AND PREJUDICE*

AND ELSWYTH THANE'S *TRYST*

The books I read when I was a girl came from the Providence Public Library—first the branch library on Rochambeau Avenue and later the main library, downtown. If only because books have to be found, discovered and collected, and brought home, the world of books has wider dimensions than the green chair. For me, then and now, the library has been the source. For there the books all were, and there I learned about the monumental pleasure of choosing them. A place devoted to books—with everybody present, both employees and customers, there on behalf of reading. In the library my passion is institutionalized: not shameful or silly. Hardly a "waste of time." A world of books; a world of readers. From the Rochambeau Branch of the Providence Public Library and a young woman named Miss Hough—a children's librarian whom I loved devotedly and who would take me around the room and introduce me to first one, then another author—to the spanking new and glamorous Boulder Public Library, where the staff all know me because I'm there so much, reading for me has been inextricably associated with the library.

I graduated from the Rochambeau Branch Library at an early age, or rather, I liberated myself from it. The trouble began when, at around eleven or twelve, I wanted to cross the hall from the Children's Room to the Adult Room. That required, I was told, the accompaniment of a different librarian, Miss Chase, not the good witch of the Children's Room but a very wicked witch indeed. (Miss Hough had gone—she probably got married. I know I mourned that loss a long time.) She tried to steer me to the Young Adults section, and when that failed, to censor the books I picked out. This joy of mine, choosing books, was growing tainted by someone discouraging rather than encouraging, peering critically over my shoulder, not to mention possessing the power to say no; and so, very soon afterwards, I ran away to the main library, downtown.

There I discovered the stacks. Oh yes, the stacks of the Providence Public Library: an enormous, dimly lit room, filled with rows and rows, hundreds upon hundreds, of books. All waiting for me—to choose them, claim them, bring them home and have them for my own for two weeks. Back then, when I had read so little, their lure was intense. It really was like an enchanted forest for me, the long shelves like woodland paths. It was so mysterious and huge, so filled with treasures. I would begin at the beginning, at the *A*'s, and work my way through, every time. The pile in my arms would grow heavier and heavier as I neared the *M*'s and the *N*'s, but I was daunted only by the limit of ten books that the library placed on adults. (I had to persuade my father to accompany me on my biweekly visits, because I wasn't old enough for an adult card. He would wait, not so patiently, in the reading lounge, and I would try not to let my knowledge of his growing displeasure impede my work.) All the way to the *W*'s I went, to the *Y*'s and *Z*'s, unless I had filled my quota already with some rare finds.

How did I choose? The title of course; then a swift glance at the opening page, a paragraph or two from the middle . . . Never, never the ending! To know what happens—it has always horrified me that some people actually look, spoiling the adventure before it begins. You have to take a chance—that's part of the deal. If something seemed right, the book would be added to the growing pile. And "right" meant, well, a feeling that I would like to be in that book, that there was something there just for me. Something having to *do* with me. This surreptitious tasting is the best method I know. I don't want to read and read while still at the library and find out too much, because that would spoil what is to come later, when I settle down with the book at home. I still do it. Although today I usually confine myself to the New Books section, sometimes I give myself the pleasure of a long, slow meander through the stacks, always receptive to a new discovery.

Thus there is a literal conduit between the private space of reading and the public space of the library. My mind, the book, the chair and the room, the stacks and the circulation desk. This was important to me then, and it still is, if only because reading is about trying to make connections, find relationships, a community, what I have been referring to here as a "world." I've always made friends with the librarians. I wonder what they thought of me back then, that eager little girl, standing there with all those books in her arms. I saw them as women who belonged to the books, the high priestesses of the library. Words from them were almost magic—that's why the betrayal of that one branch librarian has stayed with me for forty years.

Looking back on those years of discovery and pleasure at the library, I see how I was forming a template for the life in books that I still live. I learned to identify the feeling that the right books gave me, and I learned how to look for the right kind of story. Two novels from that time can serve as examples for all the others that I remember today with a proprietary tingle of happiness. They're my books; I belong to them, I always will. Jane Austen's *Pride and Prejudice* has come with me all the way into my career as a professor of literature, although the way I love it seems to have little to do with the way it was taught to me in graduate school. The other novel, *Tryst* by Elswyth Thane, has never made it on any college reading list that I have ever seen. Yet it was probably my favorite novel of all from my teenage years. Not surprisingly, the two have a great deal in common, for they both tell that particular tale of love and identity, the story of true love, that I have come to desire so deeply. And yet upon re-reading I see complications that, significantly, don't exist in my memory of them. I remembered just the delight, the content-ment—having suppressed anything that might qualify or question such happiness. Interestingly, Austen as the author of *Pride and Prejudice* is the one who works hard to see that I don't need to question, while Thane builds problems into the very structure of her novel. If Austen waves a magic wand and tries to convince me that it isn't magic at all, Thane makes the magic at once in-finitely desirable and pointedly obvious. What does it mean that the fantasy of the hero-as-mother is just that, a fantasy?

꿎

I am not alone in my abiding predilection for Jane Austen, and for *Pride and Prejudice*. Romance aficionados, if not literary scholars, *know* that Austen is the mother of their favorite genre: "we are all familiar with the best known of those who have writ-ten romances such as Jane Austen [and] the Brontës," writes Eileen Fallon in *Words of Love: A Complete Guide to Romance Fic-tion*. I would imagine that of all of Austen's novels, *Pride and*

Prejudice is the most beloved. The responses of women I know indicate this in telling ways. Recently a friend who came to dinner said, "When things are all confused or falling apart, I reread *Pride and Prejudice.*" Another woman said to me, "I feel at home in Austen novels . . . She has always been a haven for me." Anna Quindlen's article, "Feeling at Home in a Favorite Book," which I have already mentioned, was sent to me by another friend. *Pride and Prejudice,* writes Ms. Quindlen, "is the book that makes me feel most that everything is going to be all right, that the world is a hospitable place and that, as Anne Frank once said, people are really good at heart." She continues:

> Why it should do this when it was published in 1813 and those feelings in the late 20th century are so patently untrue, I do not know. Part of it is that "Pride and Prejudice" has been with me for a long time, since I was 12. Part of it is about a young woman named Elizabeth Bennet, who I have always felt would have been my best friend if she hadn't been fictional. Part is that it is about the right things happening in the wrong way—chance meetings leading to rapprochements, misunderstandings leading to marriages—in just the way you wish would happen in real life.
>
> Most important, I feel at home in this book. . . . I feel I could just slip unnoticed into "Pride and Prejudice." Elizabeth and I could sit around jawboning about what a pain Mr. Darcy is, while all the time I'd be secretly thinking he is just the guy for her. (p. 1)

The recurrence of the word "home" in these remarks is noteworthy. We feel at home in *Pride and Prejudice* because it so successfully creates for Elizabeth Bennet and for us a facilitating environment, bringing us into the presence of the mother in powerful ways. "Home" is a word for comfort and especially for safety: the excitement is there, the challenge and the danger, but it is, significantly, danger that occurs in a safe place. The happy ending and, more pervasively, the comedy that is *Pride and Prejudice*, that novel which Austen referred to as so "light and bright and sparkling," generate Quindlen's "patently untrue" feelings that everything is going to be all right. It's not bad or naive to want to feel this—especially in the version Austen gives us, in which the happy ending for the heroine and hero occurs in a social context that is anything but idealized. Elizabeth Bennet and Fitzwilliam Darcy achieve their felicitous marriage in a corrupt and patriarchal culture where good marriages are not at all the rule. The author gives to them and to them alone the chance for maturation along maternal lines, so that they incarnate our fantasy within the setting of the real world as we know it. This is a central component of Austen's skill and strategy: she makes us believe in the possibility of love and identity, the chance for true love, because she shows it happening, not in some fairy tale world but in the very midst of the forces that have traditionally worked against it.

I love *Pride and Prejudice* especially because of its comic quality. I love the combination of wit and romance, of intelligence and sentiment, each element informing, amending the other to produce in me a feeling of particular exhilaration and delight. I am also a fan of *Much Ado About Nothing* and of *Private Lives*. It's not so much the warring couple part of it that gets to me but the clever warring couple—and the clever loving couple. Wit is absolutely sexy, as Austen knew quite as well as Noël Coward. I think this special pleasure has its roots in the yearnings of that smart and bookish girl to be loved for what she was—not to have to play the dumb blonde, the shallow cheerleader. To be attractive because you were smart! And to find a lover who was like that too: dashing and debonair, quick-witted and fast on his feet. Then to meet and match him, word for word, step for step, sparks flying. Such a man may not sound much like a mother: not soothing, not gentle. But that is exactly where the fantasy resides—that from the matching up of intelligence and wit, the excitement and challenge of the intercourse, the intimacy, the care, would come the tender recognition of one another. Of course, I am describing Elizabeth and Mr. Darcy. Yes, I love the throes of passion in which Catherine and Heathcliff flail, and more will be said of them later; but I love, even more, the charm and grace and humor of the clever couple.

Elizabeth Bennet is no orphan, or so it appears at the start of her novel. She's got a mother, although the woman is a little dimwitted and foolish; she's got a smart and bookish daddy who loves her best of all his children, all of them unfortunately daughters. But no, she is indeed orphaned, we soon discover, for she has neither a mother nor a father who sees her and loves her for who she is. Mrs. Bennet wants her to be a blonde cheerleader, and Mr. Bennet, more perniciously, wants her to be himself. That is, he has picked her out among his daughters as the one most like him—intelligent and witty—and he has tried to make of her, especially because he has no son, another version of himself. As he has dealt with the failures and flaws of his culture by making fun of and withdrawing from it, so he expects the same from his daughter. Mr. Bennet married a woman who was not his intellectual equal because he found her, for a brief time, sexually appealing and malleable (the two no doubt, being linked, from his masculine perspective). He has spent the rest of his life making fun of her and belittling his responsibilities to her, to his children, and to his society. This is his legacy to his favorite daughter, one that ignores any aspirations she might have toward deep feeling, toward care, toward connection with others. This is how we find Elizabeth at the start of the novel: seeking the love her father has to offer by performing in his image.

Identifying with Jane Eyre, that pitifully abandoned child, gives us the opportunity to feel sorry for ourselves—to experience such loss in a total and drastic way. But Elizabeth Bennet has been forsaken in a secret way. On the surface she is cosseted and cared for, but what is inside her is disdained. She has developed a false self in order to protect a true self that is never recognized, never wanted. Austen's understanding of this dilemma calls up a painful identification in me. Because Elizabeth is sparkling, attractive, and apparently successful, I know her. Because she is alone and hiding within, I know her, too. Eagerly, I await what is in store for her.

Elizabeth begins her book unmothered and unnurtured, her true self in hiding. In this way she is like most young women, for the culture does not ask them to become authentic, vigorous selves. Elizabeth, however, thinks she is challenging and outsmarting the system. She thinks she is a rebel girl, not a good girl. I, of course, as a reader who thinks she is a rebel girl, identify with Elizabeth for just those impulses. Recalling what it meant to read Elizabeth Bennet for the first time, I would say that I didn't see the danger in her approach: that in identifying with her father in this way, she is exempting herself from the problems associated with traditional femaleness, but at the cost of attaining authenticity or maturity. Her true self remains unacknowledged and carefully protected: a self that needs to be loved and to love. Surely I admired her unambivalent laughter at the social system: "He is also handsome . . . which a young man ought likewise to be, if he possibly can. His character is thereby complete." (p. 62) Elizabeth seemed so sure of herself, while I was fraught with tension—between trying to prove I was above it and trying to belong to it! But we were both ignorant about the causes of our difficulties, so that for me to read her novel is to participate along with her in her psychological education.

Because of course, Elizabeth was more like me than I

thought. Her facetiousness is there to mask her own desire for romance and love, it turns out—but it must be true love, which she knows to be a rare commodity. She will protect herself from anything but, and with that I quite agree. Of Mr. Darcy, who has clearly snubbed her on their first meeting, she comments: "I could easily have forgiven *his* pride, if he had not mortified *mine.*" (p. 67)

Didn't we all dream of the handsome stranger across the crowded room? Didn't Elizabeth? Once you find him, you should never let him go. But the first time Elizabeth meets her handsome stranger, he snubs her, and she laughs at (hates) him. The original title of this novel was *First Impressions,* and Jane Austen is very, very clear throughout about the dangers of what is advocated in the Rodgers and Hammerstein lyric: love at first sight. That's what (almost) happens between Elizabeth and Mr. Wickham, between Mr. Wickham and Elizabeth's sister, Lydia. For the latter, there are (almost) disastrous results. But for Elizabeth and Mr. Darcy, a change is rung on the patriarchal version of true love. If you meet that stranger and never let him go, you are *in love* with a fantasy, a surface, and not with a person. In this way "love" has nothing to do with selfhood but with objectification—of both people. Elizabeth and Mr. Darcy are going to have to go through a long process of confrontation and understanding. Another Rodgers and Hammerstein song fits better here: "Getting to Know You." But for this even to begin to happen, a different kind of fantasy, a female one, has to be put into place. The notion that a nicely socialized, manly sort of man would *want* to love a woman for herself, as herself, in a tender and nurturing kind of way rather than in a possessive, controlling manner—*that's some fantasy!*

Elizabeth meets Mr. Darcy again, at another dance. She's busy nursing her anger at him; but Austen has a surprise in store for Mr. Darcy. True, he has been thinking about Elizabeth ever since the last time they met, but even so, the 180-degree turn in

33

his *understanding* of her can be accomplished only through authorial legerdemain. Not only so we may see what is happening but also so we will *believe* it, Austen allows us access into Mr. Darcy's consciousness, just at the crucial moment:

> Mr. Darcy had first scarcely allowed her to be pretty; he had looked at her without admiration at the ball; and when they next met, he looked at her only to criticize. But no sooner had he made it clear to himself and his friends that she had hardly a good feature in her face, than he began to find it was rendered uncommonly intelligent by the beautiful expression of her dark eyes. To this discovery succeeded some others equally mortifying. Though he had detected with a critical eye more than one failure of perfect symmetry in her form, he was forced to acknowledge her figure to be light and pleasing; and in spite of his asserting that her manners were not those of the fashionable world, he was caught by their easy playfulness. Of this she was perfectly unaware;—to her he was only the man who made himself agreeable no where, and who had not thought her handsome enough to dance with. (p. 70)

This is the moment at the center of the dreams of all of us smart and bookish girls, for such a reader cannot help but take Elizabeth's felicitous experience as her own: that although "she had hardly a good feature in her face . . . it was rendered uncommonly intelligent by the beautiful expression of her dark eyes." Suddenly, right in front of us, "beautiful" becomes not a physical attribute but a spiritual one—a matter not of an upturned nose but of intelligence. "Intelligent," "beautiful," "expression," "eyes," and "face" recombine in unexpected ways to link attractiveness and recognition of self with the focus on the eyes, those mirrors of the soul. Mr. Darcy, the first person in Elizabeth's life ever to do so, sees *her,* herself, the inside as it informs the outside, and he falls in love with her for it. Now everything about her is pleasing—her manners, her figure—for he is seeing in a new way. He is seeing as a mother might, with recognition and delight: "Oh, it's *you*," smiles the mother at her precious newborn. And the baby knows that she is real.

Elizabeth, however, does not know, not at this moment, for she is too busy paying attention to her own hastily formed preconceptions about this man. But I know, I can feel it, it is happening to *me*. It feels wonderful, and so I never once question the truth of this experience. I accept its probability, its possibility, and the book becomes for me the space where the nurture I so desire can happen—to me as well as to its heroine.

But the matter of love and recognition is not going to be so simple, as Austen shows us by involving Elizabeth with not just one but three different men; three different situations for the true self, or the false self, to be tried. Mr. Collins, Mr. Wickham, Mr. Darcy.

Mr. Collins's ludicrous proposal to Elizabeth is such a beloved scene, I think, because it's such an easy victory. His treatment of her as an object is a caricature of masculine tendencies. To her emphatic refusal of his pontificating offers, he responds, "You are uniformly charming!" (p. 150) Mr. Collins, however, as Jane Austen informs us in her first mention of him, "was not a sensible man." It doesn't take much to resist these questionable charms. Elizabeth vexes her mother and pleases her father in the process, a situation she is used to; it reinforces the status quo of her emotional life. We, in turn, laugh heartily at the proposal scene, because it doesn't affect us much, either.

The matter of Mr. Wickham is more difficult. He shows up on the scene in a dashing uniform, with a great deal of easygoing small talk, and, to Elizabeth, an attractive readiness to say nasty things about Mr. Darcy. Elizabeth finds his revelations about Darcy's wickedness delightful, and she goes away smitten:

"Whatever he said, was said well; and whatever he did, done gracefully. Elizabeth went away with her head full of him." (p. 127)

All readers, I have discovered, do not respond to this part of the novel in the same way. Some people are not won over by Mr. Darcy, that avowedly stiff and proud man, just because he notices the beautiful expression in Elizabeth's eyes. They are irritated by her continual interactions with him. Mr. Wickham seems like the right suitor. Not to me; not ever, as far as I can remember. It's Wickham who is more than annoying, really: scary. I don't want her liking him; I don't want him in the book. I want her to start to like Darcy!

With Wickham, Austen is testing the patriarchal romance premise of love at first sight. This relationship is based upon superficialities, and Elizabeth, as the novel begins, is all too good at that. She prefers it, in fact. Always trying to protect her private, hidden, true self, she is not particularly interested in coming into contact with anybody else's. She likes to show off with her quick judgments. She's clever, but she isn't wise. Wickham suits her to a T, and that makes me extremely uncomfortable.

At the same time, Elizabeth is engaging in an association with Mr. Darcy: they meet, and they fight. They meet frequently, and their disagreements go on for pages. Their interactions are intense, clever, and somehow satisfying to both parties. They argue about everything, but most of all, they argue about who they are.

> "Mr. Darcy is not to be laughed at!" cried Elizabeth. "That is an uncommon advantage, and uncommon I hope it will continue, for it would be a great loss to *me* to have many such acquaintances. I dearly love a laugh."
>
> "Miss Bingley," said he, "has given me credit for more than can be. The wisest and best of men, nay, the wisest and best of

their actions, may be rendered ridiculous by a person whose first object in life is a joke."

"Certainly," replied Elizabeth—"there are such people, but I hope I am not one of *them*. I hope I never ridicule what is wise or good. Follies and nonsense, whims and inconsistencies *do* divert me, I own, and I laugh at them whenever I can.—But these, I suppose, are precisely what you are without."

"Perhaps that is not possible for anyone. But it has been the study of my life to avoid those weaknesses which often expose a strong understanding to ridicule."

"Such as vanity and pride."

"Yes, vanity is a weakness indeed. But pride—where there is real superiority of mind, pride will always be under good regulation."

Elizabeth turned away to hide a smile. (p. 102)

Reading these scenes is exhilarating. First, of course, because Elizabeth shines in them. She is bright and clever, she takes him on again and again, challenging what she perceives to be his arrogant power. Good for her! But equally important is the fact that he won't let her get away with it. He gives back as good as he gets, so that *Elizabeth* is challenged for the first time in her life. Used to the easy victories that her hasty truisms have accorded her, she is understandably irritated. And so she tries again, and harder. In the course of such verbal give-and-take, the superficial cleverness is broken down, so that Elizabeth and Darcy come closer and closer to genuine knowledge and actual intimacy.

Although their talk is all about their differences, what it reveals is their similarities. They are equally intelligent, equally articulate, and, it should be added, equally proud and prejudiced. For all the surface excitement and danger in their exchanges (lending itself to a martial vocabulary of sallies, barbs, arrows, battle), there is an underlying feeling of contentment, satisfaction, enjoyment, that derives from the mutual recognition taking place. This is the facilitating environment that the mother establishes for her infant. The self of the infant is able to grow in this environment of closeness, identification, dependence and differentiation. Here is the matching or attunement behavior that psychologists describe in mother-infant interaction. Affect and energy consistently reinforce one another, intensifying each time enough to be stimulating but not so much as to be overwhelming, stifling, or hurtful. I recall Daniel Stern's words: "equally excited, joyful, and intense."

In these long and recurrent scenes, there is pleasure and recognition both for Elizabeth and for me. I love reading them, because she is getting to do, and to be, what I want for myself. This includes the shining, but it also includes the challenge. Attunement between the two of them promotes both feelings. For when someone takes you seriously enough to confront you on your own terms, you know that you are real, that you are valued. The result is thrilling.

To call these exchanges maternal seems to be leaving out their sexual dimension. Certainly they are arousing, stimulating. But of course, so is the mother-infant bond. It can be sensual without being literally sexual. The animosity that the couple display toward one another could well be a manifestation of the energy generated by sexual attraction. Where there's smoke, there's fire, and all that. Despite herself (her false self), Elizabeth is clearly attracted to the very man she has vowed to hate. She's attracted because he sees her true self, and she's angry because he sees it. If he knows it's there, she's vulnerable: he can hurt her; he can leave her. At the same time, the author has made it clear to him exactly how attractive she is; he is "caught" by her. Right now the eroticism is latent, a potential that bespeaks possibility. In a romance novel the mother-child bond will be transformed with the happy ending into a mature sexual relationship. Now we as readers experience the promise of such a resolution.

The climax, as it were, of all of this heady interaction is the most famous, most important scene in the novel: when Darcy proposes to Elizabeth and she roundly rejects him. It's telling that this is the crucial scene and not the other proposal, at the end of the novel, when she accepts him. I think this is because it brings to a head some of the most powerful feelings associated with self-development.

"In vain have I struggled," begins Mr. Darcy. "It will not do. My feelings will not be repressed. You must allow me to tell you how ardently I admire and love you." Grudgingly, Mr. Darcy professes love for her, despite, he tells her, his sense of her inferiority. He concludes by representing to her "the strength of that attachment which, in spite of all his endeavors, he had found it impossible to conquer." (p. 221) Mr. Darcy is certainly a little confused right now at his passion, especially since these considerable changes in his responses and behavior owe more to authorial intervention than to his usual inclinations. Elizabeth is likewise confused, and she promptly refuses him:

> "In such cases as this, it is, I believe, the established mode to express a sense of obligation for the sentiments avowed, however unequally they may be returned. It is natural that obligation should be felt, and if I could *feel* gratitude, I would now thank you. But I cannot—I have never deserved your good opinion, and you have certainly bestowed it most unwillingly. I am sorry to have occasioned pain to any one. It has been unconsciously done, however, and I hope will be of short duration. The feelings which, you tell me, have long prevented the acknowledgement of your regard, can have little difficulty in overcoming it after this explanation." (pp. 221–22)

A smart-aleck girl reader cannot help but respond with a few cheers. Good for Elizabeth! The man has insulted her, and the last thing she is going to do is agree to *marry* him, just because he's rich and powerful and she is not.

Yes, but this isn't the same thing as turning down stupid Mr. Collins. Elizabeth has just said no, in the most irrefutable way, to the man who truly loves her. My hurrahs are quickly buried beneath dismay, fear, and considerable distress. "Don't *do* this," I cry to her, but she can't hear me and goes on accusing him, berating him, insulting him. She tells him she knew he was arrogant, conceited, and selfish from the moment she met him. She tells him her dislike of him is immovable: "I had not known you a month before I felt you were the last man in the world whom I could ever be prevailed on to marry." (p. 224)

At this moment there is a real gap in me between my intellectual and my emotional response. My mind tells me that Elizabeth's saying no is important, the other side of her experience of the facilitating environment discussed by Winnicott. The feeling of sameness that their bond has already engendered needs to provoke the necessary differentiation, the not-me as well as the me. And it is because he loves her that she can tell him no, can delineate their differences. The security is there, whether she is consciously aware of it or not. This is an important moment in the developmental process, but it is far from the end of it, which is signified by marriage. Neither person is ready for marriage at this point. Elizabeth is just beginning to establish a self, and the same goes for Darcy, whose pride and prejudice are after all as strong as his love. They both have a long way to go—obviously, because this scene takes place about halfway into the novel.

What I *feel*, however, is fear—because her hasty anger has driven him away; fear of abandonment, because I loved him, even if she didn't know she did. Fear usually keeps me from expressing such anger, because I am sure that if I did, the person would never come back. It doesn't enter my mind that he could love her enough not to go away. That sort of trust is beyond me.

And yet, to pick up the novel and go on reading, in the face of these feelings, is already an act of faith that shows that Austen has gotten somewhere with me as well as with Elizabeth. After all, I have been known to turn off the TV, distressed by too many misunderstandings in so-called comedies. I certainly don't finish books if, for whatever reason, I get too uncomfortable in them. Thus, if we consider that Austen is operating as my mother as well as Elizabeth's, she has been able to win my trust. I'm certainly not placid, convinced that things will work out and the happy ending is inevitable. But I am willing to try, and this is because Austen wants me to, offering me more novel if I will just turn the page.

I do, and Darcy hands Elizabeth a letter in which he tells her he has no intentions of renewing his offer of marriage, but he does want to justify his conduct, his character. Even I know there's hope now. I don't know how things can be resolved, but he is, glory be, still *there.*

Winnicott has a great deal to say about the ability of the mother to survive the attempts of the infant to "destroy" her in anger. The baby needs to do so in order to understand that she did not create the object—the mother—but that the object has existence in the real world. But of course, contingent upon this development is the object's capacity to survive destruction. A good mother possesses this capacity. She is "essentially adaptive because of love," says Winnicott, and she has established the essential confidence related to her dependability that is needed before any further attempt to "use" the object can take place. It is only because this environment *has* been established that the infant can try to destroy the mother with anger. It is a necessary form of establishing the object's reality outside of the self and must be undertaken so that the object can be used.

Winnicott's ideas help explain not only what Austen is up to here but how I now understand my own feelings. He describes a fear of annihilation that is the response of an infant who has not experienced the prerequisite recognition and holding environment. My own feelings, often "out of proportion" to a situation, can be related to this primitive response. On the contrary, Elizabeth's reaction to Darcy is exactly appropriate in an infant for whom such a facilitating environment has been established. Her experience helps me, it must be emphasized, because I can undergo something along with her that may be new to me. When I perceive Darcy not to have *gone away*, I am encountering this possibility, perhaps for the first time, and more important, I encounter it in a context where it can make sense.

Now Elizabeth as heroine and I as reader are clearly entering a new stage. This is what Winnicott calls "transitional object relating," a space for negotiating the tricky relationship between internal and external reality. The mother now needs to let the infant know that she is not the child's own personal creation, although she remains dependably loving and nurturing. She has a reality of her own, even as, at the same time, she "belongs" to the infant. This is why she is "transitional," even as the space for this activity is likewise transitional, and safe, because it is still the maternal environment, not the outside world.

In *Pride and Prejudice*, Mr. Darcy, the mother, and symbols for him—for example, his house, Pemberley—act as transitional objects. From the moment when Elizabeth reads his letter, in which he explains his conduct to her, she begins to reevaluate the difference between how she had imagined him and how he is being revealed to her. She reads and rereads; she places what she learns up against the way she remembers it, against the way *she* interpreted it, and after this long bout with a new kind of self-consciousness, she concludes, "Till this moment I never knew myself." (p. 237)

Not long afterwards she finds herself, on a trip to Derbyshire with her aunt and uncle, visiting a famous local landmark. It is none other than Mr. Darcy's palatial Pemberley—a large, handsome, stone building on rising ground, backed by woody hills:

> ... and in front, a stream of some natural importance was swelled into greater, but without any artificial appearance. Its banks were neither formal, nor falsely adorned. Elizabeth was delighted. She had never seen a place for which nature had done more, or where natural beauty had been so little counteracted by an awkward taste ... at that moment she felt, that to be mistress of Pemberley might be something! (p. 267)

What Elizabeth sees is beauty and good taste that is based in what is natural, not artificial. Like the man himself, she learns when the housekeeper, talking about Darcy's portrait hanging in the hall, tells her what a sweet-tempered and generous-hearted person he is. "In what an amiable light does this place him!" thinks Elizabeth. "As she stood before the canvas, on which he was represented, and fixed his eyes upon herself, she thought of his regard with a deeper sentiment of gratitude than it had ever raised before; she remembered its warmth, and softened its impropriety of expression." (pp. 271–72)

When Mr. Darcy shows up suddenly, in the flesh—on the very same page—Elizabeth is now ready to look at him for what is really the first time. The blinders of her narcissistic creation of the world around her are gone, and she begins to look and see what might be there. "Never in her life had she seen his manners so little dignified, never had he spoken with such gentleness as on this unexpected meeting." (p. 273) Afterwards, for the first time ever we watch Elizabeth desiring to go beyond the surfaces: "She longed to know what at that moment was passing through his mind; in what manner he thought of her, and whether, in defiance of everything, she was still dear to him." (p. 274)

Reading, I am as much delighted by his behavior as by hers. He is back, he is clearly loving, and she is moving toward him. And I am learning. For the changes in Elizabeth are meticulously and delicately documented, so that the dawning of real love in her is shown to be a process very different from the love-at-first-sight scenario that I for one had been taught, from all those songs and movies and novels, to aspire toward.

> She certainly did not hate him. No; hatred had vanished long ago, and she had almost as long been ashamed of ever feeling a dislike against him, that could be so called. The respect created by the conviction of his valuable qualities, though at first unwillingly admitted, had for some time ceased to be repugnant to her feelings; and it was now heightened into somewhat of a friendlier nature, by the testimony so highly in his favour, and bringing forward his disposition in so amiable a light, which yesterday had produced. But above all, above respect and esteem, there was a motive within her of good will which could not be overlooked. It was gratitude. Gratitude, not merely for having once loved her but for loving her still well enough, to forgive all the petulance and acrimony of her manner in rejecting him and all the unjust accusations accompanying her rejection.

Rather than avoiding her as his greatest enemy, he is seeking her out, she thinks, and making himself pleasant to her friends, even introducing her to his sister.

> Such a change in a man of so much pride, excited not only astonishment but gratitude—for to love, ardent love, it must be attributed; and as such its impression on her was of a sort to

be encouraged, as by no means unpleasing, though it could not be exactly defined. She respected, she esteemed, she was grateful to him, she felt a real interest in his welfare; and she only wanted to know how far she wished that welfare to depend upon herself, and how far it would be for the happiness of both that she should employ the power, which her fancy told her she still possessed, of bringing on the renewal of his addresses. (pp. 284–85)

Gratitude! True love and gratitude? What can Austen mean? After all this, are we back to: "He's powerful and rich and I'm weak and poor, so I should be *grateful*"? Not at all. We have moved from surfaces to depths, from defense to openness. Gratitude is a response to care, not simply to attraction. Gratitude marks a process from appreciation to obligation—that is, from responsiveness to agency. Austen is focusing on gratitude as the site for the sort of true love that interests her, a love that develops out of a situation of care. It is a powerful challenge to the romantic ideas we inherit in our culture.

But gratitude takes some getting used to. I am deeply committed at this moment to Elizabeth's loving Darcy; I am pushing her along every step of her recognition of this love. And at the same time, I have not been brought up for true love to happen like this. So I am in an interesting conflict here. To get what I want—her to love him—I need to absorb this new way of thinking, to understand that Darcy and Elizabeth are doing something very different from my wildest fantasies—for myself.

And yet this process is a way to arrive at those fantasies—the love and cherishing for which I yearn. Elizabeth, feeling gratitude, begins to encourage Darcy in their brief meetings. And suddenly, there they are, in the middle of a tender and gratifying moment that is more emotional than anything they have ever experienced together. The scene in which Mr. Darcy comes upon

Elizabeth reading a letter from her sister Jane, telling her of her younger sister Lydia's elopement with none other than the sleazy Mr. Wickham, is no longer about wit and cleverness. It is about strong feeling.

> Her pale face and impetuous manner made him start, and before he could recover himself enough to speak, she, in whose mind every idea was superseded by Lydia's situation, hastily exclaimed, "I beg your pardon, but I must leave you. I must find Mr. Gardiner this moment . . . I have not an instant to lose."
>
> "Good God! What is the matter?" cried he, with more feeling than politeness; then recollecting himself, "I will not detain you a minute, but let me, or let the servant, go after Mr. and Mrs. Gardiner. You are not well enough;—you cannot go yourself."
>
> Elizabeth hesitated, but her knees trembled under her.

Elizabeth sends a servant, and the scene continues:

> . . . she sat down, unable to support herself, and looking so miserably ill, that it was impossible for Darcy to leave her, or to refrain from saying, in a tone of gentleness and commiseration, "Let me call your maid. Is there nothing you could take, to give you present relief?—A glass of wine;—shall I get you one?—You are very ill."

She then bursts into tears; he speaks his concern and then waits "in compassionate silence."

Finally she tells him the terrible news. He responds by pacing gloomily up and down the room. She thinks he is thinking about her embarrassing and now disgraced family and disliking her accordingly. And so the moment is "exactly calculated to make her understand her own wishes; and never had she so honestly felt that she could have loved him, as now, when all love must be in vain" (pp. 293–95).

Elizabeth discovers her love for him because she thinks she has just lost it, yes, but also because he has been overtly tender, empathetic, and deeply feeling at a moment when she is utterly vulnerable. With all of her carefully constructed defenses down, she experiences not attack, not hurt but care. Of course she knows she loves him!

I am the kind of person who never lets herself get sick but secretly yearns to have a fever, be forced to bed, clearly qualifying for some nursing. I desperately want to be vulnerable and cared for, but I am afraid of being denied if I should ask for it. I fantasize situations when it will just come, of its own accord. Naturally, I respond powerfully to Elizabeth's weakness here, and to its results. I can feel her buckling knees, his tender responses.

It's true, they are forced to part, just at this moment. Her misunderstanding again causes readerly apprehension. But it's very different from what I felt after she rejects his proposal. I just want to see what will happen to bring them together again, and my main worry is about how long it will take. In fact, Austen causes them to part because they have just entered a third stage of the developmental process, necessary so that real maturity can occur. Even as Elizabeth's prevailing concern for her sister actually initiates the separation (she sends Darcy from the room, she returns to her home at Longbourn), so we discover later that Darcy uses the time to help the erring couple secretly. Although Elizabeth recognizes just how harmful has been "the mischief of neglect and mistaken indulgence towards such a girl," the bad parenting all of her sisters have received, she responds to her sister's foolish conduct not so much with disapprobation as with love and concern. She turns toward "society" in the form of her family, profoundly imperfect as they are, because the mature adult is as much responsible for what Winnicott terms "the maintenance or the modification of society" as for her own self; because maturity demands care for both the self and the world beyond the self. Likewise, Darcy's financial intervention on behalf of the silly sister of the woman he loves and the man who has wronged him in important ways, including having tried to seduce his own sister, represents that same responsibility.

Austen concludes her description of Elizabeth's sudden comprehension of her love for Darcy with some words to me, the reader:

> If gratitude and esteem are good foundations of affection, Elizabeth's change of sentiment will be neither improbable nor faulty. But if otherwise, if the regard springing from such sources is unreasonable or unnatural, in comparison of what is so often described as arising on a first interview with its object, and even before two words have been exchanged, nothing can be said in her defense, except that she had given somewhat of a trial to the latter method, in her partiality for Wickham, and that its ill-success might perhaps authorize her to seek the other less interesting mode of attachment. (p. 296)

I am glad she has reminded me about gratitude. Now I don't question it, not at all. I know what it means now, and I feel it too.

In the final movement of *Pride and Prejudice,* the problem of the Lydia-Wickham alliance is solved as best it can be when marriage is the only solution available, a marriage that cannot possibly be happy or healthy. In its aftermath, Mr. Darcy and his friend Mr. Bingley once again come calling on the Bennet sisters, Elizabeth and Jane. Finally we get to the second proposal, and finally Elizabeth gets to accept.

The happiness which this reply produced, was such as he had probably never felt before; and he expressed himself on the occasion as sensibly and as warmly as a man violently in love can be supposed to do. Had Elizabeth been able to encounter his eye, she might have seen how well the expression of heart-felt delight, diffused over his face, became him; but though she could not look, she could listen, and he told her of feelings, which in proving of what importance she was to him, made his affection every moment more valuable. (p. 375)

If she can't look at him, I can, and what I see makes me thoroughly happy. My pleasure is only enhanced when the two go step-by-step through their relationship, explaining, exclaiming, and generally arriving at a mutually satisfying understanding of how they have come to mean so very much to one another. Their conversation indicates that theirs is at last the kind of relationship that true love according to Austen produces: mutual, unconditional, and nurturing. In this felicitous spirit we swiftly arrive at the happiest of endings, made particularly gratifying not only because Elizabeth and Darcy are living happily ever after but also because their union is notable for the care they take of others: Jane and Mr. Bingley, the rest of her family, and most particularly, his young sister, Georgiana, who comes to live with them. Badly parented themselves, they have been given the gift of self-development by their author, and now a quiet revolution is in process, in which they as parents will be able to nurture properly, the first time around.

As for me, I close the book with a happy sigh. Elizabeth is well loved and loves well; I feel her achievement. I am not Elizabeth, but I have gone through all that she has, and I understand myself and my hopes a little better for having done so. More important still, the voice and the spirit of Austen herself pervade these final chapters, as she dispenses fates to all the characters and generally lets me see how much her world this all is. Once she even speaks in the first person, a rare moment in an Austen novel. I know she is talking to me, and I am grateful for her love and guidance throughout the course of my reading.

But when I close the book and sit there for a moment enjoying my pleasure before I get up and rejoin the world, I discover another little feeling lurking in the background. It is sadness—because it is over. I have to stop being in Austen's world and having her as my mother. And I don't want just a memory; I want the real thing. True love is mutual, unconditional—and forever. I'm not too good at "introjecting" it. When the one I love isn't nearby, I have trouble feeling the forever. So yes, I need a book. I won't wait long, in the happy glow of Elizabeth and Darcy's marriage, before I start a new one. If not Austen, then, if I'm lucky, someone like her.

✿

Back when I was a teenager, Elswyth Thane fit the bill. I read all her novels, and I especially loved her Williamsburg Series, a family saga that begins in Revolutionary War Virginia and goes up to World War II. But my favorite was a little novel called *Tryst*, written in 1939, which I read and reread throughout my girlhood. My memories of it are selective but clear. The upstairs room in an English country house: tweedy, comfortable, filled with books. Sabrina: all those sensitive, unloved, bookish, gawky girls rolled into one. Hilary, whom I imagine as a cross between Leslie Howard and Gregory Peck, only he's a ghost, so no one can really see him. And the love: the tender, total, beautiful love they share in the secret room. So what if he is a ghost? The love is completely real.

I like ghost stories, I always have. But a certain kind of ghost story, one without horror or gore. No Stephen King for me. But think of *Berkeley Square, Portrait of Jenny, The Ghost and Mrs.*

50

Muir, and of course, *Wuthering Heights.* Ghost love stories, in which people go back through centuries to find their true loves—or stay more or less in this world after they have died in order to love someone. True love is forever, so where do time, and death, fit in? It helps to believe that this world is not the only one, and that time is, well, negotiable. If you are glad at the end of *Wuthering Heights* when Heathcliff dies and is finally reunited with Catherine, if you know they are together at last, if you haven't a qualm or a scruple, then ghost love stories are for you. The need for true love is stronger than the need to follow the mandates of science—at least for a person like me.

What I am remembering is the power of the love in these stories, but I am not remembering its iffyness. Certainly iffy because the lovers never get to have proper sex. That part never bothered me, because I always cared about the feeling more than the physical exercise. But rereading *Tryst* makes me see that the heroine pays other costs for getting a ghost lover than just not being able to have an orgasm. Costs that have to do with the maternal part of the lover's role. Ghosts can provide the recognition, the support and nurture that are the mother's initial task; but when it comes to the negotiation between internal and external, subjective and objective, they're on shaky ground. Literally, for as ghosts they cannot and do not live in anything recognizably "external." What happens to the developmental process if it is cut off in midstream? How can a ghost's lover grow up?

The novel begins with a tantalizing scene: "Sabrina had never picked a lock in her life, but it was done every day in books." Sabrina—no introduction, no explanation—picking a lock to the door of a forbidden room, following the model that books have given her. She steps across the threshold and closes the door, shutting herself inside. Forbidden rooms are always exciting; girls defiant enough to pick locks always appeal to me.

Yes, I discover right away as the flashbacks begin, this is my kind of book, my kind of heroine. Sabrina is around eighteen. Her mother is dead, her father is a professor who doesn't like women and finds his child boring. She has been raised by an aunt who neither loves nor understands her. She is "sensitive, self-contained, old for her years" (p. 7) and a voracious reader. Her aunt's one attempt to send her to a boarding school had been a disaster. She did not fit in: "she was the problem-child for all time of that very sane and unimaginative school" (p. 8).

Her father has rented, sight unseen, a house in the country, near a site where he is doing research. As their car draws closer to the house, Nuns Farthing, Sabrina feels a peculiar sensation of excitement and joy.

> This was a day she had been coming towards all her life. It would bring the fulfillment of some tremendous, half-dreamed desire. Ugliness and vague fears and unaccountable uncertainty had been left behind, and just ahead, at the end of this day's journey, some still inconceivable enchantment was waiting at the house called Nuns Farthing. I'm coming home, I'm coming home, she told herself over and over, and had to let it go at that. (pp. 12–13)

When her father decides to stop for tea before reaching the house, she is curiously at ease. "Whatever it was had been waiting for her for a long time, and would still be there when she came," she thinks. (p. 14)

What "it" is I, of course, do not know; I don't even try to know or to figure it out. I am so pleased with the words I have been given—"tremendous, half-dreamed desire," "enchantment . . . waiting" for her, and of course, "home"—that I don't have to know exactly. We are in my ballpark. My particular set of needs is being engaged, and I too, like Sabrina, can actually enjoy waiting to find out what it is.

It turns out to be first the house and an old-fashioned bed-room (" 'This is it,' she said simply, and for some childish reason she could not understand there was a lump in her throat and she wanted to cry" [p. 15]), and then, the discovery of the mysterious locked room. The housekeeper says that the room belongs to someone who used to live at Nuns Farthing, that it's "got his books there, mostly—and the sort of odds and ends a man collects." "Books?" asks Sabrina, and the die is cast. Naturally Sabrina wonders about the person whose room remained locked and whose things were not touched. Naturally she picks the lock—to find home.

Home is a comfortable, cozy room with well-worn furnishings and many books. "There were favorites of her own in his library, and hundreds of unknowns she meant to read. If he liked an author at all, he apparently never rested till he had got hold of everything that had ever been printed by him or her." (p. 23) The room becomes Sabrina's "secret sanctuary."

> Sometimes it almost seemed as though she knew its owner too. Sometimes it was almost as though he himself was there in the room—waiting for her to come back to him. His dominant masculine personality which had put its imprint on his room was a thing almost tangible, as real as the persistent odor of good tobacco which clung about the worn pipe he had left behind on the desk. (pp. 22–23)

Soon Sabrina is doing more than reading his books. She is searching the room for clues to the personality "which still pervaded the atmosphere like inaudible music." Now he is just a "vague tweed shape, a nice voice, and quiet laughter" (p. 26). She wants the rest of him; she awaits his return.

Masculine *and* sensitive: a reader, his room a home to a girl who has never had a home, never known parental love. Whoever this mysterious man is, he has already given this emotionally orphaned girl, by way of his room and his books, more nurture than she has ever before experienced. If she is the perfect romance heroine, he is clearly the perfect romance hero. But who *is* he? And *where* is he? We are to find out before Sabrina does.

His name is Hilary Shenstone. He is on a mission for the Home Office in India. Part II of the novel switches to Hilary, who has been for several months experiencing a nagging need to return home. Why, he cannot fathom. "Half hunch, half dream, the thing would not down." (p. 37) Against his will, he had allowed himself to be talked out of his hunch by a high commissioner with an impossible job to be done. "The impossible always appealed to Hilary because people looked so silly when he did it after all." And so, for the first time in his life, Hilary had turned his back on a hunch, "because it said 'Go home!' and India said 'Go on!' " Hilary should have listened. What we witness next is his death, out there in the desert, and as he dies he cries, "It's hard to know how to say it—but—oh, God, if I've earned heaven when I die, let me have England first—let me have England *instead*—" (p. 45)

Hilary dies on June 5, 1938. On that same day—in the following chapter—Sabrina is in the room, exploring the bedroom beyond the desk, as she had never done before. Suddenly, "a long shiver ran through her, and uneasiness like a cold draught pervaded the room" (p. 50). The room seems different, empty and strange, no longer safe and cherishing. Sabrina is frightened and ill. The doctor says it is a slight chill on the liver and leaves some little pills. I know what has happened, of course. I know that she has felt Hilary's death. Up to this point in the story, I am assuming that he will come back to his room, and there she will be, waiting for him. He is dead now, and the story has barely begun. Clearly, it's their story—so, what can happen next?

Next comes that long sequence familiar to ghost story lovers, in which the person discovers that he is a ghost. It takes time for Hilary, finding himself in London, deciding to spend the night at his club, to find out that no one can see or hear him, that for all practical purposes, he isn't there. It takes time for him to decide what to do about it in general, then how to manage the technical matters, like entering rooms, sleeping in beds. I admit to impatience. I want him to get to Nuns Farthing, the sooner the better; but Thane wants him to arrive there with a certain amount of knowledge and expertise. Especially, she wants him to observe his family—brother, mother, and fiancée Alice—and discover painfully some truths that have been hidden from him. First, that George is his mother's favorite. Second, that his mother was not happy with his father and that Hilary is just like his father. And third, that George loves Alice, who is not as faithful to him as he had liked to think. Even before the fateful telegram arrives, George, spurred on by his mother, has proposed to Alice and been more or less accepted. The news of Hilary's death is not so sad for his next-of-kin. Whatever unfinished business Hilary has, and he keeps feeling the sense of it nagging at him, it is not with these people. And so at last he comes to his favorite place, his childhood home, Nuns Farthing.

"So you've come back at last," says the housekeeper: "I can't see you, Master Hilary, but I know you're there. I've felt you homing ever since nightfall." (pp. 122–23) And Hilary is comforted. "Undemonstrative, inarticulate, indestructible, their strange friendship stretched back through the whole length of his memory, and never once had she let him down." (p. 122) In this way we know that Nuns Farthing is home to him—the house and the housekeeper rather than his literal family. But what about Sabrina? Where will she fit into his homecoming? The answer is not far away. Only a page later, he has observed with displeasure her aunt and father on the stairs and has come to Sabrina's room, where she is sleeping, the result of the doctor's little pills. "Obedient to some irresistible necessity, careless of consequences, he turned the knob noiselessly and went in."

A night-light burned on the table by the bed, where a girl-child lay asleep, her lashes dark against pale cheeks, her fine golden brows a little drawn, her wide sweet mouth tightly closed, as though even in slumber she was beset by some unchildlike worry. He saw by the length of her, from the square, determined chin to the small mound made by her feet, that she must be well into her teens, for all the delicacy of the bare arm flung above her head, and the natural silk of her fair hair.

Fascinated, soothed, and possessed by a deep contentment he had never known before, he hung over the bed watching her breath come and go as she slept. Infinitely helpless she looked to him—defenseless, troubled, and pitiably young—Sabrina, the invalid, who had gone off to sleep so nicely.

And that futile woman with the dog, and the irate old man in the study doorway—were they all she had to look after her, and why hadn't they got at whatever it was that oppressed her and wiped it out? Why wasn't somebody sitting with her, if she was ill? Suppose she woke alone and was frightened. Suppose she called out. No one could hear . . .

In her sleep she stirred and smiled, and groped with one thin hand for his, where it rested on the pillow as he bent above her. Incredulously he felt the warmth of her clinging fingers. But how could that be, when he could feel neither hunger nor fatigue . . . Journey's end . . .

He knelt beside the bed, her warm fingers cradled in his.

(pp. 125–26)

This is the moment that we remember from *Pride and Prejudice*—when the hero looks at the heroine and *recognizes* her, the wonderful "Oh, it's you!" gaze. This version has elements that are especially compelling for me. Hilary Shenstone is in his thirties; Sabrina, as Hilary's look at her so clearly indicates, is at once childlike and nubile. She is certainly much, much younger than he is, her youth underlined by her defenselessness and innocence. Clearly, his response to her is parental. But his protective, nurturing concern, his idea that someone should sit by her bed and be there in case she should call out, seems less "father" than "mother," the maternal care that Hilary notices is lacking, even as he moves in to take its place.

At the same time, however, his regard is sexual, even as he is aware that she is not really a child. The dark lashes against pale cheeks, the wide sweet mouth, the bare arm flung above her head, all attest to her physical attraction for him. The point is not that this is one thing or the other, mother or lover, but that it is both. My need as an adolescent girl was for the mother I had always wanted, the lover I had waited for, all together in one. It takes Elizabeth Bennet more than half of her book to allow herself to be vulnerable, so well has she protected her real self, but Sabrina is that self incarnate. I see her as my own hidden self, which he, the hero, has recognized and desired. When Hilary cradles Sabrina's warm fingers in his, the touch is so incredibly romantic because it is so obviously both maternal and sensual.

If Hilary's response is erotic, his version of eroticism is particularly in line with my fantasies. "Fascinated, soothed, and possessed by a deep contentment he had never known before": sex for him means coming home—"Journey's end," is how he puts it. Intimacy, peace, safety, *home*—not danger, wildness, combat. Hilary loves in the way many women want a man to love, which is not the same thing as the way many men do love. Hilary loves the way a mother would.

At this moment, I am both satisfied and excited. He has come home to her; he is home for her. The little matter that he is dead doesn't seem all that important, not when the love is exactly as I desire it. Besides, he's there in every respect but bodily. I am certain that they will be able to love one another, even if I'm not quite sure how.

Discovery, delight, affirmation: so the facilitating environment is formed. When Sabrina returns to the room the next day with the housekeeper's blessings (she thinks she has had a dream that he has returned) and all feels well again, her search to know him becomes more effective, for he is helping her. She speaks, he answers, and although she cannot exactly hear him, he guides her—to his name in the flyleaf of *Puck of Pook's Hill.* "To darling Hilary on his 12th birthday, with fondest love from his Auntie Dot. September 6, 1916." " 'Why, that's it! I've found you!' cries Sabrina with triumph and excitement." Then:

> *"You heard me!"* he marvelled. *"You must have heard me—in a way. I can get through to you. Perhaps with practice I can make you know all the things I want to tell you—because you found your way to me here. It's rather—sobering—to me."* (p. 144)

As Sabrina settles in to read the book, Hilary sits, knowing the book so well that he can almost follow her progress through the story. And he thinks about the two of them, about what would have happened if he had come home, alive; how they would have met:

> . . . those clear gray eyes, that wide, engaging smile, the warm little fingers—her implicit confidence in the man who belonged to this room . . . He would have had to exercise patience—she was so young—but she was his, and he liked to think he would not have been clumsy, or hurried her . . . Obviously, whenever, however, he came, he was to find her here waiting for him. But it oughtn't to be like this. Something had

gone wrong, out there on the Frontier . . . It was never meant
to be like this . . . (p. 144)

The next step in the process of establishing this particular facilitating environment is for Sabrina to discover that she is not waiting for Hilary to return, but that he is dead. Dead—and there, a
ghostly presence, in the room. This is accomplished by a visit
from George, Hilary's brother. Her grief at the news is finally
mitigated when she seeks the comfort of the locked room and
discovers unmistakable signs of his presence. Here their first real
love scene occurs.

> "Hilary—" she whispered . . . "Where are you? I can't see
> you—I can't hear you—but I know you're here in this room.
> I've felt it before and—and now I know. And I'm glad. But
> how do I find you?"
> *"You can't,"* he said, standing still by the mantelpiece,
> watching her. *"Not yet."*
> "Hilary—" (From where he stood half way across the room
> he could see the tiny pulse which beat in her thin throat.)
> "Hilary—who are you?"
> *"I am the man you would have married, if things hadn't gone
> wrong,"* he told her simply, knowing it now himself with diz-
> zying certainty.
> But her eyes went past him and her next words took no no-
> tice of his.
> "Can't you talk to me?" she begged, and it seemed the most
> reasonable request, with only the sentient air of that quiet
> room between them.
> *"Evidently not yet,"* he said, and wondered why, when they
> were already so close.
> "Hilary. I'm afraid!"
> *"Not of me."*

"I'm afraid of living—if you're dead. They'll always try to separate us."

"They can't do that. Nothing can."

"Oh, why didn't you come home as I planned it! I'd have felt so safe with you, whatever happened!"

"I meant to come. Something slipped—a matter of weeks—the timing went wrong."

"What did you say, Hilary—say it again—I nearly heard—"

"Don't try, my darling. I'll wait."

"Wait for me, Hilary! Don't ever go away!"

"I'll be here—always," he promised. (pp. 176–77)

The fact is, I always cry when I read this scene. I did then, and I do now. And my tears have to do both with the unconditional nature of his love for her—*"I'll be here always"*—and with the impossibility of consummating that love. At this moment in *Tryst,* the utter necessity of the fantasy and the fact that it *is* a fantasy come together irrevocably. The fact that Hilary is a ghost and not a flesh-and-blood person emphasizes the element of fantasy in the idea of a maternal male lover—in my moments of sober lucidity, I do know that. Even as I know that when Jane Austen turns Mr. Darcy into a maternal presence, that too is fantasy. But my need for love of just this kind is no fantasy, but an abiding reality. This scene wrings my heart because Sabrina is getting such love, but not fully, not "really."

We see this paradox in what happens next: "With a reckless gasp of decision she started forward, one questioning hand outstretched— *'Don't,'* said Hilary firmly, without moving. *'Don't try to touch me.'* " (p. 179) She is apologetic; she is content enough to be sure that he is there. When the housekeeper, Mrs. Pilton, encounters her a few minutes later, she sees Sabrina's radiant smile: "Like a bride, darted through the housekeeper's mind.

Like a bride on her way from the altar." (p. 180) Bride? Yes and no.

Certainly the intimacy between them, the forming of the facilitating environment, increases. Up in the secret room she keeps house for him; he leaves books off the shelf, and she reads them. He even begins to rummage out things she would never have found for herself that he wants her to see, so that she can begin to piece together his life, "as she had once dreamed that he would reveal it to her if he returned" (p. 201).

Then a shift occurs. One day she has a cold and does not come. Instead, he goes to her room. There she is, reading on her bed in a pink dressing gown. She reacts to her awareness of his presence by "an instinctive clutch at the folds of the dressing gown which fell open across her breast" (p. 208). Recognizing then that he is there, she laughs and invites him in. Hilary, responding to her dawning sexuality, is "enthralled." During their tea party, Sabrina and Hilary both speculate about the next stage: what might happen after the facilitating maternal environment has been established.

Sabrina thinks about books—about how in them she had always sought "something to steer by, trying to find clues to the puzzle of living . . . She had a touching faith in the printed word. These people who wrote must know. These things must be so" (p. 211). Sabrina has clearly been using books to be parented—not a peculiar thing to do, as I have been arguing. Then, upon coming to Nuns Farthing, she had grown less confused: "Here was a life one could cope with . . . Here, tomorrow would be like yesterday, and confidence unfolded like a flower in the sun." Yes, she worries about men and marriage, and children—and divorce. But Hilary would know the answers, she thinks. "One wouldn't have been afraid to say anything, try anything, go anywhere, with Hilary. The thing was now to stay as close to him as possible, never to lose him. Here at Nuns Farthing, which was his home, one was safe." (p. 212) She thinks that Hilary himself, alive, could have provided the transition from the original world of mother and child to the outside world and to adulthood—men and marriage and children—and yet, at the same time, we see this possibility being denied her, because he has no physical existence of his own. He can never offer experience of the external world to a child, the way a flesh-and-blood mother can. Because Sabrina has been given a ghost for a mother-lover, she cannot really grow up.

At the same time, Hilary, meditating on his bodiless condition, notes that without the barriers of flesh and bone, "sensations of all kinds reached him directly, acutely, in some distilled, immediate form . . . His mind was there, alive still, his spirit, once harassed by his body, was now free and quick and very aware. The pleasures he had enjoyed as a man all remained to him, accentuated, fined down—distilled. All?"

Yes, all—for he looks at Sabrina and feels desire: "he knew a surge of singing ecstasy which took him entirely by surprise, and opened up yet another vista before him." He acknowledges his full love for her, "a love so strong and inevitable that even death had not robbed them of each other."

> Thus he must study to fulfill his fractured destiny, and to make what refuge he could for her from disillusionment and disaster; to stay with her, however he could, as long as she needed him; to make of himself a sort of guardian angel, always with her growing knowledge and consent. And some day, late or soon, it would be his privilege and his responsibility to see that she made the crossing safely and willingly and without fear, into his perpetual care.
>
> . . . He realized that to accept this state of affairs . . . was not

just making the best of things. Rather, it was to appreciate a perfection of intimacy that two people bound by flesh and blood could never know. (p. 215)

Yes but . . . Contradictions appear everywhere. How is it that the moment when he recognizes his sexual desire for her, the adult nature of his love as well as her own dawning sexuality, is the moment when he decides that their intimacy is more perfect than that of flesh-and-blood lovers? Thane has him say that he is not just making the best of a bad deal, but why has she created such a deal in the first place? It's important that this scene does not take place in Hilary's room upstairs but in Sabrina's room, downstairs, a space that belongs more in the life of the real world, a world to which she belongs. The little tea party lets me know that the pressures of the real world are there, much as I have been avoiding them up to now.

I have, for example, more or less ignored the fact that the ghost has been noticed by Sabrina's aunt—not with pleasure but with fear and worry. Aunt Effie has forbidden the room to Sabrina, but of course she has gone there anyway. Now danger cannot be avoided. For Aunt Effie has decided to send Sabrina away to a boarding school in Switzerland, and the school's acceptance arrives. Sabrina runs away. "Don't leave," I am begging, "don't leave Hilary and the house," but Sabrina is thinking that Hilary can't help her now, because she can't throw her arms around him and beg to stay with him at Nuns Farthing forever.

On the peaceful hills outside Glastonbury, Sabrina contemplates her fate. What she wants is simply to stay on at Nuns Farthing, becoming a nice old maid—"not lonely and cross and unhappy like some, because there would always be Hilary" (p. 225). But she also knows that nobody will ever let them alone, for whichever way she turns, there is no clear way to him now.

Hilary, who has followed her as she checks into a hotel, is visited with alarming doubts: "for the first time he saw himself at war with the world for her future, and he saw that it wouldn't do." (pp. 230–31) Aunt Effie and the professor find her and make her come back with the promise that she won't have to go to the school in Switzerland. But the lease at Nuns Farthing has been given up. They are going to return to London.

There follows a scene between Sabrina, her father, and Aunt Effie that demonstrates the truly dire predicament she is in. For she and we clearly see that if the developmental process initiated by Hilary as mother is cut off, then she will have no choice but to replicate the lives of the adults in her family. She looks at her cold father and her silly aunt. "Jog along alone—and forgetful—and complaisant. Get irritable, or silly, or futile. Grow old—like *these?*" (p. 242)

Now, for the first time, Sabrina's own mother is mentioned, the mother who, in her father's words, was so very like her daughter. The story of her mother's death is told first by her father, who laments that the doctors chose to save the child over the mother, his well-loved wife, his eyes "guarded and hostile and bleak." But Aunt Effie remembers the words of the doctor fighting the losing battle for the mother's life: "She isn't *trying*... She won't *help* me—!" (p. 244)

Upstairs in the room, Hilary has the same dreadful forebodings for Sabrina:

> Suddenly he was more afraid for Sabrina than he had ever been for himself in a perilous lifetime. What was ahead for her? Where would she turn in her loneliness and confusion? They would encourage her to marry some fool like George or her father. She would be frightened—she would not understand—she would not know that he was waiting—she would make mistakes and be miserable ... (p. 249)

Halfway through the process, able to see the world as it is but unable to change her own role in it, Sabrina is truly in a bad way. But when she comes to the room for the last time and, hysterically, finds his pistol and aims it at herself, not hearing his warnings and promises that he will wait for her till her life is over, he does what he has never done before—he touches her, lunging across the room and knocking the gun onto the floor by "sweeping his hand through hers." " *'I had to stop you,'* he said apologetically. *'There is some sort of pattern. Don't ever meddle with it.'* "   .

> "Answer me, Hilary, you must answer! What will become of me if I leave this house? I might never feel as though you were in the room with me again! I might get ill and die, alone! Or I might have to live till I'm eighty, without you near! Hilary, promise me that when I die you'll be there!" (p. 252)

He promises, but she can't hear. And then he deliberately tries to eradicate himself from her consciousness after that one moment's reckless contact, deserting her utterly, "for her own good," trying to set her free to have some sort of life without him.

Numbed with despair, she leaves and gets into the car, which strikes a limousine coming much too fast from the other direction. Afterwards she is lying still, facedown, in a ditch.

> *"Hilary—Hilary, where are you?"* She had reached the second flight of stairs already, on her way to him.
> *"Hilary, something's happened—I don't have to go, after all—"*
> Then she saw him. (p. 255)

My tears come from relief, happiness, but with a kind of grief mingled in. How happy I am that she has died, that they are together at last and forever. (How happy I am to see her words in italics.) And yet, I feel as well the terrible *why?* Why this way?

65

The novel concludes with one more short paragraph, echoing the ending of *Wuthering Heights*. "A generation from now, on a summer's day, three village children will come along the lane and pause at the sagging gate of Nuns Farthing, gazing in at the riot of untended bloom which was once the herbaceous border." One of them, a visiting cousin, will express a wish to pick the lovely flowers, going to waste on an empty house "where a top-floor shutter is flung wide to the sunlight, and the casement stands open in the June heat."

> "Come away, Mildred, do!" the others will advise her in lowered tones . . . "We never go there—it's *haunted!*" (pp. 255–56)

Throughout the novel, Hilary has meditated upon the discrepancy between the power of his love for Sabrina, "so strong and inevitable," and the "mistake" that occurred out there on the desert: his death. Getting to return to her as a ghost has been reparation, made "as far as it could go" (p. 215). But of course, the mistake as well as the inevitability are inventions of the author. If we translate Thane's story into developmental terms, we could read the mistake, the early death, as standing for the loss of maternal nurture in the life of a child, while the inevitable and strong love is the mother love that ought to be a child's birthright. Reparation becomes the idea of another mother who will provide a second chance, the fantasy that the male lover could be that person. But *Tryst* both develops this premise and questions it because it accentuates the fantasy element in the construction of such a figure. Whereas Austen simply renegotiates the responses of her manly hero so that he finds himself bucking the masculine system, Thane makes *her* hero a ghost. He isn't alive, he doesn't exist in the real world, and he doesn't have a body. For these reasons he can't facilitate a complete development for the heroine. Left halfway between a deprived childhood and an un-achievable maturity, the heroine dies—her death the best and only alternative to having to grow older without getting the chance to mature. This feels like a happy ending, especially be-cause it means that true love under these terms can indeed be for-ever. (We may also be happy when the heroines die at the end of Kate Chopin's *The Awakening* and George Eliot's *The Mill on the Floss,* which, while they aren't stories of true love, reach the same conclusions about the impossibility of achieving authentic self-identity in a patriarchal culture.) Yet I am discomfited nonethe-less, for good reason. We have been given the true-love feeling, 'but it doesn't lead to the right results. The heroine does not grow up.

Why *was* this book such a favorite of mine? I read it again and again. Even now, all I have to do is think about that room, and Sabrina reading the passages set out for her in his books, to get a thrill of delight. Maybe—partially, anyway—because *Tryst* is a book about reading, and because Hilary in the room is a lot like the author in the book. Sabrina can't see him, but she knows he is there. And he helps her, comforts her, inspires her, loves her, just as the mother-author does when I read in her maternal pres-ence. Reading is the site for the feeling, which is what I knew then and I still believe. The mother-author is like the ghost lover: she can't take me all the way either. I guess I know that, but I am still drawn to her. It's such a paradox: she is the real thing, but she isn't real.

One way in which *Pride and Prejudice* differs from *Tryst* is in the uses to which each author puts the underlying fantasy of true love. Austen is a much stronger authorial presence in her book than Thane is. She instructs, guides, admonishes, suggests, whereas Thane stays behind the story, letting it speak for her. When Austen moves in and changes Mr. Darcy's mind, when she asks me to trust her enough to turn the page after Elizabeth rejects him the first time, I am very aware of her presence and her power. She suggests the fantasy element in her love story by situating it smack in the middle of a real-life world where other lovers don't get the same opportunities (as if Elizabeth and Darcy were composed in color, the others in black and white), so that one plot, Elizabeth and Darcy, serves as commentary on another (say, Lydia and Wickham), and vice versa.

Still, reading Austen, I can believe that I, too, am one of the Technicolor heroines—it can happen to me. I have spent my whole life believing this, even while, at the same time, I have spent most of that life finding a special satisfaction in the world of books. Novels such as *Pride and Prejudice* and *Tryst* turned me into a romance reader when I was a girl. They validated me, responding to those acute needs unmet in other places. And they told me the story that I wanted to hear. If they also questioned the story, I didn't listen, then. Now I see how the fantasy of true love is built on tensions as well as pure desire; but these complications don't deter my appetite for romance reading. Rather, they whet it, if only because I have spent enough time in the real world by now to appreciate the interplay between the lives I lead.

2

True Love Is Forever

EMILY BRONTË'S *WUTHERING HEIGHTS*

True love as I have always imagined it is mutual, nurturing, unconditional—and forever. Oh yes, forever. Once I find it, I want it to stay. The first love, maternal love, is the best love. The fantasy of replicating or reexperiencing it later in life is a way to extend that love into adulthood: one way to have it always.

The simplest romance novels end with a kiss. We have a phrase for that fade-out: "happy ever after." I think our need for forever is so powerful because it stands for security. Winnicott describes the reliable mother who *does not go away,* by which he means whose love and care is abiding. She may leave the room, but she will come back. Most important, the infant *knows* she will come back. When the child grows up, the sense of that love and care is internalized. It forms a bedrock for the person's sense of existence. Winnicott tells us that the capacity to be alone is based on the experience of being alone in the presence of someone, and without a sufficiency of this experience the capacity to be alone cannot develop.

If the mother is inconsistent and unpredictable—if the child never knows when there will be care and when it will be gone, or what causes its withdrawal; if rules must be followed, but they are always changing; if, most significantly, the care and attention are absent for long periods of time—the child will seek forever as the proof of real love. I am speaking abstractly and generally—because it's easier. I understand the sense of being on probation all too well, of worrying constantly that I said or did something wrong, something to make the other person disapprove of me, something that will cause me to be cut off, suddenly. The template for this kind of anxiety, a persistent companion to desire and love on my part, was surely formed early.

One thing about books: they stayed put. All you had to do was reach out for them, start to read, and you could get the feeling. True, they also had to end, which was a little scary—sort of like falling off a cliff. But there were always parachutes in the form of more books. To this day, I shore them up. I can't be comfortable unless the book I'm reading is backed up by others, all lined up on the bookshelf beside my bed. I wouldn't want to be left in the lurch.

Romance fiction is dedicated to the pursuit of forever. Jane Austen's novels end with the kiss, the marriage, but she often gives us as well a sense of what will happen next. She shows us how "happy ever after" involves good parenting, which evokes another kind of forever—that of generation. This love will go on because it will lead directly to little Elizabeths and Darcys. Some romance novels carry this idea further. The sequel, the series, and especially the family saga forestall endings. In the family saga, for example—a series of novels that follow the course of one family across generations by telling many love stories—there's always another novel in the series (till the last one), and the very concept of generation, in which daughter becomes mother who produces daughter who becomes mother, defies endings. In a romance saga, the lovers may change, but the love itself goes on and on. In *Tryst* the lovers do die, but when death is translated into a world of supernatural existence, their love is sustained and maintained quite literally forever. The ghost love story is a romance genre precisely because it is an answer to the problem of forever.

I think that one reason why Emily Brontë's *Wuthering Heights* ranks as one of the greatest romances of all time is because its intricate and powerful working through of the fantasy of true love culminates in not one but three versions of forever: the happy-ever-after love story, the ghost love story, and the generational love story. Hollywood certainly did the story a disservice, no matter how exciting Laurence Olivier is as Heathcliff, when it gave us only one of the three possibilities by cutting out the second generation altogether, not to mention relegating Catherine to a minor role. No—*Wuthering Heights* is Catherine's book, because she is daughter, lover, ghost, and mother; because in the very act of probing and interrogating the fantasy of true love, Brontë writes what is perhaps the most compelling romance novel of all, precisely because it is so complex, so multiple.

In this many-faceted romance there are two heroines with whom to identify; in fact, the novel turns into something more like two novels, except that the first one does not slip neatly into the background. There is a hero who really isn't a hero, not in Mr. Darcy's terms. There is a series of narrators who make me consistently uneasy, because they don't seem to be telling the same story that I am reading. There are two endings and three kinds of forevers—marriage, death, and maternity. But despite, or maybe because of, these complications, there are for me some of the most compelling moments of empathy and excitement in all of literature. When the ghostly Catherine cries to Lockwood, "I've been a waif for twenty years . . ."; when Catherine tells Mrs. Dean, "Nelly, I *am* Heathcliff!" and then, seven years later, asks her, "Why am I so changed?"; when Heathcliff implores the dead

Catherine, "Be with me always . . . I *cannot* live without my life! I *cannot* live without my soul!"—I am, each time, every time, enlarged, intensified, and somehow, appreciated. I recognize my deepest desire, and in the process, I am recognized in turn.

The problem is that the two halves of the novel expose and respond to different desires and develop different fantasies. It is the second half, the story of Catherine's daughter, Cathy, that replicates the Austen model I love so much, where maternal nurture and care facilitates the development of two needy selves so that they can love, grow, and ultimately influence society. The story is sweet and tender, as young Cathy civilizes her half-wild cousin Hareton and he in turn cherishes her. But it's not my favorite part of the novel, not what arouses my ardor. That is reserved for the passionate attachment of Cathy's mother, Catherine, and Heathcliff, the man she understands to be her other self. This too is a tale of mutual recognition and love, but what is recognized is an aspect of the maternal that has nothing to do with society, with culture, with history. The maternal signifies exactly what is wild and uncivilized, what is not under the sway of the father or society. When Freud thought about the preoedipal stage, he compared it to "the Mynoan-Mycean civilization behind the civilization of Greece." Much traditional psychoanalytic thought sees the maternal in just this way: somewhere blurry and vague, back *before*. To disavow the mother, to embrace the father, is to enter culture, time, and history. Yet not all thinkers see the maternal as outside of culture: both Winnicott and Jane Austen think of the mother-infant relationship as very much a part of society. The first story in *Wuthering Heights* is so gripping because it is about the struggle to *stay* in the maternal wild zone—to be passionate and strong and true and free. True to something that was there first, something that is validated and reinforced for Catherine by the presence of her partner in "crime," her beloved companion and counterpart,

Heathcliff. But the first story is also about how this war between preoedipal and Oedipal is lost—because the daughter turns out to be vulnerable to the father's seduction. When the daughter believes that access to the society he represents offers her a different kind of power, a different kind of belonging, she is doomed.

Yes and no. One tale piggybacks onto the other. The myth of origins: Catherine and Heathcliff. The romance tale: Cathy and Hareton. Prehistory and history; tragedy and comedy. Catherine dies creating Cathy—and yet, Cathy perpetuates Catherine. Not only does this mother live on in her daughter's story as a ghost, her spirit haunting the house where her daughter lives, but at the exact moment when her daughter and her daughter's lover have mutually mothered one another into mature selves, she surfaces in *both* of them as part of their identity—she can be seen in their eyes!

There are two happy endings to *Wuthering Heights*. One is the marriage of two maternally identified selves who will thereby influence society; the other is the union of two ghosts who forever haunt the house where they lived together as children. The two endings are made possible by generation, by the mothering of a daughter who in turn brings her dead mother's spirit into existence. In this way three different fantasies of true love are shown to support one another, even as together they create a comprehensive vision of the meaning of female development and its perennial need for mother love.

᭐

Wuthering Heights really gets going for me in the third chapter. To that point we have encountered a strange house on a moor, wild without and neglected within, with a dark-skinned, brooding master, a surly but beautiful young mistress, and a pack of vicious dogs—all the trappings of the gothic romance. I don't particularly like gothics, so I'm not sure about this book. The narrator, a Mr. Lockwood, who is visiting these strange parts from the city, is forced by a sudden snowstorm to spend the night in an unused room. When he discovers a name carved on the ledge of an old-fashioned bed—along with a diary of sorts, written in the margins of an old book of sermons—and subsequently encounters a ghost who announces that she is trying to come *home,* then I begin to engage with the novel.

Later I will come to understand that there is a good reason for my inability to identify in any way with the narrator or with his perceptions about what is happening. In his pretentiousness and egotism, his belief in his own acumen, Lockwood is Brontë's little joke, someone who cannot possibly comprehend who these people are or what this situation is. Nonetheless, despite Lockwood, when Catherine Earnshaw Linton enters the book, I read around him, through him, whatever it takes to encounter her. What attracts *me* first is the bed. When the storm forces Lockwood to spend the night at Wuthering Heights, the servant Zillah takes him upstairs to a chamber in which, she says, the master would not willingly lodge anyone. There he sees a large oak case, with squares cut out near the top, resembling windows—a structure that turns out to be a bed contained in a little closet. The window ledge, which it encloses, serves as a kind of table, upon which are resting some mildewed books.

I am delighted by this hermetic little world—all the more when Lockwood discovers the name scratched all over the ledge, in different-sized characters: *Catherine Earnshaw,* here and there varied to *Catherine Heathcliff* or *Catherine Linton.* I know what that writing means, for what schoolgirl has not sat in class writing her name and then turning it into the name of the boy she loves? *Suzy Hecht, Suzy Juhasz, Mrs. Joseph Juhasz.* I feel a kinship with this Catherine and her bedchamber, so I find it odd that as the sleepy Lockwood closes his eyes, he is adversely overwhelmed by the name. A swarm of Catherines fills the air, "as vivid as spectres," and he rouses himself "to dispel the obtrusive name." Then Lockwood proceeds to read the writing in the books, for it turns out that Catherine, whoever she is or was, has used her books for a singular purpose, writing her own words in their margins, "covering every morsel of blank that the printer had left." (p. 62)

Catherine writes of her brother Hindley's tyranny (he is substituting for her absent father) and the comparable persecution by the servant, Joseph, who first preaches before the children for three hours and then sets them to reading the Gospels. The children respond by physically destroying the books that represent this oppression. But Catherine's desires differ from Heathcliff's. He wants to escape to the moors, to nature, but she wants to write, herself: "I reached this book, and a pot of ink from the shelf, and pushed the house-door ajar to give me light, and I have got the time on with writing for twenty minutes." (p. 64) Catherine wants to join the society that language represents—although on her own terms. She appropriates the books, using them as the very pages for her own story.

That story is, however, fragmented, chaotic, irregular: "Some were detached sentences; other parts took the form of a regular diary, scrawled in an unformed, childish hand. At the top of an extra page . . . [was] an excellent caricature of my friend Joseph, rudely yet powerfully sketched," comments Lockwood. (p. 62) Either Catherine can't write like the authors whose words her own surround, or she won't. Catherine's narrative endears her to me as much as her writing of her name, or names. All of her writing shows her trying to connect to the culture *and* create herself differently from it. The names demonstrate how feelings of emotional attachment lead to economic and political bondage, in that "Catherine" cannot exist without a man's name to give it culturally sanctioned meaning. I understand Catherine, who doesn't want to be as different as she is but who knows she needs to be different to survive at all.

It's important that the heroine is introduced as a writer, a young girl intent on representing her self in language. Especially because the actual writer of the novel seems so different. Brontë hasn't used the first person; she hasn't even used the third person. She has immediately given over her story to some silly man, a gesture that seems to stand in direct contrast to her heroine's act of altering, revising the words of men. We could think that the writer Brontë wants to create a heroine as much unlike herself as possible, except that this makes no sense. Brontë *is* a writer, as much or more so than the young girl Catherine. I think that these two initial writerly acts, the author's and the character's, are comments on one another. One female writer defaces male texts, the other one ventriloquizes them. Both call attention as the novel begins to the act of women writing and to the problem of their relationship to language when it is understood as the culture's agent.

This extraordinary scene culminates in Lockwood's so-called dream of Catherine. Lockwood sees a ghost, but he reports his experience as a dream. Lockwood doesn't believe in ghosts. So, just at this point, when he has wakened from his first dream—of a terrible sermon divided into 490 parts, each for a separate sin—he convinces himself that what happens next occurs after he has fallen asleep again. He wakes, determining that the rappings and counterrappings he hears in the chapel are "merely, the branch of a fir-tree that touched my lattice, as the blast wailed by, and rattled its dry cones against the panes." Then, hearing the fir bough repeat its teasing sound, he resolves to stop it—and encounters instead, when he opens the casement and reaches out, "a little, ice-cold hand."

I am powerfully affected by Lockwood's meeting with a sobbing child outside the window who cries, "Let me in—let me in! . . . I'm come home, I'd lost my way on the moor!" (p. 67) The lost child, seeking home—oh, I know her well. Her pain is my own, especially since for me, too, it has been at least twenty years. Thus Lockwood's subsequent violence against the ghostly child, the violence of man's fear of the female whom he takes to represent all that is repressed and despised by the civilized world, the violence of the so-called "gentleman" who has shuddered at the crudeness of Wuthering Heights, is especially hateful and repulsive.

> As it spoke, I discerned, obscurely, a child's face looking through the window—terror made me cruel; and, finding it useless to attempt shaking the creature off, I pulled its wrist on to the broken pane, and rubbed it to and fro till the blood ran down and soaked the bedclothes: still it wailed, "Let me in!"
>
> (p. 67)

There are reverberations here of all such violence against women, such denial of our most basic needs and desires: " 'It's twenty years,' mourned the voice, 'twenty years, I've been a waif for twenty years!' " (p. 67)

Lockwood insists that what has occurred is a dream, but this is not so certain. He thinks that feeling a hand when he had expected a branch means he must be dreaming, but the hand could of course be as real as the branch. Later he "wakes" from his "dream" by screaming, only to "discover that the yell was not ideal." Nor might the experience itself have been imaginary, as Lockwood himself suggests when he goes from telling Heathcliff, roused by Lockwood's cries, that he has had a "frightful nightmare" to announcing that the place is haunted, "swarming with ghosts and goblins." I think that Brontë, if not Lockwood, has alerted us to the existence of a world with ghosts in it. Indeed, when we examine the content of Lockwood's experience, we realize that there is no way he could have made up the truths that the ghost reveals: that she has been a waif for twenty years; that her name is Catherine Linton. "Why did I think of *Linton*," wonders Lockwood. "I had read *Earnshaw* twenty times for *Linton*." (p. 67) The Catherine who is trying to return to Wuthering Heights is the dead wife of Edgar Linton, dead these twenty years.

But why is she locked out? Where has she been? How has she died? I know the generic answers but not the specific ones. That the search for home will be connected with the story of true love is something I expect, and my beliefs are corroborated a few pages later, when Lockwood observes Heathcliff's reaction to the ghostly tale he has told him. Heathcliff orders Lockwood out of the house, but Lockwood, as is his wont, remains to eavesdrop. "I stood still, and was witness, involuntarily, to a piece of superstition on the part of my landlord, which belied, oddly, his apparent sense." Lockwood clearly has no idea who or what Heathcliff is, but I do, as soon as I read what happens next.

> He got onto the bed, and wrenched open the lattice, bursting, as he pulled at it, into an uncontrollable passion of tears.
>
> "Come in! come in!" he sobbed. "Cathy, do come. Oh do— *once* more! Oh! my heart's darling! hear me *this* time— Catherine, at last!"
>
> The spectre showed a spectre's ordinary caprice; it gave no sign of being; but the snow and wind whirled wildly through, even reaching my station, and blowing out the light. (p. 70)

Lockwood reacts to this anguish and grief by calling it "raving," by congratulating his own "compassion" that makes him "overlook its folly," by noting that the reasons for such agony in response to his "ridiculous nightmare" are beyond his comprehension. But not mine, and here is where I part company with Lockwood forever, knowing now that my various intuitions about his unreliability as a narrator are absolutely right. I know

who Heathcliff is, whatever else he may be or seem to be: he is
Cathy's true love—and has been, I can tell from the words in her
diary, since her childhood. Now I understand that Lockwood's
words are being used to expose a meaning different from what he
grasps. If Lockwood is a scion of the patriarchy, seeing from its
point of view, then there is another story altogether, which can be
revealed despite his impositions.

Chapter 3 has introduced me to a heroine who is a ghost,
longing for home, and also to her true love. Already I have the
ingredients I need for my kind of love story. But there is more.
For if Catherine is dead, Heathcliff's feisty daughter-in-law is
not. Before Lockwood leaves Wuthering Heights, he encounters
a quarrel between the two of them. He observes Heathcliff
threatening the young woman, and her spirited response: "I'll
not do anything, though you should swear your tongue out, except what I please!" (p. 72) Who is she, anyway—and what is
happening? I begin to wonder, in the present tense of this story,
with Cathy's story belonging to an impinging past.

Immediately, the next chapter answers my question and suggests to me that the extra ingredient in this novel is going to be
something I likewise cherish: generation. In Chapter 4 Lockwood, back at the house he has rented, Thrushcross Grange, and
ill with a bad cold, literally hands over the narration of the novel
to his housekeeper, a woman called Nelly Dean. "Well, Mrs.
Dean, it will be a charitable deed to tell me something of my
neighbors—I feel I shall not rest, if I go to bed; so be good
enough to sit and chat an hour." (p. 76) An hour turns into
many, as Nelly takes up the reins of the tale, which will be hers
until the final pages of the novel.

Nelly's first comments provide a genealogy for the characters
now residing at Wuthering Heights. The "pretty girl-widow" in
whom Lockwood is so interested is Catherine Linton, Nelly's
"late master's daughter." ("What, Catherine Linton!" exclaims

Lockwood: "But a minute's reflection convinced me it was not my ghostly Catherine.") This Catherine had married her first cousin, who was the son of Mr. Heathcliff and Mr. Linton's sister. The other young man now residing at the Heights, called Hareton, is identified as the late Mrs. Linton's nephew, and therefore, another cousin.

But Nelly's genealogy leaves out the essential connection between these people: the *first* Catherine Linton, née Earnshaw— the late master's wife, the aunt of Hareton, the childhood companion of Heathcliff, and, most important of all for this genealogy, the *mother* of the young Catherine. The crucial role of the mother is suppressed by Nelly Dean, because she wants to tell a story of fathers, not mothers. This brief interchange between Lockwood and Nelly, the exact place in the novel where the narrative is turned over to Nelly, suggestively counters Lockwood's "it was not my ghostly Catherine" with Nelly's "my late master's daughter." Catherine is present here—linguistically, narratively, and psychologically—only as a ghost. Lockwood doesn't believe in ghosts, and Nelly ignores the possibility of mothers altogether. In this way they act to erase the mother. But she is not erased; she is repressed. If she is not present, neither is she absent. Lockwood makes the essential connection between the mother and the daughter, though he doesn't know it; and the very name, repeated in Catherine's daughter, gives her mother representation, although unacknowledged.

After establishing a genealogy, Nelly begins, returning the body of the tale, if not its frame (we are always to imagine Nelly talking, Lockwood listening), to the past: "Before I came to live here . . . I was almost always at Wuthering Heights." Who is Nelly? Nelly's mother had nursed Catherine's brother Hindley. Nelly played with the children, ran errands, and hung about, "ready for anything that anybody would set me to" (p. 76). Nelly's subservience underlies all her activities: she is set in motion by the upper-class family to which she has been attached. Nelly is a creature of the culture; it inspires her actions, and her actions work to support it. Her narration is one of these actions. Brontë has handed over the telling from an egotistical scion of the culture to a menial devoted to it. Whereas Lockwood infuses everything he sees with his own version of reality, Nelly adopts a point of view that she thinks promotes the needs of her masters. Yet both narrators, belonging as they do to the culture, possess the right to speak.

In this way Brontë reverses the writerly gesture of her heroine, Catherine. Rather than writing in culture's margins, she writes its text herself—she seemingly writes "like a man." But her cross-dressing is not really for the purpose of "passing" (although the novel was published under the pseudonym "Ellis Bell"), because, as has already become apparent, the narrations of Lockwood and Nelly call their own reliability into question over and over. Their culturally approved interpretations don't quite do—for the speakers do not exactly understand the stories they are called upon to tell. Brontë is actually *parodying* the language of the culturally correct, and therefore leaving room for another interpretation—by those who can see the joke. It is no accident, I think, that some readers believe Nelly throughout and actually see her as the only "good mother" in the novel. They are reading through the lens of culture, so they don't get the joke; they don't see that there is a slippage between what is told and how it is told. In this way what is supposed to be repressed is instead represented, in the very teeth, or terms, of the dominant narrative mode.

Nelly begins her story with a significant moment in the life of the Earnshaw family, a generation ago. Mr. Earnshaw is the old master; he has two children, Hindley and Cathy. (Their mother is referred to only once in Nelly's narrative, on the occasion of her death.) Off to Liverpool, Mr. Earnshaw asks his chil-

dren what they would like him to bring back. Hindley names a
fiddle; Cathy, hardly six years old, but able to ride any horse in
the stable, chooses a whip. Instead of her whip, lost along the
way, Cathy gets "a dirty, ragged, black-haired child" who speaks
"some gibberish that nobody could understand" (p. 77). Mr.
Earnshaw has picked "it" up, starving, homeless, and "as good as
dumb" in the streets of Liverpool. Nelly calls him a "gipsy brat,"
which fits with his speaking an unintelligible tongue. But the origins of the wild child, subsequently christened Heathcliff (the
name of a son who had died in childhood), are never known.
Hindley calls him "imp of Satan"; throughout the novel, associ-
ations with the devil will be made by those who confront him.
"Heathcliff" comes to serve him both as Christian name and surname, indicative both of his lack of true genealogical connection
with any known family and of his ability, as a male, to get along
without one (remember "'Catherine" and her succession of inter-
changeable surnames).

Nelly's story thus starts with the introduction of Heathcliff
into this family of rural gentry: Heathcliff, who becomes "thick"
with Cathy. Together, Catherine and Heathcliff make a life of
heady rebellion and happiness, running away to the moors,
laughing at punishment, contriving naughty plans of revenge.
Catherine at this point in her childhood is all energy, energy that
seeks to escape any kind of containment—her spirits always "at
high-water mark."

> A wild, wick slip she was—but she had the bonniest eye, and
> sweetest smile, and lightest foot in the parish; and after all, I
> believe she meant no harm; for when once she made you cry
> in good earnest, it seldom happened that she would not keep
> you company; and oblige you to be quiet that you might com-
> fort her.

She was much too fond of Heathcliff. The greatest punishment we could invent for her was to keep her separate from him: yet she got chided more than any of us on his account.

(p. 83)

Catherine is essentially amoral—neither good nor bad. She is a self that is not culturally demarcated, defined, limited, or controlled. And she actively *resists* any attempts on the part of those around her to do so. Her most dominant trait is this resistance. "She was never so happy as when we were all scolding her at once, and she defying us with her bold, saucy look, and her ready words." (p. 83)

Catherine is a self brought into existence by a mother but then abandoned. The kind of development that maternal nurture produces has been arrested. Hers is a maternally oriented sense of existence continually beleaguered by pressures from fathers to define and delineate her according to cultural norms. Specifically, she is fending off the pressures of gender, the attempt to turn her into what the social order understands to be a "girl." In this way she reminds me of many of my other favorite heroines at the start of their stories.

But Catherine is also different from these heroines, and that difference is indicated by the fact that Brontë creates Heathcliff for her. In her unbounded state of sheer energy, in her active resistance to all that signifies culture, in her association of selfhood with what is outside of culture, i.e., nature, Catherine's identity has more to do with Freud's idea of the "Minoan" mother, presiding over a realm outside of culture. Heathcliff, in his wildness and otherness, supports the acultural maternal principle, not the kind of maternal nurture that leads up to interaction with society. He fosters not her maturation but her immature condition: wild, primitive, prehistorical. Consequently, although Heathcliff is clearly in the novel to "mother" Catherine, he is *not* like Mr. Darcy, Winnicott's "good mother," who brings the child through developmental stages into the social world.

When Mr. Earnshaw dies, his benevolent rule replaced by the tyranny of his oldest son, Hindley, this aspect of the relationship between Catherine and Heathcliff is strengthened. Heathcliff is banished from the house to labor in the fields, where Catherine joins him. "They both promised fair to grow up as rude as savages," says Nelly, her words underlining the way in which Heathcliff's class and "racial" (he is probably Gypsy-born) otherness reinforce Catherine's own sense of difference. In turn, their difference is associated with nature, especially the wild and rugged moors, because nature, like Catherine's essential energy, is exempt and apart from all of these cultural categories.

It is during this state of affairs that Catherine and Heathcliff first encounter Thrushcross Grange, the house across the moors—and with it, its two children, Edgar and Isabella Linton. It is Heathcliff who tells this story—to Nelly, and she reproduces it for us. Words become necessary, even for Heathcliff, when he has to try to deal with what he had not hitherto understood as the seductive force of the social order, the father.

Through a window Heathcliff and Catherine first see the glories of bourgeois culture: "a splendid place carpeted with crimson, and crimson-covered chairs and tables, and a pure white ceiling bordered by gold, and a shower of glass-drops hanging in silver chains from the centre, and shimmering with little soft tapers" (p. 89). The window to Thrushcross Grange both allures and separates: the image of Catherine and Heathcliff, dirty faces pressed against the glass, watching the pretty and beautifully clad Linton children, Edgar and Isabella, struggling over a little dog is unforgettable.

"We laughed outright at the petted things, we did despise them," says Heathcliff. "When would you catch me wishing to have what Catherine wanted? or find us by ourselves, seeking entertainment in yelling, and sobbing, and rolling on the ground, divided by the whole room?" (p. 89) But if there is profound difference between the relationship between Catherine and Heathcliff and that between Isabella and Edgar, so is there a difference between Heathcliff and Catherine, regardless of the fact that they do not want there to be one. For if Heathcliff is certain that he would "not exchange . . . my condition here, for Edgar Linton's at Thrushcross Grange," Catherine is not so sure. When she is bitten by the Lintons' dog, she is discovered by the master and mistress of the house and brought inside. Heathcliff, however, is sent away: "a wicked boy . . . and quite unfit for a decent house." Refusing to go without her, he remains in the garden. Now he is outside the window, she within. The vision Heathcliff sees this time, accentuating their separation, is of Catherine petted, cosseted, and served by the whole Linton family. "They dried and combed her beautiful hair, and gave her a pair of enormous slippers, and wheeled her to the fire, and I left her, as merry as she could be." (p. 92) Although he imagines "shattering their great glass panes to a million of fragments, unless they let her out," he does not do so, because Cathy does not want to be rescued.

The window between Thrushcross Grange and the world outside keeps Heathcliff out, but it lures Catherine in. For Catherine is a daughter of her father, too, while Heathcliff is an alien ("Frightful thing," cries Edgar Linton. "Put him in the cellar, Papa"). She has attachments to the culture, however much she would reject them, and she is attracted to as well as repelled by what the father signifies. Thrushcross Grange ups the ante of acculturation by emphasizing the comforts and the refinements of the father's culture and opposing them to the blatant brutality and tyranny at Wuthering Heights. Both houses are aspects of the social order (not, as some would have it, Wuthering Heights

85

standing for nature as opposed to Thrushcross Grange for culture); they give us a Janus view of the father. Catherine, who has experienced and resisted tyranny, is not so good at resisting beguilement. If Edgar had been another Hindley, there is no way that Catherine would have responded. She is drawn to the world of the father because as it separates and objectifies her, it names her "lady"—and treats her accordingly. It offers her stature and what seems like importance as well as comfort and pleasure. It seems a change, a relief from Wuthering Heights, when in truth it is another version of it. The world of Thrushcross Grange asks her to turn away not from Wuthering Heights but from Heathcliff. To love the father, not the mother—and the second-hand power the father will confer.

Catherine stays at Thrushcross Grange for five weeks before she returns to Wuthering Heights. "Instead of a wild, hatless little savage jumping into the house, and rushing to squeeze us all breathless, there lighted from a handsome black pony a very dignified person, with brown ringlets falling from the cover of a feathered beaver, and a long cloth habit which she was obliged to hold up with both hands that she might sail in." (p. 93) In response, surely, to Cathy's gender socialization and literally to her absence, Heathcliff has, in his turn, grown wilder: "if he were careless, and uncared for, before Catherine's absence, he had been ten times more so, since" (pp. 93–94). If Cathy has turned into a "lady," Heathcliff is everything that a lady is *not*. For every step that Catherine takes toward society, Heathcliff takes a step away from it, to provide her, as it were, with some balance. For Heathcliff is there, as always, to mirror the part of Catherine that is not a part of culture and therefore to permit it to live. Heathcliff does not embody what Catherine is not; he is everything she is that the culture will repress. Yet Nelly's words are worth pausing over: "careless, and uncared for." The relationship between Catherine and Heathcliff is not one-way, as no mothering relationship is. Heathcliff needs Catherine. He needs her to allow him to exist at all, as human. For the culture would deem him nonhuman, antihuman. Catherine's recognition of Heathcliff gives him selfhood.

Catherine's struggle occurs between her twelfth and fifteenth years. It takes place precisely from the onset of puberty till she is of marriageable age. One might ask why a vocabulary of early development is needed here, since Catherine's trajectory can be understood as an adolescent crisis: as the change and socialization that occurs as "girls" become "women." And yet Catherine, before her encounter with Thrushcross Grange, is hardly even a "girl." She has resisted gender identity as well as she can, with Heathcliff as her ally and other self. The onset of puberty and adolescence may be understood as a second developmental stage, a second version of the Oedipal crisis, but it doesn't seem to me that Catherine has experienced the first one yet. As in all women's romances, the drama of the adolescent period is layered over the symbolic depiction of the original developmental stage.

During this period, the contrast between the two houses is exaggerated. Hindley's town-bred wife dies soon after childbirth, and he becomes more vicious than ever. "I could not half tell what an infernal house we had," sighs Nelly. These are the chapters where Nelly tells stories of Hindley forcing a knife into her mouth—and throwing the baby, Hareton, over the banister. Compared to this environment, the Lintons cannot help looking pretty good.

Catherine, all too aware of her own struggle and where it might lead, goes about being angry at both Heathcliff and Edgar. She berates Heathcliff for his lack of gentlemanliness: "You might be dumb or a baby for anything you say to amuse me, or for anything you do, either!" (p. 110) At the same time, she torments Edgar for his lack of wildness, a want of "spirit in general." She pinches Nelly, even slaps her, just to shock Edgar. With

Heathcliff, she plays the daughter of culture; with Edgar, she plays daughter of the wild. She discovers soon enough that she cannot be both with either one of them. In other words, the pre-oedipal world and the Oedipal world do not mix, even though she now feels characteristics of each in herself. It is in this condition that she comes to Nelly—who else is there?—when Edgar proposes marriage to her.

This is the first of Catherine's great speeches. Nelly can report and interpret, but she is also forced to record these words which are *not* her own. Catherine begins by announcing that she will marry Edgar Linton: because he is handsome, pleasant to be with, young and cheerful, loves her, and will be rich: "and I shall like to be the greatest woman of the neighborhood, and I shall be proud of having such a husband." Even Nelly can tell there's something wrong with this, and with Catherine's declaration that "I love the ground under his feet, and the air over his head, and everything he touches, and every word he says—I love all his looks, and all his actions, and him entirely, and altogether. There now!" (pp. 118–19). What's wrong is not what she says, for Catherine is using the sentimental vocabulary entirely appropriate for declarations of romantic love, but the tone in which she says it, culminating in her "There now!" Her awkward use of these words points to their superficiality and inadequacy, as well as her hypocrisy. She knows they are not representing her feelings. Even though she has gone too far into the culture to turn back—she wants to be "the greatest woman of the neighborhood," which is all that her condition in this society has fitted her for, and who else in this town *could* she marry?—she knows there is an obstacle.

"In whichever place the soul lives—in my soul, and in my heart, I'm convinced I'm wrong!" The words to describe *this* feeling are not so readily available, because it has little to do with the social, economic, or even romantic reasons for marriage in culture. The feeling comes from the preoedipal, from outside of culture, but Catherine nonetheless needs language to tell it. And so she expands the symbolic with the logic of dreams, with simile and metaphor, to express that for which culture has no words.

She describes "dreams that have stayed with me ever after, and changed my ideas; they've gone through and through me, like wine through water, and altered the colour of my mind." (p. 120) Nelly resists this kind of information: she likens it to ghosts, visions, prophecy, and catastrophe—another "world." Indeed, these somatic memories are the residue of the preoedipal, which shapes and affects all that comes after, like "wine" as opposed to "water." One such dream is of being in heaven, a place that did not seem to be Catherine's home:

> ". . . and I broke my heart with weeping to come back to earth; and the angels were so angry that they flung me out, into the middle of the heath on the top of Wuthering Heights, where I woke sobbing for joy. That will do to explain my secret . . . I've no more business to marry Edgar Linton than I have to be in heaven; and if the wicked man in there had not brought Heathcliff so low, I shouldn't have thought of it. It would degrade me to marry Heathcliff, now; so he shall never know how much I love him; and that, not because he's handsome, Nelly, but because he's more myself than I am. Whatever our souls are made of, his and mine are the same, and Linton's is as different as a moonbeam from lightning, or frost from fire." (pp. 120–21)

Neither heaven nor hell, both aspects of the culture's mythology, is relevant to Catherine's need for *home.* Her home is earth, the heath on top of Wuthering Heights—the environment of Catherine/Heathcliff. Nature is home and home is mother. Her dream is a truth about identity, and it clearly challenges the socialization process to which Catherine has submitted herself. (It also foreshadows the fate of a woman caught as Catherine will be between mutually exclusive definitions of selfhood—a woman who will herself end up as a ghost, perennially seeking home.)

Marriage is a central cultural institution. In cultural terms, Heathcliff and Linton are rivals for Catherine's hand. In these terms, Heathcliff loses. To describe her love for him, she again must move outside culture's vocabulary. Not "handsome" (culture/Oedipal) but "more myself than I am" (preoedipal). Catherine's self is defined by her relationship to Heathcliff—as his is to hers. Figurative language takes over to explain the feeling, metaphors of nature: lightning and fire, moonbeam and frost. Metaphors create the sense that Catherine and Heathcliff are in some primary way joined. From this perspective, marriage isn't the operational term. Theirs is not a cultural arrangement. It is earlier, later, deeper, wider. It is not about property or social position, not even about romantic love: it is about identity.

Thus, when Nelly sees the impending marriage as a desertion of Heathcliff, Catherine is indignant. Never! She will marry Linton so as to aid Heathcliff to rise, and to place him out of her brother's power, and she tries to explain how this goal has nothing to do with satisfying her whims, or Edgar's.

> "I cannot express it; but surely you and everybody have a notion that there is, or should be an existence of yours beyond you. What were the use of my creation if I were entirely contained here? My great miseries in this world have been Heathcliff's miseries, and I watched and felt each from the beginning; my great thought in living is himself. If all else perished, and *he* remained, I should still continue to be; and if all else remained, and he were annihilated, the universe would turn to a mighty stranger . . . My love for Linton is like the foliage in the woods. Time will change it, I'm well aware, as win-

ter changes the trees. My love for Heathcliff resembles the eternal rocks below—a source of little visible delight, but necessary. Nelly, I *am* Heathcliff—he's always, always in my mind—not as a pleasure, any more than I am always a pleasure to myself—but as my own being—so, don't talk of our separation again . . ." (p. 122)

Catherine is describing the exact version of an all-powerful love that I have always, as far back as I can remember, yearned to feel. She explains true love as something very different from the romantic love that society offers us in its stead. This is not delight; it is not really even pleasure; it is much more elemental. It is the idea of the perpetuation of the maternal bond, deeper and stronger and more meaningful than anything else, for when you feel it you are powerfully, unutterably yourself because you are more than yourself. The self defined in relation extends beyond the confines of the discrete ego—to the loved one and through her/him to the world beyond, throughout time. "Nelly, I *am* Heathcliff" always brings tears to my eyes—tears of both satisfaction (someone is saying it, so it must be so) and longing, for this is not my experience, never, never quite this much, though I have sometimes pretended or deluded myself that it was. Just to *feel* it, I have created relationships that were false, with men who could never, and did not want to, be Heathcliff to my Catherine.

At this moment Brontë herself separates Catherine from Heathcliff, underlining, perhaps, the inevitability of their rupture. Heathcliff overhears Catherine's conversation with Nelly, but only up until the point where she says it would degrade her to marry him. He runs off into the night, his departure heralded by a terrible storm that splits a tree, knocking down a portion of the chimney. Catherine, distressed by his disappearance, drenches herself in the rain and becomes violently ill. However, she is eventually nursed back to health by Linton's mother at

Thrushcross Grange. With clear symbolism, Brontë indicates the radical effects of Heathcliff's loss: destruction and trauma. Nature and Catherine are wounded by it. Catherine "heals," but only by repressing and papering over her connection to Heathcliff. She is now a daughter of Thrushcross Grange, although it is worth noting that Edgar's parents catch her "fever" and die of it. Evidently it was a dangerous sort of disease. Three years later, she is married to Edgar Linton and mistress of Thrushcross Grange.

Here, appropriately, Nelly's narrative breaks off, to be briefly resumed by Lockwood, who announces his continued interest in a tale that he understands as a typical romance: "her hero had run off, and never been heard from for three years; and the heroine was married." (p. 130) He is wrong, as usual. Heathcliff is the protagonist of a different sort of love story altogether. Nelly, upon resuming her narration, glosses over in a paragraph or two the happy honeymoon months of Mr. and Mrs. Linton. The real story resumes with Heathcliff's return.

In this second stage of Catherine and Heathcliff's relationship, they must now try to play out their story in culture. Heathcliff returns—on the surface a changed man, athletic, well formed, upright, decisive, intelligent, even dignified, to use Nelly's admiring words. "A half-civilized ferocity lurked yet in the depressed brows, and eyes full of black fire, but it was subdued," says Nelly. (p. 135) Although Catherine welcomes him with unabashed delight and assumes that he will now function in their lives as a sort of family friend, she is quite wrong.

In the meantime Linton's sister, Isabella, falls in love with Heathcliff, whom she thinks of as a dashing, dark and brooding, utterly romantic hero. Heathcliff decides to cultivate Isabella's love because she is an heir to Thrushcross Grange. "I seek no revenge on you . . . That's not the plan—The tyrant grinds down his slaves—and they don't turn against him, they crush those beneath them." (p. 151) Heathcliff is living at Wuthering Heights, busily bringing about the further debasement of Hindley and little Hareton. The revenge plot thickens. But he doesn't seem to have accounted for Catherine in all of this, even as she has not quite understood him. Thus culture *has* come between them. Although each continues to believe implicitly in their love for one another, it becomes more and more unclear how this love is to function in the world in which they both now live.

Inevitably, Heathcliff and Linton fight, and Linton banishes Heathcliff from Thrushcross Grange. Catherine resorts to a peculiar defensive strategy: "Well, if I cannot keep Heathcliff for my friend—if Edgar will be mean and jealous, I'll try to break their hearts by breaking my own. That will be a prompt way of finishing all, when I am pushed to extremity!" Catherine's actual *powerlessness* as a woman in culture is revealed by her concept of self-directed violence; the idea that she can hurt others only by hurting herself—the idea that this is a form of winning. "I'd not take Linton by surprise with it," she advises Nelly: "You must . . . remind him of my passionate temper verging, when kindled, on frenzy." (p. 155)

But Catherine has underestimated Nelly at this critical juncture. Nelly has long been Catherine's confidant—this is necessary so that her story can be told at all—but she is not her friend. Nelly, aware of the degree to which Catherine is *not* entirely socialized, both condemns and is afraid of her. Nelly serves masters, not mistresses. "I did not wish to 'frighten' her husband, as she said, and multiply his annoyances for the purposes of serving her selfishness. Therefore I said nothing when I met the master coming towards the parlour." (p. 156) Instead, she tells Catherine that Linton is busy with his books, not missing her in the least.

What follows is Catherine's "mad scene," in which, thrown into a frenzy by her belief in Linton's disloyalty, she seems to hallucinate and offers a series of visions to the shocked Nelly Dean.

Catherine's great cry of loss and betrayal calls up an answering feeling in me. "Why am I so changed?" she cries, and I know exactly what she means, even if Nelly does not. Is Catherine mad or pretending? What does it matter? Or rather, as in her description of her dreams, we are again aware that she needs recourse to experience outside of culture when she tries to express or live her true self. Madness works as well as dreams for this purpose, except that it is a more dangerous discourse—appropriate to the fear that she experiences for the first time, that she is in a situation from which there is no satisfactory way out.

In her "ravings" Catherine keeps trying to return to her old room at Wuthering Heights. "Oh, if I were but in my own bed in the old house! . . . And that wind sounding in the firs by the lattice. Do let me feel it—it comes straight down the moor—do let me have one breath!" Nelly holds the casement ajar for a moment, letting in a blast of wintry air, then shutting it fast. To Nelly, Catherine is "no better than a wailing child."

But of course she is a child, or wants to be, and that powerful urge and the even more powerful frustration are the gist of her visionary words, when she tries to explain to Nelly what happened to her immediately after her quarrel with Edgar.

> "I thought . . . I was enclosed in the oak-panelled bed at home; and my heart ached with some great grief which, just waking, I could not recollect . . . most strangely, the whole last seven years of my life grew a blank! I did not recall that they had been at all. I was a child; my father was just buried, and my misery arose from the separation that Hindley had ordered between me, and Heathcliff—I was laid alone, for the first time, and rousing from a dismal dose after a night of weeping—I lifted my hand to push the panels aside, and it struck the tabletop! . . . I cannot say why I felt so wildly wretched . . . But, supposing at twelve years old, I had been

94

wrenched from the Heights, and every early association, and my all in all, as Heathcliff was at that time, and been converted, at a stroke, into Mrs. Linton, the lady of Thrushcross Grange, and the wife of a stranger; an exile, and outcast, thenceforth, from what had been my world! . . . Oh, I'm burning! I wish I were out of doors—I wish I were a girl again, half savage and hardy, and free . . . and laughing at injuries, not maddening under them! Why am I so changed? why does my blood rush into a hell of tumult at a few words? I'm sure I should be myself were I once among the heather on those hills . . . Open the window again wide, fasten it open! Quick, why don't you move?"

"Because I won't give you your death of cold," I answered.

"You won't give me a chance of life, you mean," she said.

(p. 163)

Catherine's attempts to be clear about tenses—the then and the now—are undone by a different kind of reality that condenses time to emotional and psychological truth. Yet both versions of reality reinforce our sense of Catherine's betrayal by the social order. Listening to her, I believe both that the seven years have never happened and that they are the occasion of deep and irrevocable change. They are a blank because real life was the time before them at Wuthering Heights. But even then, even there, she was not guarded from loss. It was Hindley, taking her father's place and his power, who separated her from Heathcliff. Thus, when she discovers she is at Thrushcross Grange, the seven years reassert their reality not so much as contrast but as intensification of separation and loss, the exile that was already growing at *home*. Misery turns into anguish, for Catherine understands that the roots of her betrayal were there in her own family, since fathers destroy the bond with the mother if they can. This is why she

95

longs for nature instead—the hills, the wind and the night. This is why she courts death.

Looking out the open window, Catherine sees what cannot literally be seen, the candle in the window of her room at Wuthering Heights. She speaks as if to Heathcliff of the journey home, which will take them through the churchyard cemetery.

> "We've braved its ghosts often together, and dared each other to stand among the graves and ask them to come ... But Heathcliff, if I dare you now, will you venture? If you do, I'll keep you. I'll not lie there by myself: they may bury me twelve feet deep, and throw the church down over me; but I won't rest till you are with me ... I never will!" (p. 164)

Catherine wants only to go home, and home means one thing only: reunion with Heathcliff, reunion with the mother, return to the identity that had been established in preoedipal space and time. But even as she speaks, Wuthering Heights' status as home is complicated utterly, for now she must pass through the grave for it to be redeemed. Wuthering Heights in the real world is as corrupt as Thrushcross Grange. To return to the past, the past before separation and acculturation occurred, means to live in a different reality.

Death is the bridge between the two. Death is at once the end of one reality and the beginning of another. Not heaven— Catherine has made it quite clear that heaven is no place for her. Not hell, because hell too is an idea out of culture. The spirit world, of ghosts and all that hover there, is the only remaining recourse.

We have come to the ghost love story. Brontë, like Elswyth Thane, understands all too well how difficult it is for the love of the mother to hold out against the power of the father and the culture he represents. But she also understands, as Thane did, that true love is a force that will not exactly die, either. It stays in some stronghold of memory and desire, and those who yearn for it may well try to find a way to feel it at any cost. Catherine is ready to die—not for the gift of oblivion but as a way to return to her existence and identity before it. Betrayed by time, she will seek out the space of death in the hope that it will contain the past that she has lost.

Do I believe her? Of course I do. I have felt her grief at the change toward which she eagerly went, I have experienced her longing for home. She speaks for all of us at this moment, and we do not worry if the world wants to call this terrible insight madness. I too would go back; except that I too, like Catherine, know that what I want is not to be found there. If Catherine refuses to stay where her true self cannot live, and if she is willing to try the possibility of an afterwards, I for one will not belittle her.

Catherine's death appears to be inevitable now. Nelly has neglected to tell Linton of her condition, while Heathcliff is busy with his grand revenge scheme: "I have no pity! I have no pity! The more the worms writhe, the more I yearn to crush out their entrails!" Catherine and Heathcliff have betrayed one another, corrupted by their entrance into the culture. Catherine did it first, pawn of the father's blandishments. But Heathcliff followed directly; and if she became something akin to a "woman," he became something akin to a "man." Heathcliff takes out his suffering on others, and he works out a great plan of revenge against the culture rather than attempting somehow to rescue Catherine from it. Catherine, for her part, believes its lies until too late and so has not trusted Heathcliff.

Thus they accuse one another in their final "love scene," where they strain to bring together their bodies and their souls with a violence born of the desperation that comes from knowing not only that it is too late but that it has always somehow been too late. Nelly calls it a strange and fearful picture: Catherine with her white cheek, bloodless lip, scintillating eye, clutching the hair that she has torn from Heathcliff's head; Heathcliff grasping her arm so ferociously that he leaves blue impressions on the colorless skin. They hurl reproaches even as they vow undying love. "You have killed me—and thriven on it," cries Catherine, and then, "I only wish us never to be parted." Heathcliff, in his turn, despairs, "O, Cathy! Oh, my life! how can I bear it?" even as he berates her, "*Why* did you betray your own heart, Cathy? . . . you deserve this. You have killed yourself." (p. 197) He continues:

> "You loved me—then what *right* had you to leave me? . . . because misery, and degradation, and death, and nothing that God or Satan could inflict would have parted us, *you*, of your own will, did it. I have not broken your heart—*you* have broken it—and in breaking it, you have broken mine. So much the worse for me, that I am strong. Do I want to live? What kind of living will it be when you—oh, God! would *you* like to live with your soul in the grave?"
>
> "Let me alone. Let me alone," sobbed Catherine. "If I've done wrong, I'm dying for it. It is enough! You left me, too; but I won't upbraid you! I forgive you. Forgive me!"
>
> "It is hard to forgive, and to look at those eyes, and feel those wasted hands," he answered. "Kiss me again; and don't let me see your eyes! I forgive what you have done to me. I love *my* murderer—but *yours!* How can I?" (pp. 197–98)

With words, all that is left, they make one final attempt to intertwine their souls. The preponderance and near interchangeability of the *you*'s and *me*'s in their speech make it hard to tell who is who; but the grammar of the sentences is impeccable: it shows that the two are actually quite distinct. At this, their final meeting, Heathcliff cannot look into the eyes of his beloved Catherine, the look that in romance fiction announces the recognition of the self, because he knows there is no genuine recognition to be had—for either one of them. The scene ends with "their faces hid against each other, and washed by each other's tears." As close as they can get, they cannot get as close as they were and yearn to be. The selves they were when they were together are gone; the love they feel is more memory than actuality. "That is not *my* Heathcliff," says Catherine. "I shall love mine yet; and take him with me—he's in my soul." (p. 196)

And so she dies. What else is there to do? What else would I want for her? For everything to be all right, yes, but Brontë has made it quite clear that this is not possible. Not for Catherine. Nelly says, "No angel in heaven could be more beautiful than she appeared, and I partook of the infinite calm in which she lay." So she prays, "Incomparably beyond, and above us all! Whether still on earth or now in heaven, her spirit is at home with God!" But her words, with their pat religious consolation, are called into question by Heathcliff's cry of anguish, which is its own kind of prayer:

> "May she wake in torment! . . . Why, she's a liar to the end! Where is she? Not *there*—not in heaven—not perished— where? Oh! you said you cared nothing for my sufferings! And I pray one prayer—I repeat it till my tongue stiffens— Catherine Earnshaw, may you not rest, as long as I am living! You said I killed you—haunt me then! The murdered *do* haunt their murderers. I believe—I know that ghosts *have* wandered on the earth. Be with me always—take any form— drive me mad! only *do* not leave me in this abyss, where I cannot find you! Oh God! it is unutterable! I *cannot* live without my life! I *cannot* live without my soul!" (p. 204)

99

Nelly says he is howling, "not like a man, but like a savage beast, getting goaded to death with knives and spears." She's wrong: he is howling like a child, abandoned over and over, abandoned for what seems to be the final time, all that means love and identity gone. Forever? No! How could that be? How can you stay alive for the rest of your life and never be yourself again? Because you *are* alive, this seems both impossible and the worst punishment conceivable. No God, if there is one, could be that cruel. And so Heathcliff is willing to try even God to have this most primary need fulfilled. When Heathcliff cries to Cathy, "Be with me always," we understand in a way that intensifies everything I have been saying in this book what forever has to do with true love. We understand the strength of that need. With all of culture, all of the world as we know it set up to thwart that deepest desire, the raging child-lover may not willingly submit to some therapist's admonishments to "mourn the loss and move on." No. She or he will have it, if it means madness, if it means death. Because, from this perspective, there is nothing without it.

This is the moment toward which the entire first half of the novel has been moving. This cry releases everything that I know about need, about desire, about passion, about loss. It is *not* catharsis: it is recognition, it is affirmation. It mirrors a part of me. I am not alone. Brontë has been there before me; she has made Heathcliff and Catherine so that she, but also I, will be validated.

⁜

And yet the novel is not finished. For Catherine dies in giving birth to another Catherine, her daughter, a second generation. The sentence is startling: "About twelve o'clock, that night, was born the Catherine you saw at Wuthering Heights, a puny, seven months' child; and two hours after, the mother died." (p. 201) We never even knew that she was pregnant until Nelly refers once to her condition, just before her death: "on her existence de-

100

pended that of another." (p. 172) But Brontë is ready to offer more than one solution to the problem she has set, for even as Catherine's death initiates the ghost love story, so with this birth Brontë launches the family saga, too.

Catherine has become mother, sinking into the textual background so that her daughter can take over the foreground. Catherine's "self" mutates, becomes another Catherine at the same time that it pursues its individual destiny. Both are happening at once, we realize when we recall Lockwood's experience of Catherine's haunting, occurring while her daughter lives in the house. Catherine the daughter is and is not another version of her mother; she is separate and yet she is deeply related to the mother who made her. The question of how to talk about the two heroines forces us to focus on the role of generation in the nature of selfhood. "Cathy"? "Catherine"? Often we resort to neologisms: identifying the daughter as Cathy II, or deciding that one will be "Catherine," the other "Cathy," when in fact no one in the novel distinguishes them this way. They are two and they are one, and that is always what the notion of generation tells us.

The new Cathy is, however, the product of her father as well as her mother—the result, therefore, of Catherine's move into culture.

> She was the most winning thing that ever brought sunshine into a desolate house—a real beauty in face—with the Earnshaws' handsome dark eyes, but the Lintons' fair skin and small features, and yellow curling hair. Her spirit was high, though not rough and qualified by a heart, sensitive and lively to excess in its affections. That capacity for intense attachments reminded me of her mother; still she did not resemble her; for she could be soft and mild as a dove, and she had a gentle voice, and pensive expression: her anger was never furious, her love never fierce; it was deep and tender. (p. 224)

The word "qualified" is the key to Brontë's excursion into genetic theory. In the second Cathy, the genes, or the qualities, of her mother have been tamed—domesticated—by interaction with those of her father. And whereas the story of Catherine, Heathcliff, and Edgar, in its depiction of the self's struggle between the maternal creation of identity and the paternal conquest of it, proposes a myth of the existence of a maternal site outside culture, the story of the second Cathy, Linton, and Hareton situates even the maternal *within* culture. It is a fantasy about transforming the culture rather than escaping it. But it does not exist independently of the myth of origins, the first half of the book.

When Cathy II is born, in the first paragraph of Chapter 16, almost exactly halfway through the novel, we become aware of the novel's double or mirrorlike design. We cannot experience this Cathy without knowing that she is the second Cathy. But mirroring works in both directions, each half of the book looking into the eyes of the other. Even as we are always aware that this is the second half, our understanding of the first half is now qualified by the existence of the second. The birth of Catherine sets the second generation in motion. At about the same time, somewhere near London, the child of Heathcliff and Isabella is born: Linton, "an ailing, peevish creature." The third member of this generation is already at Wuthering Heights: Hareton Earnshaw, whose father, Hindley, has recently died. The new story is now implicit: another love triangle, Linton-Catherine-Hareton.

The new story formally begins when Catherine is thirteen, just as her mother's catastrophic entry into culture took place at the same age. For Catherine, it is initiated by her discovery of Wuthering Heights, as for her mother it was the reverse: the discovery of Thrushcross Grange. Whereas the first Catherine abandoned the world of the preoedipal for the lure of the father, her daughter returns to the possibility of maternal nurture that

Wuthering Heights still holds out. In this process we see a true mirror reflection, and therefore the hope for a different answer. The mother's journey was away from the maternal; the daughter's is toward it. For Wuthering Heights, although it exists in culture, never loses its maternal potential because Heathcliff lives there. This may seem a strange statement, but Heathcliff, despite his strangling of dogs and villainous schemes for revenge, is *not* a patriarch. He is, rather, a male mother deprived of his child; the male half of the maternal matrix that was Catherine/Heathcliff. Male, he aggresses outward, in direct contrast to Catherine's masochism. And yet central to his plan for generational revenge is taking control of Wuthering Heights, even as returning there was central to Catherine's self-inflicted illness and death. Wuthering Heights stands as the site for the possibility of the maternal.

Cathy II's story is cast as a fairy tale romance, in contrast to the mythic story of her mother. (For Brontë, a fairy tale is a story about culture; a myth tells of how culture comes into being, so it necessarily includes elements of a state that is pre- or non-culture.) Cathy is the princess in the tower, who has never been outside the gates of her father's kingdom until the fatal year when she is thirteen. One day, because her father has left Thrushcross Grange to go to his sister, Isabella, in London during her last illness, Catherine escapes. She goes toward Penistone Crags, the favorite haunt of Heathcliff and Catherine when they were children, encountering none other than her cousin Hareton, who takes her to Wuthering Heights, where Nelly finds her. Heathcliff too is conveniently absent, so Cathy's first visit to the Heights involves only an encounter with Hareton, with whom she fights. She treats him as a servant, and he is surly and rude in return. Nonetheless, Hareton is moved by Cathy's distress and brings her a puppy. He "bid her wisht; for he meant naught." (p. 231)

Nelly describes the young man Hareton as well made, good-looking, healthy, even in his rough clothes: "Still, I thought I could detect in his physiognomy a mind owning better qualities than his father ever possessed. Good things lost amid a wilderness of weeds, to be sure, whose rankness far over-topped their neglected growth; yet notwithstanding, evidence of a wealthy soil that might yield luxurious crops, under other and favorable circumstances." (p. 231) Cathy is taken home, angered and shocked by the cousin she had mistaken for a servant, notwithstanding the fact that before bringing her to the Heights he had "opened the mysteries of the Fairy cave, and twenty other queer places." The devoted romance reader intuits that the stage now is set for the sort of love of which romance fiction is made. Hareton is rough but tender, clearly ripe for someone to till his psychological soil; Cathy is stirred by someone who challenges her assumptions, her sense of self. If you can imagine Mr. Darcy in homespun, Elizabeth as the daughter of a gentle devoted father rather than an acerbic devoted father, then you know exactly what story you are in.

And yet the second half of this novel, even though it is supposed to be my favorite kind of romance, is not particularly compelling for me—because the first half has existed. It is not so much that the first half trivializes the second by making us see what we have had to give up in order to find this fantasy satisfying, though that is certainly a part of it. Without the first half, as in an Austen novel, we have to accept our existence in culture and go on from there. But the problem for *Wuthering Heights* is that Catherine is not dead, not exactly. We know she is out there somewhere, the ghost of her child self, because Lockwood saw her. Brontë won't write the novel of verisimilitude for us either, in which the culture squashes the incipient female self, and that is that. She counters one romance solution with another, the ghost love story poised against the happy-ever-after one, and she complicates their relationship to one another even further by making it hinge on the promise of generation—that the second Catherine contains her mother as much as she is not her mother. For all these reasons, the first Catherine is still the heroine of the novel, and she is the one with whom I identify most.

This isn't the case for all readers of the novel, as many young women have told me. They think the first Catherine is quite simply too scary, and they don't want to be like her. We could dismiss their response by saying that the poor dears are just too acculturated for their own good, except that the second story is not about capitulation to patriarchy but about appropriating it. It is, after all, the narrative of how a female can find self-development and maturity in nonpatriarchal terms. Consequently, the second story is itself a critique of the first story, offering the potential for success in the place of a tragic heroism. The two kinds of readers may well represent two components of Brontë's own vision.

If Hareton is a toned-down Heathcliff, then Linton, the son of Isabella and Heathcliff, is a pathetic version of the first generation of Linton children. Edgar brings him back to Thrushcross Grange after Isabella's death, "a pale, delicate, effeminate boy, who might have been taken for my master's younger brother, so strong was the resemblance; but there was a sickly peevishness in his aspect, that Edgar Linton never had." (p. 235) When Heathcliff comes to claim his son and bring him to the Heights, he asks, "Where is *my* share in thee, puling chicken?" Well he might ask, for Brontë's genetic theory—in which each child of the second generation is a symbolic mix of the parents—does not hold up with Linton, who seems rather the incestuous child of the Thrushcross Grange brother and sister. Heathcliff's genes somehow didn't *take,* as if he were not a real person. Which, of course, he isn't: he is a projection of both Catherine's and Brontë's fantasy—the other self, the mother self. Catherine could exist without Heathcliff, although she would be diminished, but Heathcliff, called into being by Catherine's wish for a "whip," has no existence without her need for him.

105

Linton, because he *is* the negative representation of all that Thrushcross Grange stands for, is needed by Heathcliff because he is an heir to Thrushcross Grange. Heathcliff's plot requires that Catherine Linton marry Linton Heathcliff; only then will he be master of everything—that is, of Wuthering Heights and Thrushcross Grange, the two houses signifying the entire world. Most of the remainder of the novel is devoted to the fulfillment of his designs. Linton courts Cathy in a pathetic travesty of romantic love. They exchange secret notes and arrange secret meetings. How romantic, she thinks. Beneath the one travesty is another, for between them they enact a perversion of the mother-child relationship. She pets and cossets him, doing his bidding to avoid his nasty tantrums. "Sit on the settle and let me lean on your knee," he tells her. "That's as Mama used to do, whole afternoons together—Sit quite still, and don't talk, but you may sing a song if you can sing, or you may say a nice long interesting ballad—one of those you promised to teach me, or a story—I'd rather have a ballad though: begin." (p. 274) Two motherless children, neither can truly love the other, for neither has had the opportunity for genuine development.

And yet, even as Linton sinks from a "child which frets and teases on purpose to be soothed" to a "confirmed invalid, repelling consolation" (his decline paralleling the last illness of Edgar Linton), Heathcliff's intentions intensify. Finally, Linton begs her, "Leave me and I shall be killed! *Dear* Catherine, my life is in your hands; and you have said you loved me." (p. 299) She is caught. Her marriage to Linton soon turns into widowhood, and, her father now dead, she is a prisoner at Wuthering Heights.

For the most part, Heathcliff has been supremely uninterested in Cathy as anything but a commodity—a pawn in the economy of inheritance. This is exactly the way in which he saw his wife, and the exact opposite of the way he saw her mother.

But Cathy does have her mother in her, as Heathcliff notes for the first time when she challenges him and he looks up, "seized with a sort of surprise at her boldness, or possibly, reminded by 'her voice and glance, of the person from whom she inherited it." (p. 302) At the moment when Cathy declares she will marry Linton, which is to say the moment when Heathcliff's plot is nearing closure, she again challenges him, this time more profoundly: "Mr. Heathcliff, you have *nobody* to love you; and however miserable you make us, we shall still have the revenge of thinking that your cruelty arises from your greater misery! . . . *Nobody* loves you—*nobody* will cry for you when you die!" (p. 319)

She has hit the target, for of course Heathcliff's life plan stems from his abandonment. It is no accident that his famous description of digging up Catherine's grave follows directly upon her daughter's admonishment. I am always glad to get to that part, because then I am back again in the Catherine/Heathcliff story, which I now know has been going on all the while. It's a wonderfully ghoulish moment: Heathcliff opening the grave and seeing Catherine's face ("it is hers yet"), striking one side of the coffin loose, so that when he dies he can be put in beside her. "Then, by the time Linton gets to us, he'll not know which is which!" (p. 319) But the more interesting part of this speech for me is his description of his earlier attempt to open her grave, which took place immediately upon her death. Because it was then, for the first but not, we hear, the only time, that he encountered Catherine's ghost. He had actually tried to dig her up directly after her death but was stopped by hearing a sigh, feeling warm breath at his ear. "I knew no living thing in flesh and blood was by—but as certainly as you perceive the approach to some substantial body in the dark, though it cannot be discerned, so certainly I felt that Cathy was there, not under me, but on the earth . . . Her presence was with me; it remained while I refilled the grave, and led me home." (pp. 320–21) Since that time he has been tortured by her almost presence—teasing him, taunting him, always in the room he has just left or is just about to enter. He has sensed her most strongly near the bed they had shared as children: "I couldn't lie there; for the moment I closed my eyes, she was either outside the window, or sliding back the panels, or entering the room, or even resting her darling head on the same pillow as she did when a child. And I must open my lids to see. And so I opened and closed them a hundred times a night—to be always disappointed!" (p. 321)

Now I understand Lockwood's so-called dream, and I know exactly how the two are yet striving to be together. I have renewed hope that this will come true, and that, in some way, the story of Catherine's daughter can actually influence the story of her mother. The ghost love story, the generational love story, and the developmental romance are intertwining. The second Catherine affects Heathcliff and the resolution of his story: she has her mother's eyes. So does Hareton. Those two pairs of eyes cannot help encountering one another with recognition. After Linton's death, their love story gets under way at last. Their love, in turn, is what finally causes Heathcliff to understand the complete futility of the revenge plot and to seek his own death (which means reunion with Catherine).

The love story of Cathy and Hareton occupies the foreground of the final section of the novel. We recognize it readily. Enemies at the start, they are brought together through books, through reading. They mature through a process that begins when Cathy tries to reach for a stack of books that are too high up for her on a dresser. It is Hareton who gets them down for her and fills her lap with them. He stands behind her while she reads, occasionally pointing to certain pictures that strike his fancy (he can't read, because Heathcliff has degraded him by keeping him below the level of a servant). Then he proceeds to "looking at her instead of the book." Finally, he puts out one hand and strokes her curls, "as gently as if it were a bird." This angers her: "I can't endure you!" she cries. (p. 327) But the die is cast. His recognition of her is linked to her intelligence and her participation in the social order, symbolized by her reading. And although she has bridled at his *touch,* she has permitted his looking.

The courtship—his of her, hers of him—proceeds apace through the symbolism of reading. In this novel reading, writing, and books do indeed stand for the symbolic order, so that access to them means participation in culture. Yet at the same time, the novel subverts that order. For Cathy and Hareton, books are the path toward a socialization that is not exactly in accord with patriarchal norms. For them books have the same role as *Wuthering Heights* does in the life of its reader: they show how the culture's symbol system can be used differently.

First Hareton steals some of Catherine's favorite books and tries to teach himself to read them. This upsets her most because the passages he tries to learn are "my favorite pieces that I love the most to repeat, as if," she says, "out of deliberate malice!" In response to her scorn, he throws the books into the fire. Yet the effort, occasioned by what the narrator (it is Lockwood now) calls his "self-love," causes him "anguish": "I fancied that as they consumed, he recalled the pleasure they had already imparted; and the triumph and ever-increasing pleasure he had anticipated from them." (p. 333) The books represent to Hareton the conjunction of the self and the mother. His pleasure has come from using them to connect the mother with the culture, thereby expanding his own sense of self and of reality.

At this point the narration takes an abrupt lurch. Suddenly it is one year later, and Lockwood has unexpectedly returned to visit Thrushcross Grange, only to discover that Nelly Dean is now living at the Heights. Arriving there, Lockwood walks into the finale of the novel: Catherine and Hareton, healthy and handsome, having a reading lesson, with kisses for getting the words right, and Heathcliff, Nelly tells him, dead for three months. This is the happy ending we have been anticipating. We don't, in fact, really need the intermediate scenes to understand how the lovers came to this happiness, or to understand that Wuthering Heights, with Heathcliff dead and the young couple as mistress and master, has been turned into a happy haven of comfort and civilization: the fragrance of flowers and fruits, doors and windows wide open, a fine, red fire in the hearth. What we need to know, though, is how Heathcliff died, and what this means for the ending of the other story, the story of Heathcliff and Catherine.

Because his death is intrinsically intertwined with the new life that is represented by Cathy and Hareton, however, we are treated, for the final pages of the novel, to the whole story—which concludes with Nelly's observation of "two radiant countenances bent over the pages of the accepted book . . . the enemies were, thenceforth, sworn allies." (p. 345) Hareton has allowed Cathy to teach him to read.

Thus the lovers come to selfhood in an egalitarian and mutually loving way—Hareton mothers Cathy, she mothers him. At the same time, however, something else happens: their resemblance to the preoedipal mother, now associated with the first Catherine, intensifies. "They lifted their eyes together, to encounter Mr. Heathcliff—perhaps, you have never remarked that their eyes are precisely similar, and they are those of Catherine Earnshaw." (p. 352) The renewed presence of Catherine asks for a resolution other than the cultural subversion that is the message of the story of the second generation. The preoedipal mother demands escape from culture altogether. "It is a poor conclusion, is it not," notes Heathcliff: "An absurd termination to my violent exertions? I get levers and mattocks to demolish the two houses, and train myself to be capable of working like Hercules, and when everything is ready, and in my power, I find the will to lift a slate off either roof has vanished!" (pp. 352–53)

It is the recognition of Catherine, of his own self, of what they were and are still, that makes his plan suddenly seem so silly. It is as if the two now mother him—back to what he was before. In fact, Hareton's uncanny resemblance to Catherine makes Heathcliff see Hareton as exemplifying *himself*: Hareton appears to Heathcliff as "a personification of my youth"; "the ghost of my immortal love." (pp. 353, 354) Hareton, brought into selfhood by Catherine's daughter, is at once Heathcliff's past and his future, for Hareton's startling likeness to Catherine reminds Heathcliff that everything is connected to her. "In every cloud, in every tree—filling the air at night, and caught by glimpses in every object, by day I am surrounded with her image! . . . The entire world is a dreadful collection of memoranda that she did exist, and that I have lost her!" (p. 353)

Heathcliff's words of loss, however, are negated by the truth he has just expressed—that Catherine does exist—as a spirit that haunts the world. There is the world that culture has constructed, and there is something behind it—outside it but also before it; informing it but not a part of it. This is the spirit of the preoedipal mother, and it is Heathcliff's true self as well. "Nelly, there is a strange change approaching . . . I take so little interest in my daily life, that I hardly remember to eat, and drink . . . I have a single wish, and my whole being and faculties are yearning to attain it. . . . I am swallowed in the anticipation of its fulfillment." (pp. 353, 354)

Nelly gives us her description, not of Heathcliff's death—for he has forbidden her to approach him there in his chamber, their chamber, the bed in which Lockwood had his vision, in which Catherine and Heathcliff slept as children—but of Heathcliff dead. "I observed the master's window swinging open, and the rain driving straight in":

111

> I ran to unclose the panels . . . Mr. Heathcliff was there—
> laid on his back. His eyes met mine so keen, and fierce, I
> started; and then, he seemed to smile.
>
> I could not think him dead—but his face and throat were
> washed with rain; the bed-clothes dripped, and he was per-
> fectly still. The lattice, flapping to and fro, had grazed one
> hand that rested on the sill—no blood trickled from the bro-
> ken skin, and when I put my finger to it, I could doubt no
> more—he was dead and stark!
>
> I hasped the window; I combed his black long hair from his
> forehead; I tried to close his eyes—to extinguish, if possible,
> that frightful, life-like gaze of exultation, before anyone else
> beheld it. They would not shut—they seemed to sneer at my
> attempts, and his parted lips, and sharp white teeth sneered
> too! (pp. 364–65)

This scene mirrors Lockwood's night in the same bed, down to
the flapping lattice that has grazed the hand resting on the sill.
But now the ghost has been permitted entrance, and now the
hand does not bleed, for at the same time, the sleeper in the bed
has been permitted exit. The open windows, the flapping lattice
signify the dissolution of all those borders and barriers that the
many closed windows of the novel have represented: death and
life, surely, but much more important, the barrier between self
and other, between culture and what exists before and beyond it.
Heathcliff and Catherine are together at last, wherever together
is. His emphatically, decisively *open* eyes declare this fact: that
recognition has come at last.

We hear very little more of the young lovers Catherine and
Hareton, except that they will remove to Thrushcross Grange
upon their marriage. This seems only right. For although they
have domesticated Wuthering Heights according to the principles of the acculturated mother, in the very process they have re-

leased the spirit of the repressed preoedipal mother. Brontë's double happy ending does not repudiate one version of the mother at the expense of the other. Rather, it shows how the one produces the other as well as how the original mother is never entirely lost or repressed. Each new generation recalls her. "What is the matter, my little man?" Nelly asks a little shepherd boy, on the road to Wuthering Heights. "They's Heathcliff, and a woman, yonder, under t'Nab . . . 'un Aw darnut pass 'em."

The novel closes where it began, with the culture's interpretation of this strange story. Lockwood speaks the final words at the graves of Catherine, Linton, and Heathcliff, and they are Emily Brontë's final irony:

> I lingered round them, under the benign sky; watched the moths fluttering among the heath and hare-bells; listened to the soft wind breathing through the grass; and wondered how anyone could ever imagine unquiet slumbers, for the sleepers in that quiet earth. (p. 367)

How could they not? I always retort. Lockwood, I will not accept your version, and I do not have to, for Brontë has used it to reveal the difference between what you stand for and what I believe in. She has compelled the very language of the culture to express all that it does not want to know, to tell stories that it has sought to repress of the power of mother love. Brontë shows us how the very form that has repressed the mother may be used to call her back into being, and that is why hers is indeed a maternal text, and she is a maternal author.

Her story(s) of mothers and daughters in their quest for true love mothers me. It satisfies my own yearnings to experience true love through reading: Catherine and Heathcliff get their forever, Catherine and Hareton get their "happy ever after." More important perhaps, these two happy endings come about because if mothers give birth to daughters (and die), the daughters, in their turn, give new life to their mothers. It is not an accident that *Catherine Earnshaw* dies by becoming *Catherine Linton* but is born anew when *Catherine Linton* becomes *Catherine Earnshaw*. Now the names are put to maternal as well as paternal purposes.

Yet if I get deep satisfaction from this novel, I also am unsettled by it. The ghost love story demands the rejection of culture, its happy ending imagining a place outside of time and society. The happy-ever-after love story asks for social responsibility and suggests the appropriation of culture. If the Minoan mother, the repressed unconscious, surfaces in the mature female self, what can she have to do with social consciousness? Each happy ending complicates the other one. If I am tempted to believe that I can change the culture, I am reminded that a part of me can never fit in or belong. If I am tempted to try to escape, I am reminded that I can never do that, not really. I exist as a woman in a permanently uneasy relation to the culture, where I live but where I do not really belong. Each happy ending offers me a fantasy of desire fulfilled, but Brontë's novel shows me that each ending is only half of my desire, always shadowed by the other story, the other generation—the mother, if I am daughter; the daughter, if I am mother. *Wuthering Heights* is the ultimate romance novel, because it is both a compendium of all other romance fiction and a commentary on it.

3

Seduction and Betrayal in the

Gothic Romance:

The Fantasy of Father Love

CHARLOTTE BRONTË'S *JANE EYRE*

"Reader, I married him." Words that ought to bring a warm glow of satisfaction and pleasure to any romance aficionado. Then what makes me so *uncomfortable* when Jane Eyre marries her beloved Edward Fairfax Rochester? Jane, the ultimate abandoned child—orphaned, poor, and plain—has now achieved family, wealth, identity, and true love. Why am I not happy with this happy ending?

The pages are falling out of my Penguin *Jane Eyre* by now. I suppose I should have invested in another copy, but I never have, because I've been reading this one for so long, and it has all my little markings in the margin. They serve as a testament to my abiding relationship with this novel. For me, as for generations of women readers, *Jane Eyre* has been essential reading. How could any of us forget Jane Eyre, the newly hired governess, looking out over the skyline from the attic windows of Thornfield Hall, declaiming women's inner rebellion against their lot? Or Jane as a child, confronting her abusive stepbrother John Reed and his tyrannical mother on behalf of her right to feel, to exist? She names it liberty, the prerogative to be herself. We love Jane because she is a spokesperson for women's humanity, especially our right to passionate feeling, and the reader's own heart swells to hear her defend it.

What else about this novel remains forever etched upon my mind? Mr. Rochester, of course, dark, craggy-featured, brooding, mysterious, dangerous Mr. Rochester—endlessly desired, endlessly feared. Mr. Rochester, master and lover, the only one who can see who Jane really is, the only proper object for her love. Mr. Rochester, who tricks and deceives Jane in equal proportions to his care for her. Loving Mr. Rochester is risky business, yet surely I have loved him. Jane and I, small and not beautiful, brimming with passion and imagination, have set out together on the path to selfhood and have encountered—Edward Fairfax Rochester.

How *can* we resist him when he tells her, "My bride is here . . . because my equal is here, and my likeness"? (p. 282) How can we not thrill with understanding when Jane says to him, "Wherever you are is my home—my only home"? (p. 274) And yet Mr. Rochester is no Mr. Darcy, who may be infuriating and challenging, but who is always polite, upright, and sincere—and never, never frightening. Mr. Rochester lives in a spooky mansion replete with spine-chilling laughter and bloodcurdling screams coming from somewhere in the upper stories; strange fires are lit and visitors get attacked in the night. Mr. Rochester himself has a dark and murky secret past, a strange foreign child as a ward, and he goes away for inexplicable journeys. Mr. Rochester is suspicious and mysterious: he is exciting, powerful, and dangerous. He is so sexy.

But reading *Jane Eyre* today is different from when I was fifteen. Then, Charlotte Brontë's fantasy of true love was fine by me. My discomfort at the ending had mostly to do with the fact that Mr. Rochester got hurt in the process. I didn't see why he had to be blinded and maimed, just so he and Jane could get together. Back in those days, I wasn't the kind of girl who wasted her time swooning over Elvis. My kind of hero was Mr. Rochester. I planned to find somebody just like him to make my real life begin.

It is true that I always felt a sense of well-being reading novels that created the hero as a mother—the sort of novels and psychological homes I have been describing thus far. But in another part of my mind I lived a very different scenario. I wasn't dreaming about a gentle, compassionate, tender sort of *wimp*. I was looking for someone strong and powerful, smart, successful, impressive, in control of things: someone *just like me*. Except that, as a man, he would be entitled to be that way; and loving me, he would allow me to be that way too.

I was definitely confused about being a girl. Being smart and pushy, not blonde and pretty, I always felt excluded. I was perpetually trying to belong. I hung around "normal" girls who had no claim to fame other than that no one thought they were different. I sighed over "normal" boys with straight hair falling in their eyes and skinny asses, boys who strutted and swaggered and let you know they were already manly. I never wanted the smart, weird boys—the male equivalent of me. I wanted the legitimacy that having a boyfriend could confer upon me, and that boyfriend had to come from the center, not the periphery. So I fell in love at fifteen with a college man, no less, and married him at twenty-one, directly after I graduated from college. I had found what I thought I wanted, and I wasn't about to let it get away.

The fantasy of father love involves a strange paradox. When the mother is perceived as subjugated and powerless, she seems *un*like the ambitious daughter; thus not the proper source of identity. It is the father, with his confidence, his power, his access to the outside world, who looks like the best route to identity. Thus, on the one hand, this fantasy requires the father to appreciate the daughter's likeness to him, thereby offering her both identity and power. Recognition is at the heart of this exchange, just as it is with the fantasy of the maternal hero. However, the other piece of the fantasy is that the father stay masculine. In the fantasy of the mother-hero, a man is "feminized" in order for the requisite recognition, nurture, and maternal-style love to transpire. Recognition is thus mutual recognition, a reciprocal exchange. But in the daughter-father scenario the hero retains the distance, the separateness, and the hierarchical positioning that are part and parcel of his masculine gender identity. The fantasy of father love has a vested interest in *not* taking from the hero his patriarchal birthright of power and authority: he is desired by the daughter for just those attributes. His mystery and glamour, which make him so seductive, arise precisely because he is distant and hard to get. In such an arrangement, how could true reciprocity occur? Instead, the empathy that may seem to arise works in one direction only. He "recognizes" you in order to see how you see him.

Yes, being with a man—a man like a father—confers on you the privilege of belonging. But what you're belonging to is not what you thought you'd get. You don't get identity based in likeness, and you don't get shared power. There's power all right; but it's his. It's always his. Men don't give away power. His power is over you, and to get what you need from him, you have to comply. And as much as you are indeed like him—worthy of the kind of power he has as his birthright—you threaten him. At worst, he'll retaliate. At best, he'll push you away. Between those two words lies a range of behavior that extends from what is frustrating to what is humiliating to what is emotionally and physically dangerous. No wonder that today I find this fantasy frightening rather than attractive—and clearly at odds with the idea of maternal love to which I have devoted this book. I know too much. I know that it results not in selfhood, but in bondage, degradation, and perpetual daughterhood.

118

But this is the true story, not the fantasy. In *Jane Eyre* Charlotte Brontë tries to write the fantasy, to give herself and her heroine the father love that she herself had sought all her life. True, she doesn't quite pull it off. The very process of writing the novel seems to occasion contradictions and impasses, but nonetheless, *Jane Eyre*'s status as a great love story is based in the powerful allure of the fantasy of father love. And that is something I no longer want to experience. To read and then write about *Jane Eyre* today is to feel more anger than delight: it is to want to expose the emperor rather than worship him.

Feeling like this puts me in an edgy relationship with Charlotte Brontë the author. As a daughter-writer, she needs my complicity: for me to identify with Jane, and with her, as together they seek the love and devotion of Edward Fairfax Rochester. But whereas I am being asked to see her in Jane and to cheer them both on, now I keep distinguishing between them. Indeed, I find myself more interested in Brontë's struggle with the fantasy than I am with Jane's supposed triumph within it. Although Brontë writes her novel to make her fantasy of father love come true in a way that was impossible for her to achieve in real life, she keeps discovering, probably because she is a brilliant woman and a gifted writer, all the ways in which it will not work. I think that Brontë is ultimately such an important writer for women readers because despite her best intentions and deepest desires, she cannot sustain the fantasy. In *Jane Eyre* she finds herself documenting both the seduction and the betrayal, letting us know how and why it remains the deadliest deception of them all.

※

Jane Eyre is such a fairy tale really, so much the story of a poor, unappreciated princess who finds her prince—despite his being dark and melancholy rather than bright and squeaky clean—that it is hard to imagine at the start that Brontë is going to run into any trouble fulfilling her dearest fantasies. And what she wants is Patrick Brontë—the intelligent, learned, sensitive, brooding, exciting, all-powerful father who loomed at the peripheries of her lonely childhood. The early death of her mother, followed only four years later by that of her oldest sister, Maria, who had taken her mother's place as well as her name, was a devastating experience for the remaining four Brontë children. Biographers tell of the little Brontës huddled together for love and support, "driven in upon each other's affections, like shelterless sheep huddled together to keep out the cold." It was their father who blew in like a bracing wind from the outside and brought them the magazines and newspapers that they eagerly devoured and then tried to approximate with their own writing; their father who gave them, one famous day, the toy soldiers that became the source not only of hours of play but of imaginary kingdoms and histories about which the children were to write thousands of pages of stories, verses, and dramas. The person who taught the children about the thrilling worlds of literature and politics, who stood for literary and intellectual energy, who had himself taken up his pen, was her father. No matter that he ate all his meals alone and "did not require companionship, therefore he did not seek it, either in his walks, or in his daily life"; that his temper was so fierce that he used to vent his rage by firing pistols out the back door or sawing the backs off chairs—Charlotte admired him intensely and greatly desired his approval. Perhaps such behavior made him all the more fascinating. "Patrick Brontë stood at the center of Charlotte's life," writes Irene Taylor, in *Holy Ghosts: The Male Muses of Emily and Charlotte Brontë.* "As eldest surviving daughter she seems to have hoped that she might in some way replace her mother at her father's side."

But of course, Patrick Brontë was not available. Indeed, he was her father; he was also particularly aloof and undemonstrative as a person. Taylor comments: "Charlotte had always to see the 'beloved' as forbidden or inaccessible. This pattern is expressed in Charlotte's life by her attachments first to her married teacher and later to her charming but emotionally elusive publisher, neither of whom, she well knew, was romantically available to her." Certainly Mr. Rochester, in his remoteness and initial inaccessibility, possesses an appeal that is similar to her father's. Mr. Rochester is socially as well as psychologically out of reach for the governess, Jane, and that fact just underlines his allure. Later it will turn out that there is even more: he happens to be married. Mr Rochester's marriage is a powerful plot contrivance in this novel, serving many functions; but surely one of them is to underscore yet further a sense of distance. This is a primary stimulus to the passion that finds its antecedent in daughterly desire.

The daughter's quest for the father's love is paradoxical, but it is Brontë's goal in *Jane Eyre*. In the wake of her rejection by the enticing M. Heger, the married schoolmaster, who had sent her packing from his school in Brussels (or more probably, it was his wife who had contrived Brontë's dismissal), she sets out to write her love into existence. In her novel it will be rewarded and fulfilled. The format of the fairy tale is essential to Brontë's novel. Not only because it consistently and formally enables wishes to be granted, but also because it has its roots—and they are obvious—in the psychodynamic sources of those wishes. The schematic stages of her heroine's process are a blueprint for wish fulfillment, except for the fact that the subtle winds of verisimilitude keep blowing through them. Gateshead; Lowood; Thornfield; Moor House; Ferndean: Jane's journey is charted through a series of houses, because what Jane is looking for is *home*. At the same time, the novel breaks into four sections: before Mr. Rochester; during Mr. Rochester; after Mr. Rochester; and the finale, reunion with Mr. Rochester. Home equals true love in *Jane Eyre*—and Mr. Rochester, whatever else he may or may not be, is Jane's true love.

"Before" commences with Gateshead, the antihome, the place where the orphaned heroine discovers her status as outcast and alien: the child-whom-no-one-can-love. To the child this is the worst of all possible beginnings; the worst of all possible fates. Indeed, the Gateshead chapters plunge us into the secret places of childhood suffering so painfully familiar to many of us. If we have not been parented adequately, we feel ourselves to be isolated and unrecognized no matter what the actual details of our adult lives may be. Always, we live with the terrible pain of lacking—and longing for—love. Jane is literally what I imagined myself to be: abandoned, despised, mistreated. Her wicked stepmother, stepsisters, and stepbrother are as cruel to her as Cinderella's were, and there are no little mice around to make it feel even a tiny bit better. The opening scenes of *Jane Eyre* engage and arouse many of my secret beliefs about myself, which come out of deep places of need and desire. They are embodied so sharply and dramatically that I cannot help responding and identifying.

Immediately, I am catapulted into an extremity of childhood feelings of abandonment and misery. The very first scene in the book is of a happy mother with her darling children clustered around her. But the narrator and heroine, Jane Eyre, has been deliberately excluded from this group—because of, she tells us, her inability to acquire "a more sociable and childlike disposition" (p. 39). It is a particularly vicious circle. Because the orphan Jane cannot behave like a "contented, happy little [child]," she cannot be treated like one. She is ostracized, she is abused, she is punished.

Motherless and fatherless, Jane Eyre suffers exactly in proportion to her stepfamily's hatred of her true identity. When the malicious John Reed strikes Jane for retreating to her own private world behind the curtain, he justifies his violence as resulting from "the *look you had in your eyes* two minutes since, you rat!" (p. 42) [my emphasis] He sees and *rejects* her identity, as it is revealed in what Mr. Darcy calls "the intelligent . . . expression" in her eyes.

Reading has been her crime—"You have no business to take our books." (p. 42) His punishment is to use the book as agent for his violence. He hurls it at her, so that she falls and cuts her head against the door. Bleeding, her privacy and her very self-hood violated, Jane nonetheless recognizes oppression, and she fights back: "Wicked and cruel boy! . . . You are like a murderer—you are like a slave-driver—you are like the Roman emperors!" (p. 43) Even as I cheer, she is punished yet more cruelly by her wicked stepmother ("Did ever anybody see such a picture of passion!") and shut up in the haunted Red Room.

More childhood terror. Literally abandoned, she is left alone in the Red Room, an eerie, silent, unused chamber where the late master of the house had died. This is the setting for Jane's "consternation of soul." She knows that what she is experiencing is "insupportable oppression," but the mental battle, she attests, is fought in darkness and ignorance. She cannot answer "the ceaseless inward question—*why* I thus suffered." (p. 47) In the mirror, a "visionary hollow," she sees a "strange little figure . . . with a white face and arms specking the gloom, and glittering eyes of fear moving where all else was still." (p. 46) She thinks it is one of the tiny phantoms, half fairy, half imp, from the folk tales she has heard. Is this vision her true self or the "uncongenial alien" that the family at Gateshead find her to be? Or are these one and the same? The child doesn't know, of course. How can at least a part of her not believe what others tell her she is? So that terror builds and builds as the afternoon wanes and the darkness comes in. When she sees a ray of light on the wall gliding up to the ceiling and quivering over her head, she breaks down and shrieks wildly, bringing the adults to the room. But as she pleads for release from the room, her aunt rebukes her: "Silence! This violence is almost repulsive." (p. 49) In response to her frantic anguish and wild sobs, she is shut back into the room, where she has, she supposes, a "species of fit": she loses consciousness.

In this nightmare world of childhood trauma, there is neither safety nor recourse. Not in the private world of the imagination and the mind, represented by her reading, nor in external action. In the former she is "sneaky"; in the latter she is "passionate." Both are crimes against the society represented by the Reed family. The scene in the Red Room is so terrifying because her very strengths are turned against her. Introspection becomes paranoia; self-defense becomes hysteria. In the Red Room she falls victim to society's definition of herself.

But she does not succumb, which is why she is Brontë's and our heroine. She continues to fight back, crying out to Mrs. Reed:

> "You think I have no feelings, and that I can do without one bit of love or kindness; but I cannot live so, and you have no pity . . . People think you a good woman, but you are bad, hard-hearted. *You* are deceitful!" (pp. 68–69)

Jane identifies this defiant release of passion with "the strangest sense of freedom, of triumph I ever felt. It seemed as if an invisible bond had burst, and that I had struggled out into unhoped-for liberty." (p. 69) From the start, Brontë seeks victory for Jane, victory in direct proportion to her early victimization and suffering. Brontë understands the connection between this kind of triumph and the need to establish and fight for the integrity and sheer potential of the spirit. Liberty! Jane's character is built upon this ability to strive for true selfhood. Her intelligence and her passion, reviled and feared by her false mother at Gateshead, are actually the resources she possesses that could lead her to this goal. At this juncture, "liberty" of a certain sort is indeed the result of her efforts. For, out of fear and hatred as much as anything else, Jane's wicked stepmother sends her away to school. In this way her life in the world beyond the false home commences.

⁂

Lowood is a charity school for girls, based directly upon Cowan Bridge, the school where Charlotte's sisters Maria and Elizabeth died. Jane's "escape" from Gateshead catapults her into another arena for suffering, as the patriarchal oppressions of the outside world are painted in pre-Dickensian detail. The Lowood chapters offer an unmerciful depiction of the indignities and physical hardships suffered by the children under the pious and sadistic tutelage of the "black pillar," the Reverend Mr. Brocklehurst. Most important of all, they rehearse the death of Charlotte's own substitute mother, her sister Maria, incarnated here in the character of Helen Burns. The early chapters of *Jane Eyre* are significant for the way in which they reject all of the women with whom Jane comes into contact as real sources of nurture. Orphan Jane is, and orphan she will remain, at least until she meets her intended lover.

Charlotte was five when her mother died, soon after the birth of her sixth child. Charlotte's only memory of her mother was of "a shadowy image seen on the single occasion." Biographers tell of the fierceness and passion of the children's mutual devotion in response to the "terrifying sense of insecurity awakened in them by the early death of their mother." This dependence upon one another characterized the Brontë sisters and brother for all of their lives; but at this time, one was "mother," and that was the oldest daughter, Maria. However, only four years later, Maria too was dead, of a fever that probably resulted from the poor sanitary conditions at Cowan Bridge.

In *Jane Eyre*, Jane's only friend at Lowood, the saintly Helen Burns, dies from similar causes, while she and Jane sleep in one another's arms in Helen's small crib. Yet in the novel Charlotte mitigates the importance of that second death, as if to shield herself and us from its trauma. She stresses Helen's spirituality, which makes her both suited for death and unable to embody the qualities that would help a daughter deal with the vicissitudes of real life. I sense anger as well as pain in Brontë's rendition of Helen's death: anger at women who are strong only in their passive acceptance of precepts that suppress their vitality and agency. Both Charlotte's mother and her sister were such women, and their deaths, as well as depriving her of maternal nurture, deprived her of a sense that women could be appropriate "mothers" to a daughter like her.

At Lowood, therefore, Jane must surmount the influence of both Helen and another good woman, the loving teacher, Miss Temple, from whom Jane had "imbibed . . . something of her nature and much of her habits; more harmonious thoughts; what seemed better regulated feelings . . . I was quiet; I believed I was content; to the eyes of others, usually even to my own, I appeared a disciplined and subdued character." (p. 116) As soon as Miss Temple marries and leaves the school, however, Jane undergoes a "transforming process": "my mind had put off all it had borrowed of Miss Temple . . . now I was left in my natural element, and beginning to feel the stirring of old emotions." (p. 116)

Jane needs a better mother: a mother who can recognize her true self, a self not in accord with society's dictates for women. Again, she names her need the desire for liberty:

> . . . for liberty I gasped; for liberty I uttered a prayer; it seemed scattered on the wind then faintly blowing. I abandoned it and framed a humbler supplication. For change, stimulus. That petition, too, seemed swept off into vague space. "Then," I cried, half desperate, "grant me at least a new servitude!"
>
> (p. 117)

Liberty is juxtaposed against servitude, as if both could be possible metaphors for self-identity. And yet it is precisely this tension that underlies the romance of a woman with a passionate spirit and a man who loves her as a father would.

When Mr. Rochester rides up on that horse, falls off, and is rescued by the governess, Jane, I know this is what I have been waiting for. Who else could he be but her true love—especially when she announces that it is his frown, his roughness that keeps her there, despite his admonitions for her to leave him be; the darkness, strength, and sternness of his face that keep him in her memory after the episode is over. He is clearly powerful, strong, and dangerous; on the other hand, he had needed *her:* "My help had been needed and claimed." (p. 147) The father is recognizing the daughter, seeing in her the companion and help-meet she imagines herself to be—and imagines that he is seeking. Oh yes!

Avidly, I follow the seduction scenes between Jane and Mr. Rochester. I cannot deny myself the pleasure that these moments bring. For the hope for recognition is always my temptation. "He had been looking two minutes at the fire, and I had been looking the same length of time at him, when, turning suddenly, he caught my gaze fastened on his physiognomy." (p. 162) The narrative of their intense interaction concentrates upon their eyes. She watches him ("he had great dark eyes, and very fine eyes, too—not without a certain change in their depths sometimes, which, if it was not softness, reminded you, at least, of that feeling" [p. 162]); he looks back: "My eye met his as the idea crossed my mind: he seemed to read the glance, answering as if its import had been spoken as well as imagined." (p. 166) In fact, their conversation having become more and more interesting to them both, Mr. Rochester concludes it by looking even more deeply, past Jane's grave, quiet restraint to her true nature: "I see at intervals the glance of a curious sort of bird through the close-set bars of a cage: a vivid, restless, resolute captive is there; were it but free, it would soar cloud-high." (p. 170)

This certainly feels like maternal recognition, set in clear contrast to the moment when John Reed had disavowed "the look you had in your eyes . . . you rat!" Mr. Rochester sees past the false self and demands the true self: "I think you will be natural with me, as," he continues, "I find it impossible to be conventional with you." (p. 170) What he means by "conventional" has to do with hierarchies—between employer and employee, mature man and young girl, nobleman and commoner. He finds himself desiring to bridge these gaps because of her "innate sympathy" for him, which enables him to "proceed almost as freely as if I were writing my thoughts in a diary" (p. 167), and because she is honest and forthright with him: "I don't think, sir, you have the right to command me, merely because you are older than I, or because you have seen more of the world than I have; your claim to superiority depends on the use you have made of your time and experience." (p. 165) "Humph! Promptly spoken," he replies, clearly enjoying her initiative and intelligence.

Yet here is where I begin to see that this "recognition" has hooks attached. For even as Jane's true self is being discovered and coaxed into the open in an interchange that smacks of maternal empathy—at the same time, this man who is questioning Jane, badgering, even bullying her into having a serious, spirited, and stimulating conversation with him—prompting her to speak the truth, about him, about herself—is no mother at all. What he is telling her is: Jane, you understand me because you are *like me,* and I applaud you for it! He is not saying, "Oh, it's you!"—i.e., I understand who *you* are—but rather, you understand who *I* am. She can understand, because she is like him— not because he has become womanly but because, it must follow, she can be manly. This seems the greatest of compliments, despite the fact that it is contingent not upon mutuality but upon dominance and control: his.

It is there in the very shape and form of their interaction. There is all the difference in the world between this exchange and the witty dialogue between Elizabeth Bennet and Mr. Darcy. Here Jane rises to the bait he has thrown to her, but there is no vice versa. Elizabeth and Darcy egg one another on; their interaction is really mutual, despite the social gap that exists between them, too. Here, Mr. Rochester is always in control, no matter that Jane can rise to his level and can even challenge him to higher—or deeper, or truer—heights. He is in control, because he has set the tone and the form for the interaction: question and answer, even though she is entitled to ask as well as answer. He is the teacher and she is the brilliant pupil, and he is the kind of teacher who likes that. He is the father and she is the clever daughter—and he is the kind of father who likes *that.*

In this way Brontë fuses what looks like maternal recognition with paternal authority. Who *needs* a mother, she seems to be saying, when fathers can give you everything? This reparational fantasy gives the daughter both empathetic warmth and access to power. By means of it, Charlotte Brontë gets Patrick Brontë to love her in exactly the way she wanted to be loved. And what about me, daughter of the culture that I cannot help being? Oh yes, I too feel the delight of his recognition as it is bound up in the erotic pull of his power. For erotic it is. All my life, I have seen such power effortlessly exercised by the men around me. Professors, chairmen, deans! Boyfriends, lovers, husbands! What I had always wanted from them is the kind of recognition that means I have it too. The idea of one of them wanting me for that, rather than for being sweet and nice, pretty and good; wanting me for being his peer—what a thrill! What other response was there than to do exactly as Jane is doing now—to fall in love with him?

Jane understands what is happening to her in terms of the

conjunction of growth and love: "So happy, so gratified did I become with this new interest added to my life, that I ceased to pine after kindred: my thin-crescent-destiny seemed to enlarge; the blanks of existence were filled up: my bodily health improved; I gathered flesh and strength." (p. 177) And yet as I read on, I wonder what sort of development can be occasioned by this particular brand of "empathy," which seems to have more to do with the parent than the child. For the central ingredient of their many conversations is Mr. Rochester's revelations about himself, as he gradually places (parts of) the story of his life before her. "Strange that I should choose you for the confidante of all this, young lady; passing strange that you should listen to me quietly, as if it were the most usual thing in the world for a man like me to tell stories of his opera-mistresses to a quaint, inexperienced girl like you." He attributes this rare communion to the quality of her mind: "it is a peculiar mind: it is a unique one . . . The more you and I converse the better; for while I cannot blight you, you may refresh me." (pp. 174–75) Jane and Charlotte and I, deprived daughters all, respond excitedly to the presence of empathy; it is hard to see that it is in this instance a perverse form of control. Not only is it being utilized for the self-aggrandizement of the parent, but his ability to know who we are in our secret hearts becomes a way to enslave a daughter in this unequal relationship.

For if Mr. Rochester is motivated by the good that Jane is doing for him, Jane is motivated by—the same thing. What she understands as helping herself is to help him. Her sense of growth is intertwined with emotional servitude. It facilitates her falling in love better than anything else can.

> And was Mr. Rochester now ugly in my eyes? No, reader: gratitude and many associations, all pleasurable and genial, made his face the object I liked best to see; his presence in a room was more cheering than the brightest fire. Yet I had not

forgotten his faults; indeed, I could not, for he brought them frequently before me. He was proud, sardonic, harsh to inferiority of every description: in my secret soul I knew that his great kindness to me was balanced by unjust severity to many others. He was moody, too, unaccountably so; I more than once, when sent for to read to him, found him sitting in his library alone, with his head bent on his folded arms, and, when he looked up, a morose, almost malignant scowl blackened his features. But I believed that his moodiness, his harshness, and his former faults of morality (I say *former*, for now he seemed corrected of them) had their source in some cruel cross of fate. I believed he was naturally a man of better tendencies, higher principles, and purer tastes than such as circumstances had developed, education instilled, or destiny encouraged. I thought there were excellent materials in him; though for the present they hung together somewhat spoiled and tangled. I cannot deny that I grieved for his grief, whatever that was, and would have given much to assuage it. (p. 178)

What excites Jane is the belief that she is going to be responsible for bringing this man to his better self, a self of better tendencies, higher principles, and purer tastes. She and she alone will save him, or so she thinks. He has chosen her, given to her this perilous mission of helping him.

But that is only part of the excitement here. The other part is the strong attraction of his badness. Lovingly she lingers over how harsh he is, how morose and even malignant. True, she is going to save him from all this eventually, but right now, it's thrilling. His badness indicates his primal power, his paternal power—his essential *maleness;* so when Jane says that his kindness to her is balanced by unjust severity to many others, that kindness is all the more wonderful because it comes from a cruel man. Loving him, serving him, she plans to have her cake and eat it too: she can

131

at once save him and become him. She will remain female (i.e., good), but at the same time realize her own aggressive, ambitious, passionate (i.e., bad, male) tendencies by experiencing his. Or so she thinks. This familiar impulse is actually quite confusing, but then, so are gender configurations in our culture.

Mr. Rochester's seduction of Jane is truly masterful—he has quite an array of cards up his sleeve. Jealousy, for example. Provoking Jane's jealousy is one sure way to make her want him even more. Jealousy is a stock component of the romance plot. Jane Austen, for example, frequently uses it to bring a character to the awareness that she or he loves—to recognize feelings that have, for one reason or another, been buried. Mr. Knightley in *Emma* understands his love for her when he becomes jealous of Frank Churchill. And, at the climax of the novel, Emma understands she loves Mr. Knightley when she becomes jealous of her own little protégée, Harriet Smith: "It darted through her, with the speed of an arrow, that Mr. Knightley must marry no one but herself!" But there is a great difference in how Austen and Charlotte Brontë deploy this powerful emotion. Mr. Rochester is *not* in love with Blanche Ingram. We, and Jane, don't find this out until well into the novel, but in fact, all the time, he has been flaunting their so-called relationship before Jane, inspiring jealousy where it need not be, just to trap her into intensifying her feelings for him despite the obvious social improprieties of their attachment. If we remember that this particular version of true love is modeled on the Oedipal situation, then we won't be so surprised that the daughter's desire for the father is helped along by sexual jealousy—of her mother, who has his sexual love (the opportunity for intimate acquaintanceship with the magic penis) when she doesn't. The daughter has to learn to distrust, dislike, and generally disavow women in favor of men. And this is what happens to Jane Eyre.

First with Blanche Ingram, who is a lady, whereas Jane is just a governess. Mr. Rochester spends a lot of time dining and dancing with Blanche amid brilliant company, with Jane watching from the wings. And yet, as much as Jane tries to convince herself that someone like Mr. Rochester would hardly "waste a serious thought on this indigent and insignificant plebeian" (p. 191), her growing attachment to him makes her defy these social facts, invoking a more primary bond:

> He is not to them what he is to me . . . he is not of their kind.
> I believe he is of mine—I am sure he is—I feel akin to him—I
> understand the language of his countenance and movements:
> though rank and wealth sever us widely, I have something in
> my brain and heart, in my blood and nerves, that assimilates
> me mentally to him . . . I know I must conceal my sentiments:
> I must smother hope . . . and yet, while I breathe and think, I
> must love him. (p. 204)

This is quite a speech. It makes Jane and me hunger to overcome all that rank and wealth nonsense. When there is something in the brain, heart, blood, and nerves that binds two people together (as if he were—gasp—her mother, not her father at all, since fathers stand for all that rank and wealth nonsense), then that is primary, that is everything. Again, Brontë has tried to merge the preoedipal with the Oedipal, even while the principles of the Oedipal experience prevail.

And so Jane rapidly moves from worrying about the propriety of her relationship with him to glorying in its profundity; Miss Ingram can't bring out his true devotion, whereas she can. And as she progresses, jealousy her mentor, she is more and more attracted by his mystery, his profound otherness—the secret in his soul.

As for that vague something—was it a sinister or a sorrowful, a designing or a despondent expression?—that opened upon a careful observer, now and then, in his eye, and closed again before one could fathom the strange depth partially disclosed; that something which used to make me fear and shrink, as if I had been wandering amongst volcanic-looking hills, and had suddenly felt the ground quiver, and seen it gape; that something, I, at intervals beheld still, and with throbbing heart, but not with palsied nerves. Instead of wishing to shun, I longed only to dare—to divine it . . . (p. 217)

Now the truth about our love for fathers is clarified—how fundamental is his separateness, his difference. For all that Jane and Rochester have been reveling in their kindred souls, these similarities are peripheral when cast against his profound otherness and the daughter's deep attraction to it. That is his secret, the enigma she wants to solve, even though (even because) she knows she never will. In this way Jane, who has longed for liberty and enterprise, has curtailed her idea of adventure to a scenario of servitude, in which the volcanic-looking hills she will dare to explore are the dangerous inclinations of his soul.

These dangers are real, they are ever present, and they are incarnated not by the insipid Blanche Ingram but by the mysterious denizen of the manor's third story, the creature whom Jane initially thinks of as "Grace Poole." For if Jane and Mr. Rochester have been having quiet little heart-to-heart chats in the library before bed, afterwards, in the deep of the night, there have been more lurid and exotic goings-on at Thornfield Hall. From her first arrival at Thornfield, from that very evening when she had stood leaning over its battlements thinking about "the tale [my] imagination created, and narrated continuously; quickened with all of incident, life, fire, feeling, that I desired and had not in my actual existence" (p. 141), she has heard, as if accompanying her thoughts, the "tragic," "preternatural," "eccentric" laughter of someone whom the housekeeper has identified as Grace Poole. Soon after she and Mr. Rochester begin their ever growing intimacy, she hears the "demoniac laugh—low, suppressed, and deep" at the very keyhole of her chamber door. It alerts her to the smell of smoke, and rushing from her room, she discovers Mr. Rochester's bed curtains on fire as he lies sleeping; she quenches the flames with her water jug. For a second time she has saved him, to his grateful "I have a pleasure in owing you so immense a debt." (p. 182) "Grace's" presence—inexplicable, ominous, maybe even supernatural—has from the first shadowed Jane's relationship to Mr. Rochester. When "Grace" actually attacks a visitor to the house, a Mr. Mason, and Mr. Rochester calls on Jane to assist him in treating the man, Jane's apprehension, and curiosity, increase tenfold.

> What crime was this, that lived incarnate in this sequestered mansion, and could neither be expelled nor subdued by the owner?—what mystery, that broke out, now in fire and now in blood, at the deadest hours of night? What creature was it, that, masked in an ordinary woman's face and shape, uttered the voice, now of a mocking demon, and anon of a carrion-seeking bird of prey? (pp. 239–40)

By this time most readers have recognized that we are deep in the heart of gothic country, although we have to remember that *Jane Eyre* is the mother of the contemporary gothic romance, the very first of those novels whose covers depict a young woman with hair flowing and dress alluringly undone, poised before a gloomy, foreboding castle or château. Charlotte Brontë did not invent the gothic novel, which came into being in the eighteenth century, but she did bear major responsibility for turning it, in the nineteenth century, into the modern gothic romance. The great, isolated, scary mansion with a secret has become a stock ingredient of the romantic gothic, along with the mysterious master of the house, the virtuous-seeming other man, the housekeeper, the child, and the governess-style heroine. And pages of critical speculation have been devoted to explanations for such an irresistible formula.

If we think of this drama as incarnating what Freud called the "family romance"—and most contemporary commentators on the female gothic do—then the necessary mystery and fear it creates have something to do with the child's early emotional experience. Especially, I would add, if we understand the novel to be a *retelling* of this story, repeated out of the need of a grown-up child to whom it didn't feel right the first time around.

Of course there's an enveloping but vast house in which all adventures are contained. And of course, although a man may own the house, its secrets are entwined with the house's association with a mother. As gothics superimpose the marriage plot over the romances of both preoedipal and Oedipal love, they play out a struggle *between* mother and father for the child's devotion and sense of identity. In this way they differ significantly from the Harlequin, that other formulaic romance genre. In the Harlequin, which is really a version of the maternal story of true love, the hero is transformed into a good mother. In such a process, the negative power of both the bad mother and the ordinary father is vanquished. In the gothic, on the other hand, the choice turns out to be between a bad mother and a good father—there is no concept of a feminized male. This is because there is no concept, anywhere, of a good mother, be this figure female or male. This is the dogma of father love, the principle behind the Oedipal drama. If a girl is going to be induced to turn from her identification with the mother to desire for the father and for all he represents, then everything connected with the person most immediately and directly like her must be sullied, defiled. As

136

Jessica Benjamin points out, "The myth of a good paternal authority that is rational and prevents regression purges the father of all terror and . . . displaces it onto the mother, so that she bears the badness for both of them." Thus the "mystery" in the house of gothic romance usually stands for the dangerous power of a bad mother, from whom the daughter can be saved if she cleaves to the so-called good father.

The mystery at the heart of Thornfield is not "Grace Poole" but Bertha Mason: the crazed and violent, debased and bestial wife of Mr. Rochester—the infamous madwoman in the attic. Bertha is hidden in the house because she is Mr. Rochester's secret. His secret wife, yes, but also his secret crime, as Jane terms it. When Rochester confesses all to Jane, he attributes Bertha's condition to her "intemperate and unchaste" behavior, "excesses [which] prematurely developed the germs of insanity." (p. 334) But of course, he has incarcerated her in the depths of his home, loathed and feared her, comprehended her not as a person but as a beast—in Jane's prescient words, "a mocking demon . . . a carrion-seeking bird of prey." Excess has been her crime, excess manifested in passion, with lunacy as its end result. If Bertha plays the role of the bad mother in the gothic scenario, we need to understand that "bad" is a term given by the dominant culture to a person who is a woman, not a beast, whose human characteristics are repulsive and threatening to society. That Bertha plays the role of "mother" to Jane can be understood not just because she is Mr. Rochester's wife but also because she and Jane are alike—both passionate, both striving for something beyond the realm of true womanhood.

In Brontë's iconography, however, there are good mothers and there are bad ones. This is called, in psychoanalytic language, "splitting." As Nancy Chodorow writes, "as a defense against ambivalence toward its mother and feelings of helplessness, the infant may split its perception of her and internalize only the negative aspect of their relationship. Or, it may internalize the whole relationship and split and repress only its negative aspect." Brontë (conveniently) likes to project all her notions of good onto her dead mother, represented in *Jane Eyre* by Helen Burns. The anger she feels at her mother for abandoning her, for being weak and passive and letting herself die, is split off from the good mother and locates itself in the idea of a bad one. And the bad mother becomes a projection of all the qualities she sees in herself that her good mother did not have: the passionate feelings of rage and love, the wildness, the ambition. These kinds of energies are "good" only when they belong to men; in women, they are scary and dangerous. The daughter is seeking to love the father so that he can recognize those qualities in her and label them just like him—and not like "her." He is meant to rescue the daughter from her association with the bad mother. If the idea sounds confusing, that is because it *is* confusing. How can a woman be loved by a man as a woman if he thinks she is just like a man? And how can she hate the bad mother for those very qualities in herself that she wants the father to appreciate and love? How can she escape the fate of the bad mother, which is to be rejected by father and daughter alike? The confusion represents what happens to women, and indeed, to men, in the throes of our culture's gender system, which is as illogical as it is harmful. But Bertha Mason, the "crime . . . that lived incarnate in this sequestered mansion," has a bigger role to play in Brontë's gothic romance than simply to be rejected. When she recognizes and is recognized by her daughter, Jane, the seduction of the father becomes a more iffy procedure altogether. And for all that Brontë, in her drive to win the love of the father, may be angry and frustrated by the truths that she uncovers in the gothic mansion, she is of course the one who put them there.

In the very midst of striving toward her fantasy of father love, Charlotte Brontë starts to show how problematic that fantasy is.

It is her book, her story, and still she cannot get it to happen properly. Once she has created Mr. Rochester, she cannot keep from developing his character realistically—and so he turns into what he always was: a dominating, narcissistic father. At the same time, Brontë knows on one level that *something* is wrong with her denial of the mother, her sacrifice of maternal love in the service of paternal power. As the relationship develops between Jane and Mr. Rochester, the novel begins to swarm with "presentiments . . . sympathies . . . [and] signs," elements from some other realm that are there to offer Jane a different kind of information. "Signs, for aught we know, may be but the sympathies of Nature with man." (p. 249) These include Jane's recurrent dreams of an infant, her visions of a motherly moon, and the presence of Bertha Mason at Thornfield Hall.

Bertha Mason's visibility in the novel becomes more and more pronounced as Mr. Rochester's courtship of Jane becomes more overt. Soon after setting fire to Mr. Rochester's bed curtains, Bertha attacks the mysterious visitor from the West Indies, Mr. Mason, who turns out to be her own brother. Mr. Rochester calls upon Jane to care for the man while he seeks the doctor.

"She sucked the blood; she said she'd drain my heart," moans Mr. Mason. Jane is left alone with him in the third story, "fastened into one of its mystic cells; night around me; a pale and bloody spectacle under my eyes and hands; a murderess hardly separated from me by a single door." (p. 239) This is Jane's most exciting adventure yet in voyaging into Mr. Rochester's secret interior. And indeed, the result of her coming so near to Bertha is yet another "confession" from Mr. Rochester; one, however, that he again manipulates so that her interpretation will further their intimacy rather than her knowledge.

For he masks an explanation of the crime—his word for it is "error"—with an avowal of love, and he turns the whole thing into an exercise in sympathetic imagination: Jane, imagine you are me! He woos her, thus, by calling upon her desire to be like him and upon the empathetic connection between them that is at the very heart of her love for him.

> "Suppose you were no longer a girl well reared and disciplined, but a wild boy indulged from childhood upwards; imagine yourself in a remote foreign land; conceive that you there commit a capital error, no matter of what nature or from what motives, but one whose consequences must follow you through life and taint all your existence. Mind, I don't say a *crime;* I am not speaking of shedding blood or any other guilty act, which might make the perpetrator amenable to the law: my word is *error*." (p. 247)

He asks her to imagine herself to be him so that she will therefore condone his aspirations for her, the one who will rescue him from his hopeless life of "heartless, sensual pleasure," who will "revive and regenerate" him: "To attain this end, are you justified in overleaping an obstacle of custom—a mere conventional impediment which neither your conscience sanctifies nor your judgement approves?" (p. 247)

This is pure and persuasive narcissism: it is *his* version of the experience, which turns crime into error; *his* version of salvation. Using Jane as his narcissistic object, something she is all too willing to be, he attempts to intensify her love for him by making it an aspect of his love for her.

But Bertha Mason, the occasion of Mr. Rochester's anxiety, represents more than Mr. Rochester's crime or error. She stands as well for his devaluation of and competition with women. If the secret at the heart of the gothic mansion is the bad mother, then her presence can reveal something about the father, too. Jane does not actually see Bertha in person until after she has agreed to be Mr. Rochester's wife—until the very night before the wedding. Until this point, Jane has understood Bertha from Mr. Rochester's point of view, as she has begun to see almost everything.

Their courtship culminates in one of the most wonderful love scenes of all time: "My bride is here," cries Mr. Rochester, "because my equal is here, and my likeness. Jane, will you marry me?" (p. 282) His triumphant assertion of identification and equality is guaranteed to send chills down the spine of a devotee of true love. This is, as well, the scene in which the heroine is given some of her finest lines: "Do you think, because I am poor, obscure, plain, and little, I am soulless and heartless? You think wrong!—I have as much soul as you—and full as much heart!" And again, "I am not talking to you now through the medium of custom, conventionalities, nor even of mortal flesh: it is my spirit that addresses your spirit; just as if both had passed through the grave, and we stood at God's feet, equal—as we are!" (p. 281)

And yet—oh, and yet. The problem, the deep unease I feel even while my heart beats quicker, is revealed by the very juxtaposition of her words and his. For why should she have to *say* those things, if he feels as he does, if they are really so "equal"? And why does he tease her, torture her, deceive her—continuing to perpetuate his charade about Miss Ingram by telling Jane that she must leave Thornfield, that he is about to take a bride, to take Miss Ingram to his bosom, to send Jane to Ireland! What am I to do with my discomfort, distaste, and downright fear—in tandem with my delight in his powerful love for her? How can I—why *should* I—entertain both kinds of feelings?

Oh, he gets what he wants from it: Jane declares her love for him, first. She can no longer hide her feelings and her needs: "it strikes me with terror and anguish to feel I absolutely must be torn from you for ever. I see the necessity of departure; and it is like looking on the necessity of death." (p. 281) Only after her declaration does he confess that he could never marry Miss Ingram, then propose to Jane over and over and vow to guard, and cherish, and solace her. "Is there not love in my heart, and constancy in my resolves? It will expiate at God's tribunal. I know my Maker sanctions what I do. For the world's judgement—I wash my hands thereof. For man's opinion—I defy it." (p. 284) Whereupon a storm rushes down upon them, thunder and lightning. Next morning, the chestnut tree under which they had stood is split in two, struck by lightning soon after they had quit the scene.

This is clearly a portent. Despite their declaration of mutual love, all is not well. And what is not well, not well at all, is the relationship itself. For even as Mr. Rochester has gone public, with Jane as his avowed fiancée, so he has gone public with his dominance and control, as he imagines the transformation of "Jane Eyre" into "Jane Rochester." He wants to put diamonds around her neck, load her fingers with rings, make the world acknowledge her as his. Jane's response is "something that smote and stunned: it was, I think, almost fear." (p. 287) Suddenly, Jane realizes that what is at risk is "myself." After a trip to town, after the silk warehouse and the jeweler's shop, she burns with "annoyance and degradation": "I thought his smile was such as a sultan might, in a blissful and fond moment, bestow on a slave his gold and gems had enriched." (p. 297)

As the images of slavery and potential "mutiny" amass, Brontë shows us what a monster she has created in Mr. Rochester. The entire rest of the novel, two hundred pages' worth, is now set to the task of finding a solution to the problem she herself has created: How can "Mrs. Rochester . . . a person whom as yet I knew not" (p. 303) come into being? How can Jane marry her true love? On the other hand, how can she not? Brontë is writing a love story. The novel yearns for a happy ending. However, Brontë has arrived at the realization that marrying the man who stands in for the father is a way to lose identity, not gain it.

Now is the moment for the final appearance of Bertha Mason, this time in Jane's very bedroom, in the dark of night—the night before Jane's wedding day. Jane wakes from disturbing dreams to confront a figure who first puts Jane's wedding veil on her own head, then rips it in two. Jane sees the face, wearing the veil, reflected in the mirror: a savage face with red rolling eyes and blackened and swollen lineaments. It reminds Jane, she tells Mr. Rochester, of a vampire. After tearing the veil and trampling on it, the figure thrusts her candle close to Jane's face, fiery eyes flaring at her. As the "lurid visage flame[s]" over her, Jane loses consciousness: "for the second time in my life—only the second time—I became insensible from terror." (pp. 311–12)

The connection between Jane and Bertha Mason, both brides of Mr. Rochester, is unavoidable. Bertha makes it, vividly and tangibly. But of course, Bertha *is* the legal wife of Mr. Rochester, Jane the imposter—exactly what would be the case if Bertha were literally Jane's mother, Mr. Rochester her father, and the daughter were attempting to supplant the father's love for the mother by claiming it for herself. In her double gesture, that of wearing and destroying the wedding veil, Bertha claims her own relationship to Jane: they are same and different, for Bertha is mother, Jane daughter. Bertha's presence, and fate, are a warning to her daughter that the patriarchy will rename, ostracize, degrade, and transform "passion" into "madness."

Jane herself associates this moment with her vision in the Red Room so long ago. Then, too, Jane had seen in a mirror a spectral shape, a supernatural version of herself. Then, too, she had lost consciousness. In each case, Jane saw a self the world will not condone, a woman unhampered by social requirements: a woman who is thus "monstrous." And yet, not to acknowledge this self is also dangerous, Brontë tells us. Disavow her and you turn into the sultan's slave.

The marriage must not take place. Nor does it, for as Jane and Mr. Rochester stand before the altar on the following day, an impediment to their union is announced by a solicitor from London. The groom is married already, to Bertha Antoinetta Mason, the madwoman in the attic. Bertha thus becomes the rationale, both impediment and protector. Her existence, bestial and crazed as Mr. Rochester demonstrates her to be—for his first act after the wedding is stopped is to bring the clergyman; the solicitor; Bertha's brother, Mr. Mason; and Jane to Bertha's chambers and reveal her to them in all her horror—allows Jane to see at last the secret at the heart of the gothic mansion. But Bertha is not the crime; she is its victim. For the crime is Mr. Rochester's misogyny and duplicity: he "was not to me what he had been; for he was not what I had thought him," laments Jane. (p. 324)

Bertha's existence serves to focus Jane's shock on the condition of her love for Mr. Rochester and its relation to her own identity. There is a terrible connection between her sudden awareness of blighted, arrested growth—"Jane Eyre, who had been an ardent, expectant woman . . . was a cold, solitary girl again . . . A Christmas frost had come at Midsummer; a white December storm had whirled over June" (p. 323)—and her understanding that Mr. Rochester can no longer nurture her, if nurture her he ever had. "I looked at my love: that feeling which was my master's—which he had created; it shivered in my heart, like a suffering child in a cold cradle: sickness and anguish had seized it; it could not seek Mr. Rochester's arms—it could not derive warmth from his breast." (p. 324) The fantasy underlying the entire novel is unraveling before our very eyes, as the father is revealed to have been no mother at all. Jane's development toward womanhood, predicated upon this love, is now "struck with a subtle doom": "ice glazed the ripe apples, drifts crushed the blowing roses." (p. 323) If love and nurture are needed to bring the self into existence, then the so-called self that Mr. Rochester's false mothering had created is indeed struck down. Will Jane then die, or can she be reborn? If so, into what manner of self?

And in the process, what will happen to her love for Mr. Rochester?

Her mind tells her to leave: "you shall yourself pluck out your right eye; yourself cut off your right hand: your heart shall be the victim . . ." (p. 325). If Mr. Rochester has been a part of her (a diseased part), then something remains—whatever the girl Jane had possessed, the "thin crescent" she had been before she loved him. And this is the strength on which she draws in the excruciating scene in which she leaves him.

Strength? When I used to read this scene, I would hate Jane Eyre, hate Charlotte Brontë. How could they do this to me? There is Mr. Rochester ("ignorant, raw, and inexperienced"), duped by the Mason family in Jamaica into marrying a beautiful woman cursed with a family inheritance of madness and idiocy, the result, supposedly, of her father's marrying a Creole woman ("Her family wished to secure me because I was of a good race"). Poor Mr. Rochester, discovering too late that he has married a woman "at once intemperate and unchaste," with a "pygmy intellect" and "giant propensities," whose "vices sprang up fast and rank." Poor Mr. Rochester, returning to England, hiding his mad wife ("her excesses had prematurely developed the germs of insanity") in his attic, looking for true love, falling under the various sexual spells of French and Italian mistresses, at last discovering Jane: "You are my sympathy—my better self—my good angel." (p. 342) Hasn't he paid for whatever part in all of this might have been his fault; doesn't he love her truly? "I am bound to you with a strong attachment. I think you good, gifted, lovely: a fervent, solemn passion is conceived in my heart; it leans to you, draws you to my centre and spring of life, wraps my existence about you, and kindling in pure, powerful flame, fuses you and me in one." (p. 342) For words like that (he's back to the old motherly rhetoric again), I would have forgiven anyone. (Sexism? Racism? Who noticed? Who cared?) And so, it seems, would Jane: "Reader, I forgave him at the moment and on the spot. There was such deep remorse in his eye, such true pity in his tone, such manly energy in his manner: and besides, there was such unchanged love in his whole look and mien—I forgave him all: yet not in words, not outwardly; only in my heart's core." (p. 326)

And yet, knowing that he loves her, she is bent on leaving him anyway. Resisting her desire to care for him at the expense of herself ("soothe him, save him, love him . . . Who in the world cares for *you?* or who will be injured by what you do?"), she cries: "*I* care for myself. The more solitary, the more friendless, the more unsustained I am, the more I will respect myself. I will keep the law given by God; sanctioned by man." (p. 344)

I couldn't care less, then or now, about the laws and principles she invokes. She loves him; he loves her. He needs her. All that rhetoric about "solitary" and "unsustained" has never done much for me. Yet this time I see elements in the scene that I missed before, taken up as I always was by the feeling—of love, and even more, of loss. Myself, I would do almost anything to avoid parting and separation. Living with my true love as his mistress because he happened to be legally married to a madwoman (no matter how or why she became that way) would be inconsequential. But now—now I watch the scene as an encounter having to do with control, and with power. Now I see Jane attempting to change the power arrangements between them—beginning with the way they talk together.

Early in the scene, in response to her will to leave, Mr. Rochester threatens violence. At this moment Jane suddenly understands how she might assert control. The idea thrills her.

The present—the passing second of time—was all I had in which to control and restrain him . . . But I was not afraid: not in the least. I felt an inward power . . . The crisis was perilous; but not without its charm: such as the Indian, perhaps, feels when he slips over the rapid in his canoe. I took hold of his clenched hand, loosened the contorted fingers, and said to him, soothingly—

"Sit down; I'll talk to you as long as you like, and hear all you have to say, whether reasonable or unreasonable." (p. 330)

From this moment on, even as they argue back and forth, she is the one who controls the terms of the conversation. The subtext of their struggle is finally articulated directly when, much later, he cries, "It would not be wicked to love me." Her answer is, "It would be to obey you." (p. 343) The slave has overthrown the sultan.

But at what cost? "Oh, Jane! my hope—my love—my life," he sobs in anguish as she walks away. When she turns back, "Up the blood rushed to his face; forth flashed the fire from his eyes; erect he sprang; he held his arms out." Still she leaves. " 'Farewell!' was the cry of my heart as I left him. Despair added, 'Farewell, forever.' " (pp. 345–46). Yes indeed, withdrawal is control; leaving is control. But Mr. Rochester has not changed because she has found a way to have power over him. Given half the chance, his old attractiveness will reassert itself—that flashing eye and general *erectness*. This is what Jane loves. She loves a father. She may gain control of the situation by leaving him, but it will not alleviate her own suffering, since it does not alleviate her love.

Would that he did not exist at all, I think. As long as he does, he is a problem, now that she has realized two irrevocable and contradictory truths: that he is not a mother and that he is the one she loves. For Brontë has discovered that Jane needs a mother—needs some way to grow and to develop apart from Mr. Rochester. To this end, she gives to Jane, first, a vision of the moon as mother, and then, the Moor House episode.

On the night following Jane's farewell to Mr. Rochester, she has a dream in which she reexperiences the long-ago events in the Red

147

Room at Gateshead. Now the light that had terrified her into fainting changes character. It glides up the wall to the ceiling, whereupon the roof opens to reveal the sky, and the gleam becomes "such as the moon imparts to vapours she is about to sever."

> I watched her come—watched with the strangest anticipation;
> as though some word of doom were to be written on her disc.
> She broke forth as never moon yet burst from cloud: a hand
> first penetrated the sable folds and waved them away; then,
> not a moon, but a white human form shone in the azure, in-
> clining a glorious brow earthward. It gazed and gazed on me.
> It spoke to my spirit: immeasurably distant was the tone, yet
> so near, it whispered in my heart—
> "My daughter, flee temptation."
> "Mother, I will." (p. 346)

The gleam that Jane had seen so long ago in the Red Room is now revealed as the presence, within the very bastions of the patriarchal culture, of the idea of the good mother. What terrified her then may well have been her own impulse toward succor. This revelation twice-removed—it is the dream of a vision—is the best that Brontë can do in this novel regarding good mothers. No earthly woman can function this way for Jane, but the vision remains as an indication that mothers are somehow necessary.

At this point and for the rest of the novel, the basic premise of the gothic romance is repudiated: that in the contest between mother and father for the daughter's identity, the father must and should win out. This is why, when later gothic romances make lavish use of the elements of *Jane Eyre* in their stories, they never refer to the Moor House sequence. It is, after all, meant to contradict the tale of Thornfield Hall with a maternal paradigm for development.

Unfortunately, it comes a little too late in the proceedings and a little too halfheartedly to be very effective. Even I, who can ferret out a maternal tale in the most unpromising of novelistic environments, feel next to nothing for Jane's discovery of a new home with the Rivers family—Diana, Mary, and St. John. It is far too theoretical, too schematic an endeavor on Brontë's part. By balancing the Gateshead experience neatly with two loving sisters and a loving brother, who turn out to be blood relatives just like the original trio, and by giving Jane the chance to work with and care for these three, Brontë lets her begin again. In the process, she has Jane's uncle die in Madeira, leaving her all his wealth, so that she is able not only to make a pretty home for her cousins but also to know that she is not and never will be poor again. Jane works as a teacher in a rural school; she develops independence and integrity.

Yet through it all, we think of, we yearn for, who else but Mr. Rochester? I don't feel maternal nurture; I feel frustration. Let's get this over with, I urge, turning the pages as fast as I can, and get back, somehow, to Mr. Rochester. Especially when Brontë makes St. John Rivers a cold and calculating suitor for Jane's hand (nobody seems to mind that he's her cousin), I grit my teeth with fear, the first time through; annoyance thereafter. Jane's life at Moor House feels less like a rebirth than an exile, and certainly an impediment.

And yet, as a reader, I'm not exactly out of line with Brontë's intentions here. Because, as much as she wants Moor House to mean maternal nurture for Jane, she also contradicts that impulse throughout the episode. First, because Jane's independence as schoolmistress makes her not "gleeful, settled, content" but, she confesses to us, "desolate." She vows to overcome these feelings, to get the better of them. But, as St. John Rivers notes early on in their relationship, "human affections and sympathies have a most powerful hold on you. I am sure you cannot long be content to pass your leisure in solitude, and to devote your working hours to a monotonous labour wholly void of stimulus." (p. 382) The word he uses for her nature (he "reads it in [her] eye") is, significantly, "impassioned." And the existence of her never vanquished passion turns out to be at war with what Moor House finally comes to symbolize. For passion (à la Bertha Mason) is now what connects her to Mr. Rochester. After a day spent in "honourable exertion" among her pupils, she has strange dreams:

> . . . dreams many-coloured, agitated, full of the ideal, the stirring, the stormy—dreams where, amidst unusual scenes, charged with adventure, with agitating risk and romantic chance, I still again and again met Mr. Rochester, always at some exciting crisis; and then the sense of being in his arms, hearing his voice, meeting his eye, touching his hand and cheek, loving him, being loved by him—the hope of passing a lifetime at his side, would be renewed, with all its first force and fire. (p. 393)

The old fantasy simply will not, or cannot, die—not at this point in the novel, or in Brontë's life. Every time reason points to its foolishness and indeed dangerousness, reason itself is attacked.

And this is precisely what happens via Jane's romance with St. John Rivers. Suddenly, the maternal mode of Moor House is connected, with St. John as its advocate, with reason and not feeling. Jane begins to see that "with me . . . it is fully as much a matter of feeling as of conscience: I must indulge my feelings; I so seldom have had an opportunity of doing so." (p. 413) St. John, on the other hand, is all white and cold, with "his lofty forehead, still and pale as a white stone." (p. 418) In relation to his ice, Jane is fire: "as his wife—at his side always, always restrained, and always checked—forced to keep the fire of my nature continually low, to compel it to burn inwardly and never utter a cry, though the imprisoned flame consumed vital after vital—*this* would be unendurable," she thinks. (p. 433) Clearly, this marriage would be a living hell.

And yet, the fire imagery with which Jane herself comes to portray passion is linked as much to Bertha Mason, with her penchant for setting fires at Thornfield Hall, as it is to Jane's love for Mr. Rochester. The connection is especially apparent when St. John recoils from this aspect of Jane's nature—"his lips and cheeks turned white—quite white," calling her words to him "violent, unfeminine, and untrue" (p. 438). He deems her unwomanly because of her passion, as Mr. Rochester had done regarding Bertha. This is why Bertha had been cast as bad mother. Thus, what happens in the Moor House episode is not so much a rejection of "maternal" on behalf of "paternal" as it is a rejection of the good mother on behalf of the bad one. Bertha is bad precisely because she is not womanly in cultural terms, and in having Jane embrace her qualities Brontë is in effect rewriting the gothic myth yet again. Jane does not repudiate the mother to love the father, but rather, she *becomes* the bad mother and in this way is able and ready to take her place in the original marriage.

Which it soon becomes possible to do. Up to this point in the novel, the domination of the father has been somewhat and sometimes countered by forces operating from outside of society—dreams, visions, and nature—which have always been associated with some kind of maternal power. But now the bad mother in Jane becomes the source of such powers, even as Mr. Rochester, the bad mother's consort, becomes their focus. At last Jane, in visionary fashion, hears him calling her: "Jane! Jane! Jane!" "I had heard it—where, or whence, for ever impossible to know! And it was the voice of a human being—a known, loved, well-remembered voice—that of Edward Fairfax Rochester; and it spoke in pain and woe, wildly, eerily, urgently." (pp. 444–45) "I am coming," she cries, breaking from St. John, who would have detained her. "My powers were in play and in force."

And so we arrive at the famous ending of *Jane Eyre,* which is as controversial as endings come in literary history. What is going on? everybody asks and then answers variously, when Jane, leaving Moor House posthaste to search for Mr. Rochester, finds Thornfield burned to the ground (by Bertha, of course, who kills herself in the fire) and Mr. Rochester not dead but, she is told, gone away to his forest retreat, Ferndean, stone-blind and crippled from the fire.

The Moor House episode has as much been preparing us for this conflagration as it has been trying to offer Jane some kind of self-development away from Mr. Rochester. When Jane affirms the Bertha in her own soul, there is no need for the first Bertha to be alive. Jane can take her place. And yet there is more to it, for the new marriage cannot possibly exist on the same terms as the old. We do not expect Jane to turn into a madwoman in an attic. Then how can Brontë allow Jane to be herself (i.e., a powerful, passionate woman) and marry a powerful, passionate man? We are back to the original dilemma. For Bertha was after all *mastered* by Edward Fairfax Rochester, who had all of the power of the patriarchy behind him as he turned her from woman into beast. And Brontë, if only because she has split the idea of mother into good (weak and feminine) and bad (strong and unfeminine), cannot entertain the idea of making the hero maternal. She won't take from him the maleness that has made him so attractive in the first place, but neither can she put Jane—no matter how full of self-knowledge—at the mercy of that masculinity. Therefore, rather than defusing his paternal power by giving him maternal qualities, she reduces him physically, cutting out an eye and chopping off a hand. This makes him not a woman but not quite a man. He is not emasculated, not "castrated," as many would have it, but reduced to being something closer to a child.

Jane finds Mr. Rochester at Ferndean: his "port was still erect, his hair was still raven black, nor . . . could his athletic strength be quelled or his vigorous prime blighted." (p. 456) But there is a change: "his countenance reminded one of the lamp quenched, waiting to be re-lit; and alas! it was not himself that could now kindle the lustre of animated expression: he was dependent on another for that office." (p. 464) The "powerlessness of that strong man" touches Jane's heart to the quick.

It has always been about power, all the time; Brontë cannot imagine love and power as separate. Now it is Jane's turn: she teases him, she makes *him* jealous, and only then does she declare her true love. "I love you better now, when I can really be useful to you, then I did in your state of proud independence, when you disdained every part but that of the giver and protector." (p. 470) And Mr. Rochester complies: "Jane's soft ministry will be a perpetual joy."

"Reader, I married him." And having married him, Jane brings Mr. Rochester back to life.

> I was then his vision, as I am still his right hand. Literally, I was (what he often called me) the apple of his eye. He saw nature—he saw books through me; and never did I weary of gazing for his behalf, and of putting into words the effect of field, tree, town, river, cloud, sunbeam—of the landscape before us; of the weather round us—and impressing by sound on his ear what light could no longer stamp on his eye. (p. 476)

Later a London specialist helps him recover sight in one eye. Nonetheless, he can never see distinctly or read or write much. A child is born to Jane and Edward Rochester, but I can't help thinking that Jane has not one but two sons. For what is she to Mr. Rochester but his mother? If it is too dangerous for Mr. Rochester to be Jane Eyre's father, then what is left for him to be but her child? It seems that Brontë can imagine only one love relationship, parent and child. There is no such thing as a marriage between peers, coming out of and fostering equality. There is no such thing as love between adults—not when the writer is herself a daughter. And of course, it is no accident that Brontë imagined this "solution" at the moment when she herself had assumed care of and control over her own blinded father; we can only imagine the satisfaction (and confusion) her role must have brought her.

I am left adrift by this happy ending. I always have been, even when I, too, loved Mr. Rochester and wanted only for this marriage to occur. Then, I felt creepily uncomfortable, for I couldn't, I just couldn't identify with Jane at Ferndean. I didn't want to be Mr. Rochester's mother! I probably wanted to remain his daughter—even if the suffering went on and on. I don't know. But now it's worse. I am bothered by the whole thing. Mr. Rochester is a travesty as a child, and Jane is a travesty as a mother. Not only wouldn't I want to be in a marriage like theirs, I wouldn't want to be in a parent-child relationship like theirs—on either side. How can Brontë create Jane as a mother when she has never received anything approximating good mothering herself? Jane as mother is a badly mothered daughter's fantasy of one: the person with all the power. Jane dispenses the largess—graciously, lovingly, but despotically nonetheless, and the child Edward is totally dependent upon her for it. She is as much the perfect narcissistic mother as he was in his time the perfect narcissistic father. The Bertha in Jane has indeed had her revenge. Rather than his mastering her, she has mastered him. But at a peculiar cost. For the wildness and the passion have had to be repressed once again. Jane has to pretend to be a good mother in order to be a bad one. Nothing remains of her dreams of liberty and adventure, much less her need for romantic passion. They are as quenched in Jane as they were distorted in Bertha. If this is domestic bliss, I wouldn't touch it with a ten-foot pole.

There is a desperation to this happy ending that I didn't use to see. As the novel draws to a close, with its seemingly peripheral emphasis on St. John Rivers's impending death in the service of God, I am less interested in my own feelings—I am pretty much distanced from the story by now—than in Brontë's predicament. Maybe the story swerves to St. John's path—sexless and pure, passion sublimated from the body to the soul—as a last-ditch alternative to Jane's. The villain turns into a weird new hero. "Firm, faithful, and devoted, full of energy and zeal, and truth, he labours for his race . . . He may be stern; he may be exacting; he may be ambitious yet . . . but his is the ambition of the high master-spirit, which aims to fill a place in the first rank of those who are redeemed from the earth—who stand without fault before the throne of God, who share the last mighty victories of the Lamb, who are called, and chosen, and faithful." (p. 477) The last lines of the novel are actually a prayer—"Amen; even so, come, Lord Jesus!" For Charlotte Brontë, religion and religious devotion could and often did take the place of her confused yearning for true love. Yet if this is the final message, it isn't very convincing in the context of all that has gone before.

By the end of *Jane Eyre,* Charlotte Brontë has painted herself into a corner. The writing has brought her to a completely unclear sense of what female selfhood means—of how ambition and passion might be reconciled with the need for love. And if I am dismayed, confused, and pretty much alienated, where is she? The best I can do is to say, still a brilliant writer; still a daughter. Her novel has not brought her to a maturity that knows how to deal with father love. On the other hand, it has most definitely raised all the problems and issues involved, even if it cannot solve them. I can watch the struggle and can see that Brontë is left with a war between *her* reason and passion. Reason may well be on the side of seeking some other path, but passion persists in loving the father. It is an impasse—for as long as you desire the father's seduction, you cannot grow beyond it.

4

The Magic Circle:
Fictions of the Good Mother

LOUISA MAY ALCOTT'S *LITTLE WOMEN*
AND GLORIA NAYLOR'S *MAMA DAY*

After all this time spent with Jane and Mr. Rochester, it is with a sigh of relief and pleasure that I turn to some of the best reading of all, those novels that do even more than transform a lover into a mother for the needy heroine, more than offer the needy reader the wise and devoted presence of an author-mother. These fictions incarnate the good mother in the flesh. She is not just an idea, an imaginative transformation: not the hero, who is *like* a mother; not even the felt presence of a maternal author. She is a person in the story; indeed, she is the very center of a work from which her power and love emanate as warmth and light spread out from the hearth in the center of a room. She is Marmee in Louisa May Alcott's *Little Women;* Mrs. Todd in Sarah Orne Jewett's *The Country of the Pointed Firs;* Mrs. Ramsay in Virginia Woolf's *To the Lighthouse;* Mama Day in Gloria Naylor's recent novel of the same name. And as there is an immediacy in experiencing her in a novel where she is literally present, so it is easier to believe in her, for these books take as their subject

156

the absolute importance of maternal nurture. "Mothers are the *best* lovers in the world," says Jo March to *her* mother, the beloved Marmee of *Little Women,* and this is a truth that readers of fictions of the good mother know full well.

Reading these novels gives me the feeling of being safe and sound in the magic circle of mother love. Safe, sound, because I belong. No longer an outsider, no longer on probation; not having to gauge, to test the waters: Am I alone, or is she there? Does she want me, or not? Will I be hurt, or is it safe to love? The good mother never goes away, and she loves you always; that is the joy of belonging to the magic circle. I was one of the thousands of girl readers since 1868 who have lived in and through *Little Women,* that cherished novel which has been passed down from mother to daughter over all these generations. Along with Jo March, I have learned to grow in the protected yet stimulating world that Marmee made. When I read that novel today, I still curl into its warmth and love. And yet there is a new ingredient to my reading, because I have a daughter who has been Jo too. Like many mothers before me, I gave this book to Alex, my reading daughter—one among many I have offered to her, one of the ways I know how to give her both lessons and love. Today I still read as Jo, because this is after all a daughter's text. The mother is not subject in her own right (as she is in some novels, such as Gloria Naylor's *Mama Day*) but exists as the object of a daughter's love. However, my experience of the magic circle is magnified by my love for my own daughters, my pain over the changes being wrought in the circle that I created with and for them. As a daughter, I come to the circle because I need Marmee's love for myself; as a mother, I find in the circle that is Marmee plus Meg, Amy, Beth, and Jo the affirmation of what I came to know the second time around.

Mama Day is also a fiction of the good mother. In Gloria Naylor's contemporary novel there is another magic circle to enter, an actual island—set apart from the mainland, not on any map. Yet here the person to whom I relate most is not the daughter, Cocoa, but the mother (literally a great-aunt), Miranda— Mama Day. I at once want her and am her. This maternal culture is emphatically black, and I am white, and whereas I never forget these differences, I nonetheless identify with the characters, drawn along by the pull of maternal feeling. Reading *Mama Day,* in fact, helps me to see that there are times when I read as a mother: if there is a mother in the text with her own subjectivity, someone with whom I can empathize.

For me to write about fictions of the good mother is to bring into this book the other dimension of my experience of the mother-daughter bond and thus to experience the heroine's romance plot from another perspective. I have three daughters, grown now, in their twenties, living far from me. One is in college, one in graduate school, one just starting her career as an assistant professor. I am becoming a long-distance mother, and I do not particularly like it. Why should I, when in pivotal ways mothering took the place of being mothered for me; gave me the chance to try again for love and recognition? Mutual recognition—isn't that the best of all? I love it that when Jessica Benjamin begins her discussion of this idea, she offers as example a picture of the daughter recognizing the mother, rather than the more traditional one of mother recognizing child: "As she cradles her newborn child and looks into its eyes, the first-time mother says, 'I believe she knows me. You do know me, don't you? Yes, you do.'" When Alex, Jenny, and Antonia have regarded me, I have come to know myself. Even as, I believe, I have recognized each of them. When I was a young mother, I hadn't read any psychoanalytic theory. I invented two guidelines: Love her always, and let her know she isn't you. Out of my own need (which produces knowledge, after all) I tried to give what I thought a daughter needed—and discovered that this particular process gave me a sense of my own identity in return. There is such a familiarity and excitement in being with them. We're so alike, yet we're different. Both parts of the exchange make me know I am really there.

Nursing a baby: lips at my breast, sucking, pulling, like an eager lingering kiss; eyes gazing absorbedly into mine. The sweetness of flesh, soft and pressing. The surge inside of joy, peace, desire. I am giving this to you, and you are giving this to me. We belong. This is the earliest magic circle. This is love.

When I divorced their father and moved into my little house—the stone cottage with a huge (ineffective) fireplace, an apple tree, a porch swing—and we were all together there, no husband to stand between us, to field my love with his own insistent demands, I felt the magic particularly strongly. True, Alex had to sleep on the couch in the living room and dress in a corner of the basement, and Jenny and Toni were crammed into one little bedroom, and I was struggling with how to keep a house running and always be the one to pick them up at gymnastics. But I remember all of us sitting around the narrow table, coloring Easter eggs, while white spring snow fell outside the window; trimming the little fat Christmas tree with ornaments we'd just made for it, dancing to the carols on the phonograph. In and out, back and forth, breakfast and dinner, nights breathing quietly as we slept—especially valuable because of the other, empty nights when they were gone to their father's house. A circle. Then one by one they went away, each to college in the east. A second marriage, and a new and bigger house, did not replace their presence in my heart. Or my need for them.

The novels I write about in this chapter are not simply good-mother fictions, like, for example, Virginia Woolf's *To the Lighthouse* or Sarah Orne Jewett's *The Country of the Pointed Firs*. They are also romances: that is, novels that alter Austen's romance pattern by giving to the heroine a good mother, rather than a bad or inadequate or dead mother. With this difference, however, problems arise. If in the Austen-style romance the function of the hero is to become a mother to the unmothered heroine and thus provide an opportunity for the development she never had, what is there for him to do if she's already had a mother? There's an obvious answer: marry her, have sex with her, so that true love is seen as an adult, sexual alliance enabling the daughter to move beyond the family romance into another home, where she in her turn can become the mother. But where does maturation fit in? Is it necessary? In what form might it occur? Why bring true love into the developmental drama at all, if a woman, either the biological mother or an adult woman who will act as a surrogate, can nurture the heroine—with much less imaginative sleight-of-hand?

That's one issue. Another is whether the hero can even compete with the mother as the best lover. Jo March does say to Marmee, after all, "Mothers are the *best* lovers in the world," even as she adds, "but, I don't mind whispering to Marmee, that I'd like to try all kinds." The love of the good mother comes first. It can, I've argued, serve as the paradigm for all to follow, so that romantic love replicates its processes and adds adult sexuality into the mix. But what if the love affair doesn't measure up? What if the fantasy of the mother-hero turns out to be just that, a fantasy? What does it mean to leave the magic circle?

And what about the mother? Once we grant her a subjectivity of her own, she now exists as a real agent in the daughter's life: i.e., the mother-daughter bond consists of mother as well as daughter. What needs of the mother get met when the daughter "tries all kinds"? Or to put it another way, what is there for a mother to *do* in romance fiction, the story of the (second) true love?

Bringing sexuality into the picture helps to suggest both why women writers might want to combine two needs and how they might have problems doing so. One need is to have a good mother; a second is that romantic love, although it is sexual, will be an emotional extension of mother love. To write about a good mother nurturing a daughter without including romantic love leaves the daughter's future, the novel's ending, hanging. What happens afterwards? The happy-ever-after ending of the story of true love intimates the rest of the heroine's life. The developmental goal of the well-nurtured daughter is to become an adult— that is, a mother, not a daughter. The first home should be left so that a new home can be made. Once this has been achieved, there is the sense that the rest of the heroine's life will be all right, whatever turns it may take. As a daughter-reader, I always want a love story in the book. I want to have the intense emotions it engenders when mother-type love and erotic love come together, but I also need that ending. Because then I don't have to worry about this heroine anymore, and for as long as that feeling lasts, I don't have to worry about myself.

And yet when the romance occurs in tandem with the story of a good mother, so that the lover is distinct from the mother, uneasy questions surface regarding the compatibility of the lover's role and the mother's role. In Rosamund Pilcher's early romances, to which she referred in unnecessarily disparaging terms as "frightfully wet little novels," there is always a warm and wise older woman, always a homey and welcoming house where she lives, and always a young couple—the heroine and hero—*both* of whom are nurtured by the good mother. It's as simple as that. Reading, you get all the good feelings, and you don't much worry about what isn't there, because just having these feelings is so delightful that you don't look for more. But of course, the very lack of complications is what makes these books minor fiction, which Pilcher herself surely realized when in her sixties she wrote *The Shell Seekers*, which places the good mother center stage, understands that the mother herself still has strong needs and developmental issues to resolve, and gives the story of true love both to the young heroine who is being mothered and to the mother herself.

Pilcher's solution is comforting, but it is not characteristic of many fictions of the good mother that include the story of true love. In both *Little Women* and *Mama Day*, friction occurs exactly where mother love and true love collide. In these novels, true love's happy ending is not guaranteed. From the time (after the publication of Volume I of *Little Women*) when Alcott was besieged by letters from readers asking whether Jo would marry Laurie, readers have almost unanimously, as far as I know, felt painfully betrayed when she refuses him and marries the middle-aged German Professor Bhaer. I know I do. This romantic resolution is a sticking point in the reading of *Little Women*—every time. In *Mama Day*, an equally dismaying sticking point is the death of the heroine's loving husband near the end of the novel. He is devoted to her, she to him. How can he die? And there are other difficult places in these stories, related to the power and appeal of the magic circle itself. The fact is, my tears come most readily in *Little Women* at those moments when I feel the loss of that childhood shared by the four sisters before they had to marry—anybody! When Jo goes up to the attic and finds the four little chests that belonged to the sisters when they were girls, my heart is torn.

How *do* good mothers and good lovers fit into the same book, the same life? "You don't want me living in your basement for the rest of my life," said my daughter Alex. One day I asked her why, if I had indeed been a good mother (I had my fingers crossed), she too was a passionate reader. It was she who helped me see that not only badly mothered daughters seek maternal nurture in true love—well-mothered daughters do, too. Because they have actually known the experience, they want to repeat it, never want it to end. But not with the original mother, for "living in the basement" means no sexuality, no adulthood, no home of her own.

I nodded sagely—good mothers always do. But I thought, "Actually, I wouldn't mind if you lived in the basement. You could have your lover there, too . . ." I would rather she didn't live two thousand miles away. I don't want her to be twelve forever, and I don't want to take from her or from her sisters their delightful growth and adulthood, but not having them in my daily life anymore makes a pain in my heart that is hard to live with. What do mothers need? *Not* to lose their daughters, not if the mother-daughter relationship nurtures both participants. The pop psychology slogan that learning to let go is good for us seems to me a simplistic response to complex matters. If the nurturing has been good—that is, if the mother has not narcissistically used the daughter, living through her rather than with her, and if the relationship has been interactive and interdependent, growing and changing with the people in it—then there seems no reason why it should be minimized, or cut off. Yet it can't stay the same, either; I know that. Changes are required: the word "boundaries" keeps coming up. And what boundaries mean to newly adult children may not be in sync with a mother's well-established desire.

Where does the magic circle go? Is it broken, transformed, reestablished? Today I am as vulnerable to these issues as a mother as I am as a daughter. I read fictions of the good mother today from both sides, looking for answers as well as feelings.

❦

Reading *Little Women* over and over during my childhood, I got the chance to be Jo March. *Little Women* is, after all, a story for children: it is what is called, either happily or disparagingly, a "girls' book." Jo is fifteen in the first volume, but I wasn't that old when I read it for the first time—I was probably ten or eleven. Jo was like me: bookish and boyish, smart and funny, awkward and ambitious, a misfit. Nonetheless, she was the heroine, because someone like her wrote her for someone like me. *Little Women* is the kind of novel where girl readers who don't belong find a world where they do. And if that world is not, as Alcott makes perfectly clear it isn't, the "outside world," then the family circle in which Jo is loved and appreciated is all the more wonderful. For Jo is not alone. She belongs to her family; and regardless of the fact that she is special and particular in her own right, her very identity is interdependent upon theirs. It is so very gratifying to be Jo not only for herself but for her place in the circle of sisters and mother that defines the central world of *Little Women*.

I learned much later, when I started to teach *Little Women* in college courses, that not every reader identifies with Jo. There were Megs in the room, Amys, and even the occasional Beth! I have to say that I was shocked, but it was a good lesson, not only about me but about the way in which Alcott created the novel. For of course, there are four sisters, and from the opening words of the book, they are granted pretty much equal time. It's important that they be. You remember how it goes:

> "Christmas won't be Christmas without any presents," grumbled Jo, lying on the rug.
> "It's so dreadful to be poor!" sighed Meg, looking down at her old dress.
> "I don't think it's fair for some girls to have lots of pretty things, and other girls nothing at all," added little Amy, with an injured sniff.
> "We've got father and mother, and each other, anyhow," said Beth, contentedly, from her corner. (p. 7)

Each girl has a particular personality and a particular role to play: "boyish" Jo is gruff, honest, and adventurous; Meg is traditionally feminine, sweet and kind but ambitious for social stature and its material rewards; pretty Amy is vain and selfish; Beth is good. Alcott based them directly on her own sisters and herself, yet as a foursome they manage to encompass many of the possible traits and propensities that girls might have. Meg and Amy and Beth, in other words, are extensions of Jo. And vice versa. Alcott makes this arrangement even clearer by dividing the girls into pairs as well: Jo's special sister is Beth ("Beth is my conscience," she says); Meg's special sister is Amy. When Beth dies, Jo "grows" by taking some of Beth's traits into herself: "Brooms and dishcloths never could be as distasteful as they once had been, for Beth had presided over both; and something of her housewifely spirit seemed to linger around the little mop and the old brush, that was never thrown away. As she used them, Jo found herself humming the songs Beth used to hum, imitating Beth's orderly ways."(p. 532)

There is something very satisfying about Alcott's simple and schematic way of creating the four sisters. The division into four organizes how they behave and what is said about them in each chapter as well as how the chapters are arranged, with each girl getting to be the main character in succeeding chapters. Thus the structure establishes over and over, from the smallest to the largest narrative units, the web of connection as well as distinction that defines them. Just compare the beginning of *Little Women* to *Jane Eyre*. If I identify with Jane because I feel I am so like her, alone and bereft, unloved and unrecognized, then I identify with Jo because although she is like me, she nonetheless *has* exactly what I want and need—love, recognition, support, and belonging. Almost everyone I have ever talked with about this novel says, "I wanted to be in that family, and while I was reading the story, I was." All the fun—the plays they act together, the clever newspaper they write together; all the love, despite hard times and hard work—the very being together draws us in and makes us glad to be there.

But the sisters by themselves don't complete the circle. The circle needs a center, and the center is the "stout motherly lady, with a 'can-I-help-you' look about her which was truly delightful," who enters Chapter 1 as soon as the girls have come alive for us. "She wasn't a particularly handsome person," writes Alcott of Marmee, "but mothers are always lovely to their children, and the girls thought the gray cloak and unfashionable bonnet covered the most splendid person in the world." (p. 14) Because there is a mother, there can be a magic circle, and Alcott describes it with the picture that has come to emblematize the Marches throughout the years: "They all drew to the fire, mother in the big chair with Beth at her feet, Meg and Amy perched on either arm of the chair, and Jo leaning on the back." (p. 16)

They are, in fact, reading a letter from Mr. March, away serving as a chaplain in the Civil War. For almost all of Volume I, the father is absent; even after his return, he has a most marginal role to play. Although we are assured that Marmee has a wonderful marriage and loves and respects her husband very much, he doesn't *do* very much in the story. He isn't in the circle—he exists in a vague way outside of it. The magic circle of love and identity is for women. Four sisters plus a mother make a world that is complete in itself.

And yet, although fathers are excluded, the circle does open up soon afterwards to include another person, a kind of honorary sibling: a boy named Laurie. "The Laurence boy" lives next door to the Marches, in a grand house that belongs to his grandfather, the wealthy Mr. Laurence. Jo meets him at a dance, where she feels "as out of place as a colt in a flower garden," especially with a burn mark at the back of her dress, but Laurie and she make friends in a natural and simple way: "Laurie's bashfulness soon wore off, for Jo's gentlemanly demeanor amused and set him at his ease, and Jo was her merry self again, because her dress was forgotten, and nobody lifted their eyes at her." (p. 40)

Laurie is a lonely orphan, who soon confesses to Jo that "sometimes you forget to put down the curtain at the window where the flowers are; and, when the lamps are lighted, it's like looking at a picture to see the fire, and you all round the table with your mother; her face is right opposite, and it looks so sweet behind the flowers, I can't help watching it. I haven't got a mother, you know." (p. 65) Laurie pokes the fire to hide a little twitching of the lips that he can't control. Jo's response is immediate: "The solitary, hungry look in his eyes went straight to Jo's warm heart . . . Laurie was sick and lonely; and, feeling how rich she was in home-love and happiness, she gladly tried to share it with him." (p. 65)

Jo and Laurie have recognized each other and offered each other nurture. Jo recognizes his sensitivity, his sadness, his loneliness—those qualities that as a boy he is supposed to suppress. She takes him into the circle, to share with him her sisters and her mother. At the same time, because he is male, he recognizes in her that aspect of her identity not traditionally feminine—hence "boyish" or "manly." Laurie is a real boy, and Jo is a pretend boy. She wants to be a boy because she doesn't want to be a girl, not the way girls are supposed to be in the culture she observes around her, and because she doesn't have any other word, or any other model, for the sort of girl she really is. But when Laurie becomes a member of the magic circle, his maleness becomes diffused. He isn't a brother, exactly; he's more like an honorary sister—a pretend girl, whereas Jo is a real girl. Jo and Laurie are so much alike, such best friends and "soulmates," because neither can be defined by the usual gender stereotypes. Laurie is a girl boy, Jo a boy girl, as the names they bear indicate. Most important, their special love and closeness takes place within the magic circle; it belongs to the world of childhood which in this novel exists, a realm that is distinct from the culture at large. For the circle is the domain of the mother. It is maternal space, where qualities and values associated with mothers, not fathers, can be nourished and celebrated.

Marmee is its source and guiding spirit, the hub at the center of the wheel. Nothing happens to any of its spokes without her. Her work is to teach her children to grow, with wisdom and loving kindness. All of the most famous episodes—Amy and the limes, Meg drinking too much champagne, Jo cutting her hair, Beth and the gift of Mr. Laurence's piano—teach a lesson, a lesson that Marmee lovingly explains at the end of the chapter. This is truly danger in the space of safety, an orderly and circumscribed kind of space suited to a child's reading needs. Curled up with *Little Women* long ago, I knew the adventures couldn't ever get really out of hand. Even when angry Jo allows Amy (who has burned up one of Jo's stories) to skate on thin ice and fall into the freezing water, I am pretty sure that it will be all right. It is: Jo goes back and rescues Amy. And for her reward, there is a private talk with Marmee, in which her mother confesses to her own unruly temper: "I have been trying to cure it for forty years, and have only succeeded in controlling it. I am angry nearly every day of my life, Jo; but I have learned not to show it; and I still hope to learn not to feel it, though it may take me another forty years to do so." (p. 101) I'm not so sure I believe in this philosophy; what appeals to me is the way the exchange shows how alike Jo and her mother are, even with regard to their "faults." Each developmental incident (which has to be at least a little dangerous, because it leads to change) is capped by both interpretation and deepening intimacy with the mother.

When Beth comes down with scarlet fever and Marmee is away, the stakes are particularly high. This is frightening, because we are not all that sure that Beth, too gentle, too shy, too *good,* is not destined for death. (She is—that's why. But it doesn't happen until the second volume.) This time Beth is saved, Marmee returns, and the terrible fear that has been engendered in all of the family as well as in the reader just makes the return to health and happiness all the sweeter, as Beth wakes, her fever broken, to see her mother's face. Each of the sisters has been affected by Beth in the days when they thought they might lose her. Meg, for example, feels herself rich in things more precious than money can buy; Jo learns "to acknowledge the worth of Beth's unselfish ambition, to live for others, and make home happy by the exercise of those simple virtues which all may possess, and which all should love and value more than talent, wealth, or beauty." (p. 226) The others respond in like fashion. It is a cautionary tale, and a developmental one. In her illness Beth becomes even more a part of the other three sisters than she has been before. The circle deepens, as its members grow into selves who are also profoundly connected to one another.

Yet while Marmee's methodology teaches the importance of connectedness and communality, of love and intimacy—what we may wish to call maternal values—the texts of her teachings are quite patriarchally oriented. For Marmee is grooming her daughters to become good citizens of the culture at large.

> "I want my daughters to be beautiful, accomplished, and good; to be admired, loved, and respected, to have a happy youth, to be well and wisely married, and to lead useful, pleasant lives . . . To be loved and chosen by a good man is the best and sweetest thing which can happen to a woman; and I sincerely hope my girls may know this beautiful experience."
> (p. 123)

Marmee calmly intimates that maternal and patriarchal mores are not mutually exclusive, yet the novel her daughter writes questions such an assumption.

Especially because an increasing strain develops between life in the circle and life beyond it. There is one danger that Marmee cannot make right. It is part and parcel of her motherly work. Growing into adulthood, maturing—these processes eat away at the very foundations of the magic circle. Growing means growing *up*. It is Jo who is particularly sensitive to this hidden threat, who avoids growing up like the plague, since it brings with it all those menacing aspects of culturally defined femininity: "I don't know anything about love, and such nonsense! . . . In novels, the girls show it by starting and blushing, fainting away, growing thin, and acting like fools." (p. 249) Meg, on the other hand, has been rushing toward womanhood as fast as she can. She is the first to encounter love and romance, in the person of Laurie's tutor, John Brooke. And Jo is appalled, for the danger is clear to her:

> ". . . she'll go and fall in love, and there's an end of peace and fun, and cozy times, together. I see it all! they'll go lovering round the house, and we shall have to dodge; Meg will be absorbed, and no good to me anymore; Brooke will scratch up a fortune somehow,—carry her off and make a hole in the family, and I shall break my heart . . ." (p. 250)

Jo's solution is as clear as it is impossible: "I just wish I could marry Meg myself, and keep her safe in the family." Although Jo responds to the crack in the magic circle with dread and horror, Marmee is more equivocal: "It is natural and right you should all go to homes of your own, in time; but I do want to keep my girls as long as I can; and I am sorry that this happened so soon, for Meg is only seventeen." (p. 251)

The first volume of *Little Women* ends with Meg's engagement, and with another picture of the circle—but it now includes Mr. March, who has returned from the war, John Brooke, Laurie's grandfather, and Laurie.

Father and mother sat together quietly re-living the first chapter of the romance which for them began some twenty years
ago. Amy was drawing the lovers, who sat apart in a beautiful
world of their own, the light of which touched their faces with
a grace the little artist could not copy. Beth lay on her sofa
talking cheerily with her old friend, who held her little hand as
if he felt that it possessed the power to lead him along the
peaceful ways she walked. Jo lounged in her favorite low seat,
with the grave, quiet look which best became her; and Laurie,
leaning on the back of her chair, his chin on a level with her
curly head, smiled with his friendliest aspect, and nodded at
her in the long glass which reflected them both. (p. 290)

The picture is indeed equivocal, for as much as it represents an
expanded circle, it also reflects estrangement: Meg and John in
their own little world, and, what is more disturbing, Mr. and
Mrs. March in theirs. Marmee is not at the center of her daughters, not here, not now, when she is focused on *her* love affair
with her husband. Immediately before Alcott describes the scene,
Laurie asks Jo, "Don't you wish you could take a look forward,
and see where we all shall be [in three years]? I do." Jo's answer
betrays her apprehension: "I think not, for I might see something
sad; and everyone looks so happy now, I don't believe they could
be much improved." (p. 289)

Yet even though Alcott offers a moment of stasis with her
family portrait, her authorial impetus is clearly toward change:
"So grouped," she concludes the volume, "the curtain falls upon
Meg, Jo, Beth, and Amy. Whether it ever rises again, depends
upon the reception given to the first act of the domestic drama,
called *Little Women*." (p. 290) For all that Alcott had resisted
writing a girls' book in the first place—"I don't enjoy this sort of
thing," she wrote in her journal: "Never liked girls or knew
many, except my sisters; but our queer plays and experiences may

prove interesting, though I doubt it"—she is clearly prepared for a sequel.

As were Alcott's young readers. "The second series was anticipated with the eagerness of a bulletin from the war and the stock market," writes Edna D. Cheney in her 1890 biography of Alcott. For me, it's more of a dilemma. I want more, we all do, just because I loved it so much. But like Jo, I do not want it to change. What I have loved the most is being in the circle; I never want to leave it. I am as apprehensive as I am eager to know what changes the second volume will bring.

"But unlike Miss Alcott herself," continues Cheney, "the children took especial interest in the love-story, and when poor Laurie was so obstinately refused by Jo, 'they wept aloud, and refused to be comforted,' and in some instances were actually made ill by grief and excitement." Alcott commented in her journal, in what is now an infamous remark: "Girls write to ask who the little women will marry, as if that was the only end and aim of a woman's life. I *won't* marry Jo to Laurie to please anyone."

The second volume of *Little Women* is unlike many of the sequels in children's series, like *The Bobbsey Twins* or *Nancy Drew,* where nobody ages and the same wonderful adventures just go on happening. Alcott is committed to some sort of realism, and so the characters need to grow up. She herself commented, "As I can launch into the future, my fancy has more play." The fancy of this professional writer, who never married herself and who wrote for remuneration so that she could contribute to the upkeep of her family (with her impractical philosopher father and her beloved mother called Marmee), is particularly complex regarding the matter of what growing up means for a woman—and its relation to her mother.

Volume II begins three years later, with this comment from the author: "If any of the elders think there is too much 'lovering' in the story, as I fear they may (I'm not afraid the young folks will make that objection), I can only say with Mrs. March, 'What *can* you expect when I have four gay girls in the house, and a dashing young neighbor over the way?' " (p. 293) For all that Alcott addresses the matter of vocation—Jo wants to be a writer, Amy wants to be an artist—the emphasis of her second book is on love, romance, and marriage. Surely this has to do partly with the fact that she is trying to please her young readers. But there seems to me to be more to it. First, it suggests a little bit of wish fulfillment, for if Jo is just like Alcott, Jo is going to get what her creator didn't: a loving husband and a brood of sons. More important yet, I think, is the proposition that maturity has more to do with love—with being able to give, receive, and use it— than with worldly successes. This is a maturity conceived along maternal lines.

Volume II opens with a wedding. Meg's marriage to John Brooke is such a perfect moment because it is such a family affair. They are married in the family garden. No gifts are on display, since they are already placed in the little house down the street that is waiting for the young couple. Everyone participates in the simple ceremony, with Jo, Amy, and Beth looking "just what they were—fresh-faced, happy hearted girls, pausing a moment in their busy lives to read with wistful eyes the sweetest chapter in the romance of womanhood." (p. 309) When Meg is ready to walk with John to their new home, she tells her parents, "Don't feel that I am separating from you, Marmee dear, or that I love you any the less for loving John so much . . . I shall come every day, father, and expect to keep my old place in all your hearts, though I *am* married." (p. 314) This makes me cry, every time, as I do when Meg, "looking straight into her husband's eyes," says " 'I will!' with such tender trust in her own face and voice, that her mother's heart rejoiced, and Aunt March sniffed audibly." (p. 310) I guess I want it all: that Meg should have her true love, and that she really will never leave. But as I watch her tell her mother that they are not separating, I can't tell if I am weeping because I know that it isn't true or because I think, since Meg is saying so, that it *is* true. In either case, the possibility of having true love *and* staying in the magic circle of the original mother-daughter matrix is raised at the very opening of this volume, to become a crucial theme underlying all that happens afterwards.

Although this book too has its share of "edifying adventures," for Jo in the world of ladies' teas and newspaper writing, for Meg in learning to be a good wife (experiences that take place between herself and John, no matter that Marmee has wise things to say afterwards), the focus of my reading now is on the romances (for Meg, Amy, and Jo)—and on the death. Because Beth has to die; there is no help for it. Not only because the sister upon whom Alcott modeled her did but also because Beth has been specifically created in contrast to her sisters as a person who cannot grow up. Beth's is indeed a cautionary life, and death, regarding the power of the magic circle.

For Beth has never wanted to leave it. She is like Jo (her alter ego) in this respect, except that their characters have enacted the impulse to stay in the circle in opposite ways. Jo wants to be out in the world. She goes off to New York to experience life. But she doesn't want to stop being boyish, for that would make her girlish (and susceptible to sex and time). Beth, on the other hand, asks never to go away. In Volume I, in the chapter called "Castles in the Air," when the sisters and Laurie describe their dreams for the future (Laurie wants to be a famous musician in Germany, Meg to have a lovely house, Amy to go to Rome and be an artist, Jo to do something splendid and heroic, and to write books and be rich and famous), Beth says, "Mine is to stay at home with father and mother, and help take care of the family . . . I only wish that we may all keep well, and be together; nothing else." (p. 178) Beth is true heir and victim of the magic circle. Not to leave, cautions Alcott, is to die.

Thus Beth's protracted illness and death are so moving not only because the death of a child is always intolerable (too young, too innocent) but also because in this instance it carries with it all our conflicted yearnings around the idea of never leaving. Jo tells Beth, "I used to think I couldn't let you go; but I'm learning to feel that I don't lose you; that you'll be more a part of me than ever, and death can't part us, though it seems to." (p. 513) Beth replies: "I know it cannot, and I don't fear it any longer, for I'm sure I shall be your Beth still, to love and help you more than ever. You must take my place, Jo, and be everything to mother and father when I'm gone. They will turn to you—don't fail them; and if it's hard work to be alone, remember that I don't forget you, and that you'll be happier in doing that, than writing splendid books, or seeing all the world; for love is the only thing that we can carry with us when we go, and it makes the end so easy." (p. 514)

I can't accept this version of never leaving. This time I weep out of anger as well as sadness, as finally the morning dawns when the room is very still and spring has come. Then what remains for Jo, the other daughter who wanted never to leave? Meg tells her that marriage is "just what you need to bring out the tender, womanly half of your nature, Jo. You are like a chestnut burr, prickly outside, but silky-soft within, and a sweet kernel, if one can only get at it. Love will make you show your heart some day, and then the rough burr will fall off" (p. 533). After Beth's death and Jo's struggles at home, she herself tells Marmee: "It's very curious, but the more I try to satisfy myself with all sorts of natural affections, the more I seem to want. I'd no idea hearts could take in so many—mine is so elastic, it never seems full now, and I used to be quite contented with my family; I don't understand it." (p. 537) "I do," says Marmee, and smiles her wise smile.

Beth's legacy includes the imperative that Jo must expand her loving beyond her family, so that she might not suffer Beth's fate. Alcott is preparing us for Jo's romance. However, she will not give her Laurie. Why *not?* It doesn't seem to make any sense. If Jo weren't to have anyone, if she were to become an unmarried writer like her creator, this would be a message that there are various possibilities for adult women. But if Jo is to marry, why is Laurie off limits? Why must Alcott go to all the trouble of inventing a warm and bearish, middle-aged and caring German professor, whom Jo meets in New York, where she goes ostensibly because she thinks that Beth's secret is loving Laurie (it isn't; it's her knowledge that she is dying) and she, Jo, wants to be out of the way so that Beth can have him? Why can't Jo marry Laurie?

Because Alcott makes Laurie grow up too, in Volume II, turning him into a frivolous, fun-loving college student—charming but rakish. This fellow clearly isn't as wonderful as he was in the first volume, but we love him anyway, no matter what he does, because he's Laurie. Still, Alcott has changed him just so that Jo can think, "You're very charming, but you've no more stability than a weather-cock, so you needn't write touching notes, and smile in that insinuating way, for it won't do a bit of good, and I won't have it." (p. 399) Alcott *masculinizes* Laurie along cultural lines, as she had formerly ungendered him, so that he could belong to the magic circle. For if Jo doesn't want the circle broken, Alcott—at least a part of her—does. Our plea for Jo to marry Laurie is part and parcel of our yearning that the circle stay in place—the circle that has made us feel as loved and wanted as it has Laurie, and Jo.

But Alcott won't have it. And so she creates for Jo someone from outside. Or so it seems. A German professor whom Jo meets in New York. Definitely not another sibling. And yet Alcott's maneuvers are not so simple, because the most important thing about Professor Bhaer is that he is really more motherly than loverly. Alcott replaces Laurie, who is Jo's other self, with an older man who is, well, like Marmee. It is Marmee who tells Jo that Laurie is not right for her, saying "You are too much alike." She adds: "Too fond of freedom, not to mention hot tempers and strong wills, to get on happily together, in a relation which needs infinite patience and forbearance, as well as love." (p. 407) In other words, she means that Laurie and Jo are both "daughters." Yet what Jo gets is not a father (not Mr. Rochester—heaven forbid!) but another mother.

The power of the paradigm of mother love prevents Alcott from imagining a manly man (like John Brooke, or like the person Laurie has become) for Jo. Alcott, like all writers of maternally oriented love stories, knows the dangers that scions of the patriarchy represent. But she isn't comfortable with transforming manly men into maternal heroes either, perhaps because that fantasy most often comes into play when the original mother has been bad, not good. So the stout, bearded gentleman professor, happy-hearted and benevolent, cheery and strong, with a large heart and baggy pockets, who comes along to teach and to cherish Jo, is like another mother. This is one way to imagine that the circle can hold, because Professor Bhaer can be understood as an extension of Marmee.

But it is a poor compromise, since Professor Bhaer is neither Marmee not Laurie; he seems a second-rate version of both. It's hard to watch Jo give their place in the center of her life to him. Brokenhearted, Laurie goes on to fall in love with not Beth but Amy. In the process these two mature and grow, but who cares? When Professor Bhaer proposes to Jo under the umbrella, he seems sweet enough. But when Laurie comes home from Europe with his bride, Amy, and sits down with Jo on the old shabby couch where they always used to be together, and asks Jo to go back to the old times, when she was like his sister (now that Amy is his lover), and Jo replies that "the happy old times can't come back, and we mustn't expect it. We are man and woman now, with sober work to do, for play-time is over . . . I shall miss my boy, but I shall love the man as much, and admire him more" (p. 546), I want to kill her.

I want Laurie. I want the old days back. I don't want the future for which Alcott has been resolutely preparing me. And I don't think that she herself is very clear about what she wants, for Jo or for me. Surely one of the most heart-wrenching moments in the whole book is when Jo goes up to the attic, in the lonely months after Beth's death, and finds there the "four little wooden chests in a row, each marked with its owner's name, and each filled with relics of the childhood and girlhood ended now for all." (p. 538) Can it be an *accident* that this moment is reprised right in the middle of the love scene in the rain with Professor Bhaer? The good professor has brought along a poem he's found in the newspaper, a little verse that, he says, "seemed to call me." He asks Jo to read it aloud. It is her poem, "In the Garret," and it begins:

> Four little chests all in a row,
>   Dim with dust, and worn by time,
> All fashioned and filled, long ago,
>   By children now in their prime.
> Four little keys hung side by side,
>   With faded ribbons, brave and gay,
> When fastened there with childish pride,
>   Long ago, on a rainy day.
> Four little names, one on each lid,
>   Carved out by a boyish hand,
> And underneath, there lieth hid
>   Histories of the happy band
> Once playing here, and pausing oft
>   To hear the sweet refrain,
> That came and went on the roof aloft,

In the falling summer rain.

(pp. 585–86)

Does Alcott mean the love of the professor to offset *this?* Even Professor Bhaer seems to sense it can't. Certainly it never does for me. Even if I have been enjoying the scene, I am caught up short by these words, these images and memories. Oh, the past—when they were all together, when everything was right. When they were safe and happy and their real selves. Those lines of verse evoke all of the much read first volume of *Little Women* for me, the world where I so wanted to be. God knows I don't long for my own childhood. I spent all those years in Providence trying to get away, to start what I thought would be my real life. No, what it makes me think of is another set of sisters, three not four—my own little girls, when they were all safe with me in their childhoods, three sisters now gone excitedly on their way into the future.

When I read *Little Women,* I do not read as a mother: no one could. Marmee is so wonderful because she is seen through a daughter's eyes, a daughter who is never angry with her but who finds her "the most splendid woman in the world." Marmee moves through *Little Women* in a nimbus of wisdom and love but at a distance from the characters with whom we identify, who are the daughters, even as Louisa May Alcott is a daughter writing this story of herself and her sisters and her mother, the original Marmee. Like all daughter-writers, even those who write the romance of mother love rather than the seduction of father love, Alcott is not mothering me. She is letting her mother character do that. She is pulling me into her own psyche, her own needs.

And her desires are entirely conflicting. Jo wants to leave; she wants to stay. She comes to believe that having her own romance and starting her own family extends the circle instead of severing it. This is the image with which Alcott ends the novel, at a March family gathering with all the daughters and their husbands and children gathered round to celebrate Marmee on her sixtieth birthday, "sitting enthroned among her daughters, with their children in her lap and at her feet, as if all found help and happiness in the face which never could grow old to them." (p. 601) And yet for me, this scene is shadowed by the image of the four little chests in the garret, and the painful longing for what has gone and can never be regained. That too is written into this story, although perhaps I feel it more intensely now just because I am a mother and so do not trust that "solution" to the problem the way a daughter might.

As a mother, my involvement in the daughter's need has more to do with her than with me. I empathize with her eagerness; I know that a part of my own charge is to help make it possible for her to feel it. I sent my daughters to colleges that were far away not only because they were the right schools for them but because as young women, they needed the experience and responsibilities of living on their own, so as to follow the course of their individual lives. *I* did that, to be a good mother. But for me this brought loss, and it always has, from the first time I waved goodbye at the airport and suddenly my oldest daughter did not live at home anymore.

Maybe I read *Little Women* differently now because I am in my life doing what Marmee did, trying to "annex" the daughters' lovers and make them part of my circle, even though I know it isn't really the same. I'll bet I'm not the only one who cries at the poem about the little wooden chests. There's more to it, though, because *everybody* wants Jo to marry Laurie. Nobody is satisfied with Professor Bhaer. The tug between staying in the magic circle and losing it by growing up is a real tension in the novel and in life, for daughters as well as mothers. It is a dilemma that daughters may try to solve by believing that they can indeed have it both ways, and mothers may try to solve by . . . well, by giving their daughters *Little Women* to read. When Alex read *Little Women* as a child, I was giving her my own young self and also the best portrait of the magic circle that I knew, for her to belong to, to carry with her as a model for something she would want to keep. It promoted my wish as a mother that she would cherish the bond between us and between her sisters, and it told her something about why I would understand these matters in just this way. It reinforced the pull of the magic circle in our lives, then and for the future.

۞

True love is supposed to be forever. The feeling of loss and long- ing that I'm describing in *Little Women* comes from the sense of being cheated out of forever. "If only it would last," writes Emily Dickinson in a poem that continues, "And I, for glee, / Took Rainbows, as the common way, / And empty Skies / the eccentricity—" (poem 257). Louisa May Alcott struggles with this need, but, perhaps because she writes as the daughter of a good mother, a security that it will indeed last propels her eager- ness to test the waters beyond the circle. Still, the longing for for- ever is real enough, and, as I have discussed, a great deal of energy in romance fiction is devoted to trying to satisfy it. Novels that come in series, for example, like the family saga, offer less ambiv- alently than Alcott does the concept of generation, of daughter becoming mother producing daughter becoming mother, to off- set the betrayal of time. But as a reader, you pay a certain price for this balm. You have to give up your love for one heroine on behalf of the next. And, as I have discussed in *Wuthering Heights,* that isn't always easy to do. Still, when female identity is under- stood as fluid rather than rigid, as process rather than stasis, the permutations from daughter into mother into daughter suggest the principle of forever in a way that is both satisfying and excit- ing. For the mother as well as for the daughter. Gloria Naylor's

181

1988 novel, *Mama Day,* is another fiction of the good mother that includes the daughter's romance with a man. While it too finds this second love story problematic, it renders the magic circle far less equivocally than Alcott does: as stronger, wider, and more elastic; as deeply powerful. In response, I find myself not wanting so much to hold on tight to what was. I begin to sense how the magic circle might hold despite the changes wrought by growing up.

Naylor's story takes place on the contemporary although imaginary island of Willow Springs, somewhere off the coast of North Carolina or Georgia, its people having lived on this spot since pre–Civil War days. Willow Springs is a world of secrets and mysteries. The novel's introduction makes this clear from the start. It is also a world of insiders and outsiders. Everyone cannot understand; everyone cannot belong. I am a white woman, a white reader, and yet I want to enter. How might this be possible? The introduction sets out some terms. It is emphatic about people like me—people coming from beyond the bridge, people who "gotta be viewed real, real careful"—people who can't listen right and can't understand at all.

The collective speaker—a "we" that turns out to be the inhabitants, perhaps even the very spirit, of Willow Springs—tells the cautionary tale of the son of one of their own people, Reema's boy, who "came hauling himself back from one of those fancy colleges mainside" with notebooks and tape recorders, all excited and determined to put Willow Springs on the map. But Willow Springs isn't on the map—because Willow Springs isn't in any state. "Look on any of them old maps they hurried and drew up soon as the Union soldiers pulled out and you can see that the only thing connects us to the mainland is a bridge—and even that gotta be rebuilt after every big storm." (p. 5) Reema's boy brought another worldview to the island (he talked of "asserting our cultural identity" and "inverting hostile social and political perimeters"), and consequently, he couldn't listen, he couldn't hear the right answers to the wrong questions he was asking.

But the introduction also give clues for doing it right:

> . . . someone who didn't know how to ask wouldn't know how to listen. And he coulda listened to them the way you been listening to us right now. Think about it: ain't nobody really talking to you. We're sitting here in Willow Springs, and you're God-knows-where. It's August 1999—ain't but a slim chance it's the same season where you are. Uh, huh, listen. Really listen this time: the only voice is your own. But you done heard about the legend of Sapphira Wade, though nobody here breathes her name. You done heard it in the way we know it, sitting on our porches and shelling June peas, quieting the midnight cough of a baby, taking apart the engine of a car— you done heard it without a single living soul really saying a word. Pity, though, Reema's boy couldn't listen, like you, to Cocoa and George down by them oaks—or he woulda left here with quite a story. (p. 10)

Although I am in many respects like Reema's boy, I don't have to be. I am willing to listen properly. Reading this introduction, I am gathering a lot of information, but it doesn't quite make sense. (And that's the point.) About Sapphira Wade, who "don't live in the part of our memory we can use to form words"; about "18 & 23"—"there's 18 & 23, and there's 18 & 23—and nobody was gonna trifle with Mama Day's, cause she know how to use it"; about Cocoa and George, talking about "that summer fourteen years ago, when she left, but he stayed," talking for a good two hours or so—"neither one saying a word." The introduction, spoken not only in a different season but from another kind of knowing, offers me the rudiments of a way of listening, and of reading—an invitation into the world of Willow Springs. If I am willing to "know" by shelling June peas or quieting a baby's cough, if I am willing to use the part of my mind that doesn't form words, if I am willing to accept Cocoa's "talking" to her husband who has been dead for fourteen years, if I am excited by the mysterious allusions to Sapphira Wade and must have more, then, I too can enter what turns out to be a magic circle just as compelling as that of Jo, Meg, Beth, and Amy, with Marmee at the center—the world of Willow Springs (which isn't really there), the legacy that Sapphira Wade left to her great-granddaughter, Miranda Day, that Miranda will leave to her great-niece, Ophelia. This is a maternal world, after all: I sense it from the start. As a mother and a daughter, I am eager to take part.

Sapphira Wade: "She could walk through a lightning storm without being touched; grab a bolt of lightning in the palm of her hand; use the heat of lightning to start the kindling going under her medicine pot . . . She turned the moon into salve, the stars into a swaddling cloth, and healed the wounds of every creature walking up on two or down on four." (p. 1) She is where the novel begins; she is the legend that "everybody knows but nobody talks about." A legend having something to do with her marriage to a white man, Bascombe Wade, her seven sons, his freeing of the slaves and deeding his land to them, his murder, her escape—to Africa, or to death, or into a burst of flames. Sapphira Wade is the mother of this island, and if this is about mothers, it is a story that puts its emphasis on maternal *power*. I am grateful to the voice of Willow Springs, which tells me that if I can read outside of the dominant culture—which is white and male, the world beyond the bridge—I too can participate in the heritage of Sapphira Wade.

And yet the story proper doesn't open in Willow Springs at all, but up north in New York City; and the narrator is no mother, but a tough, slangy young black woman called Cocoa, who notices an attractive man in a coffee shop on Third Avenue, a man whom she encounters again when he interviews her for a job. I am in familiar territory here, the prelude to romance, a contemporary urban tale of two lonely people who are going to rub each other the wrong way (of course) because they are destined to fall in love. I see my favorite plot starting up, as the narration switches to his point of view and thereby provides the moment of recognition I know so well. As he interviews her, he thinks:

> Yeah, I knew your type well. And you sat there with your mind racing, trying to double-think me, so sure you had me and the game down pat . . . [Yet] all I wanted was for you to be yourself. And I wondered if it was too late, if seven years in New York had been just enough for you to lose that, like you were trying to lose your southern accent. It amused me the way your tongue and lips were determined to clip along and then your accent would find you in the space between two words—"talking about," "graduating at." In spite of yourself, the music would squeeze through at the ending of those verbs to tilt the following vowels up just half a key. That's why I wanted you to call me George. There isn't a southerner alive who could bring that name in under two syllables. And for those brief seconds it allowed me to imagine you as you must have been: softer, slower—open . . . So I had the same myths about southern women that you did about northern men. But it was a fact that when you said my name, you became yourself. (p. 33)

This latter-day Mr. Darcy is George Andrews, product of the Wallace P. Andrews Shelter for Boys, currently a rising young engineer, another hero who seeks to know the heroine's true self.

Indeed, as the romance develops between them—as we knew

it would—we watch the slowly growing love and trust between them chipping away at the protective armor—the false self—that each one has developed. With Cocoa it is easier to see. Her fast-talking, hard-ass attitude is so defensive, so self-protective that we delight in watching it slowly crumble. Yet George has his difficulties too (after all, he suffers from a congenital heart disease). Even after Cocoa finally allows herself to be vulnerable to him, things still aren't right, because he won't do the same with her. Although Cocoa has revealed her deepest fears and feelings, George offers, "Only the present has potential" and "deal with the man in front of you." Cocoa worries:

> I thought you didn't trust me enough to share those feelings. A person is made up of much more than the "now." I had opened up to you about the frightened little girl inside of me because I'd finally come to believe that you would never hurt her. And the more I did that, the more you shut yourself off.
>
> (pp. 126–27)

After a bitter quarrel, George leaves. Cocoa spends a night with someone else. George, who has returned to propose to her only to see her leave her apartment building, follows her and waits all night outside the strange building. When she emerges he slaps her, saying, "My mother was a whore. And that's why I don't like being called the son of a bitch." He drags her to Harlem, to the brownstone that used to be a whorehouse where he was born. His fifteen-year-old mother had left him wrapped in newspapers, and the man who found him called the shelter for boys where he grew up. "And how do I *feel* about all of this?" He goes on, bitterly explaining his abiding sense of abandonment. No mother. And Cocoa asks him to marry her. He has finally given her his feelings, and his true past: his mother. But he has also tried to show her why he needed to bury his origins and to go beyond them. His mother has betrayed him utterly; he will not claim her again.

The narrative of Cocoa and George, a story of nurturing love, is, however, only half of the opening movement of the novel. It exists in counterpoint to events on Willow Springs, narrated by the plural voice of the island. After her mother died and her father ran off, Cocoa (her real name is Ophelia) was raised in Willow Springs by her grandmother, Abigail, and her grandaunt, Miranda, whom everybody calls Mama Day. She and George have, in fact, similar origins—the difference being that whereas in New York City there was only the Wallace P. Andrews Shelter for Boys, for Baby Girl, the "crib name" she is called by the two old women, there are many more possible mothers. She belongs to the family of Days, whose original mother was Sapphira Wade herself. She comes from an island where maternal power rules.

This is what I experience as I enter that world, guided by the voice of Willow Springs into the mind of Mama Day, the current ruler of Willow Springs. To Mama Day, Cocoa is a "little ball of pale fire," who "kicked her right in the eye as she brought her up to her lips to suck the blood and mucous in her nose." Mama Day not only raised Cocoa, she delivered her, since Miranda is the local midwife and "alternative" doctor, a woman who has a professional relationship of respect and division of labor with the island's white male M.D. Now we see the daughter from the mother's position—of love, empathy, and exasperation. Mama Day doesn't have much to say for those big cities where Cocoa goes to seek her fortune, even though she watches Phil Donahue daily so she can understand what it's like up there. She figures Chicago and New York are pretty much all of a piece. Especially because the cities seem to be *keeping* Cocoa from her destiny, for, as she had told her grandniece, "I plan to keep on living till I can rock one of yours on my knee." (p. 35) Cocoa is the only girl left alive in this generation to keep the Days going.

As Mama Day gathers fresh eggs, bakes her welcome-home cakes, consults with Bernice, a young wife who wants Mama Day to help her get pregnant, we begin to understand a little of what Mama Day means when she tells Bernice, "The only miracle is life itself." Mama Day's maternal work—she is nobody's biological mother, but she is in charge of nurturing all of Willow Springs and Cocoa in particular—is exactly that, life. In her wisdom, her humor, her frankness, in the way she makes of the everyday something deeply and powerfully resonant, Mama Day is wonderful. I begin to love her: to want to be her and to be cared for by her, all at once.

Therefore, when Mama Day first sees Cocoa upon her return to Willow Springs this year—when, in other words, I see Cocoa through the eyes of the mother—I encounter someone very different from that cool New Yorker.

> A sunflower . . . the sweat flowing from the reddish gold hair and absorbing every bit of available light to fling it back against those high cheekbones, down the collarbone, on to the line of the pelvis, pressing against the thin summer cotton . . . *the* baby girl brings back the great, grand mother. We ain't seen 18 & 23 black from that time till now. The black that can soak up all the light in the universe, can even swallow the sun . . . it's only an ancient mother of pure black that one day spits out this kinda gold. (pp. 47–48)

I see beauty here, but I also see connection and heritage. Baby Girl is not only herself; she exists in a line of women. She is like Jo in *Little Women,* belonging to a family, her very identity dependent upon theirs. But there is more, for Cocoa is the one who brings back the "great, grand mother." She has a potential and an obligation that contradict her independent search for fortune in northern cities. Or does it? For Cocoa always knows that Willow Springs is *home.*

> Home. It's being new and old all rolled into one. Measuring your new against old friends, old ways, old places. Knowing that as long as the old survives, you can keep changing as much as you want without the nightmare of waking up to a total stranger . . . Home. You can move away from it, but you never leave it. Not as long as it holds something to be missed.
>
> (pp. 49, 50)

As the New York sections of Part I develop Cocoa's love and marriage in the "real world" beyond the bridge, the Willow Springs sections create the life of home, of the magic circle that is always there although the daughter has fled. The circle is resonant with the ever-present past: "Living in a place like Willow Springs, it's sorta easy to forget about time." Mama Day pieces a quilt for Cocoa and George that shows us how the past stays alive. Mama Day's rags come from "the other place," the first homestead of the Day family. "A bit of her daddy's Sunday shirt is matched with Abigail's lace slip, the collar from Hope's graduation dress, the palm of Grace's baptismal gloves . . . Her needle fastens the satin trim of Peace's receiving blanket to Cocoa's baby jumper to a pocket from her own gardening apron . . . The front of Mother's gingham shirtwaist . . . Put a little piece of her in somewhere." (p. 137)

But the gingham is almost dry rot and doesn't cut well. Mama Day looks for something to back it with and finds a piece of faded homespun, much older than the gingham. "Coulda been part of anything, but only a woman would wear this color." The homespun is wrapped over and basted along the edge of the gingham. And as Mama Day makes careful stitches, she feels a chill.

She tries to put her mind somewhere else, but she has only the homespun, the gingham, and the silver flashing of her needle . . . It doesn't help to listen to the clock, 'cause it's only telling her what she knew about the homespun all along. The woman who wore it broke a man's heart. Candle Walk night. What really happened between her great-grandmother and Bascombe Wade? How many—if any—of them seven sons were his? But the last boy to show up in their family was no mystery. He had cherished another woman who could not find peace. Ophelia. It was too late to take it out of the quilt, and it didn't matter no way. Could she take herself out? Could she take out Abigail? Could she take 'em all out and start again? With what? Miranda finishes the curve and runs her hand along the stitching. When it's done right you can't tell where one ring ends and the other begins. It's like they ain't been sewn at all, they grew up out of nowhere. (p. 138)

Cocoa's destiny is connected to the first mother, because she belongs to her family, which has formed her as surely as the bits and pieces of all their clothing go to form the quilt. And Sapphira Wade broke a man's heart. Mama Day's moments of insight, or prophecy, come upon her frequently as she goes through her day, moments when knowledge comes to her through her fingers and through her heart, and yet they remain as puzzling to me, following her, wanting to be guided by her, as they are resonant with significance. I keep trying to figure out the mysteries of this family, as they are woven through the narrative of daily life in Willow Springs, even as they are woven into Cocoa's quilt.

There is Candle Walk, a ritual that the people of Willow Springs have practiced every December 22 since the beginning. They take to the road, holding some kind of light in their hands, even if nobody remembers why anymore.

Candle Walk night. Looking over here from beyond the bridge, you might believe some of the more far-fetched stories about Willow Springs: The island got spit from the mouth of God, and when it fell to the earth it brought along an army of stars. He tried to reach down and scoop them back up, and found Himself shaking hands with the greatest conjure woman on earth. "Leave 'em here, Lord," she said. "I ain't got nothing but these poor black hands to guide my people, but I can lead on with light." (p. 110)

Another piece of the mystery is the now empty house called "the other place." There Mama Day goes for nourishment, and for magic. Especially on Candle Walk.

She tries to listen under the wind. The sound of a long wool skirt passing. Then the tread of heavy leather boots, heading straight for the main road, heading on towards the east bluff over the ocean ... And the humming—humming of some lost and ancient song. Quiet tears start rolling down Miranda's face. Oh precious Jesus, the night wasn't for her—it was for him. The tombstone out by Chevy's Pass. How long did he search for her? Up and down this path ... Up and down this path, somehow, a man dies from a broken heart. (p. 118)

What does it mean that someone died of a broken heart so long ago? Why couldn't her own mother "find Peace" (her dead child)? Why is it scary that Cocoa's real name is Ophelia? And what does all this have to do with George, who interests Mama Day greatly? After she and Abigail have talked to him on the phone, she comments: "He said—'She has all I have.' That means sharing. If he got a nickel, she's got a part of it. He got a dream, he's gonna take her along. If he got a life, Abigail, he's saying that life can open

191

itself up for her. You can't ask no more than that from a man."
(p. 136)

Somehow, it's all connected. And that is the reason it's as ex-hilarating as it is mysterious. It catches you up; it makes you feel you're a part of something that never ends and has a meaning that's always a little bit beyond you. Because there's magic in it, magic that is accepted, understood to be real. Everyone on the is-land, even the "medical" doctor, Brian Smithfield, knows that Mama Day, along with her enemy, the evil Miss Ruby, and the comical hoodoo man, Dr. Buzzard, all use some version of magic. Magic denotes powers and processes that are alternative to what organizes the mainstream, or in this novel, "mainland" culture—which is male-dominated and white. Yet in this novel magic, as well as the forever of generations, will come into conflict with true love as it happens in the patriarchal world.

In Part I the love story, which takes place beyond the bridge, is separate from the magic circle of mother love, which is situated on an island that simply doesn't exist from the perspective of the outside world. Cocoa crosses back and forth, finding nurture both at home, in the world of the mother, and from the maternal hero who functions as a surrogate mother in the alien mainland world. Not until Cocoa and George have been married for four years—not until they have finally decided to try to have a baby (at George's insistence)—does Cocoa bring George home.

She is asking that the two worlds be brought together, and the reason for "crossing over" (Cocoa's phrase) is her decision to become a mother. Mama Day has been thinking about grand-children for years. We might write this off as an old lady's old-fashioned dodderings (as opposed to Cocoa's modern ambitions for career and independence), except that as the novel progresses it becomes clear that Mama Day's own death hinges upon the birth of Cocoa's children:

> She had it all planned for herself: something nice and simple.
> A warm flannel gown with ruffles on the sleeves. Propped up
> in bed with extra pillows at her back. Her windows wide open
> to let in whatever season of air it was. And Baby Girl's children
> bringing her little sips of soup, cups of tea, and heaping dishes
> of pistachio ice cream. She couldn't with all certainty put Baby
> Girl in the middle of that picture, but the children she'd get
> from that boy, having only half his heart, would be there for
> their old auntie. (p. 203)

Until those children come, she will simply live on, no matter
how old she gets.

When they are in Willow Springs, Cocoa's explanation to
George of the inheritance patterns of the Day family clarifies
Mama Day's desire: "Some kind of crazy clause in our deed. It's
always owned two generations down. That's to keep any Day
from selling it." (p. 219) Cocoa doesn't own the land—it belongs
to her unborn children. These children are necessary for the
Days to continue, and Mama Day, the ruling mother, can die
only when they have been born. Cocoa's children belong to Willow Springs, so once George tosses her diaphragm over the
Brooklyn Bridge, he too, as the father of these children, must
find his way there.

But an overwhelming question now arises: Can the maternal
hero—that fantasy women create so that true love is possible for
us as grown women living in a patriarchal culture—function in
the alternative world, the magic circle of the good mother herself?
Is he needed? Can he do it? The wrenching conclusion of *Mama
Day,* toward which the whole of Part II builds, answers these questions in a way that many readers find shocking and devastating.

As soon as George and Cocoa arrive on the island, the *difference* between them is underlined. George is an engineer who tries

to prepare for his journey by reading his atlas, to figure out "whether a raincoat would be in order or not, a light pullover for evenings." But "where was Willow Springs? Nowhere. At least not on any map I had found. I had even gone out and bought road maps just for South Carolina and Georgia and it was missing from all those islands dotting the coastline. What country claimed it? Where was the nearest interstate highway, the nearest byroad?" (p. 174) Cocoa thinks: "Your maps were no good here . . . but you still came, willing to share this with me." (p. 177) For she knows that "regardless of how well you thought you knew me, it was only one part of me. The rest of me—the whole of me—was here." (p. 176)

George's love for Cocoa is what makes this joining a possibility, George whom Mama Day thinks of as "a good-hearted boy with a bad heart." Cocoa decides that she need not worry, that she is fortunate in belonging to him *and* belonging to them.

George is certainly eager and willing to try. He takes exhausting hikes with Mama Day through the East Woods, he plays cards and gets drunk with Dr. Buzzard, and he tries to understand the strange history of the Days when Mama Day and Cocoa explain it to him. Mama Day shows him the solitary grave of Bascombe Wade, keeping his vigil for the slave woman to whom he deeded his island: "When the wind is right in the trees, you can hear him calling and calling the name that nobody knows." (p. 206) Cocoa shows him the other graves, tombstones of varying heights with no dates and only one name. George muses, "You explained they were all Days, so there was no need for a surname. But what, as in your case, if a woman married? You live a Day and you die a Day. Early women's lib, I said with a smile. A bit more than that, you said." He learns more:

You showed me how they were grouped by generations: the seven brothers and then the seven before them. The sizes of

the headstones represented the missing dates—but only in relationship to each other. There was a Peace who died younger
than another Peace and so her stone was smaller. There was
your mother's stone—Grace—and she had obviously died
younger than her sister Hope. Mama Day, you said, would
have the tallest stone. She'd already lived longer than any Day
before her. The closeness of all this awed me—people who
could be this self-contained. Who had redefined time. No, totally disregarded it. (p. 218)

George grasps how different all this is from the world beyond
Willow Springs. But he can comprehend it only intellectually.
When Cocoa tells him the story of the solitary grave of
Bascombe Wade, she adds that the woman was her grandmother's great-grandmother. "But it was odd the way you said it—she
was the great-great, grand, Mother—as if you were listing the attributes of a goddess. The whole thing was so intriguing, I wondered if the woman had lived at all. Places like this island were
ripe for myths, but if she had really existed, there must be some
record. Maybe in Bascombe Wade's papers: deeds of sale for his
slaves." (p. 218) Magic equals "myth"; history can be verified
with documents. Is it enough that George wants to belong?

The climax builds irrevocably. I read faster and faster, anx-
iously. Too much danger now. It is everywhere: storm, death;
black magic; sickness and madness. First comes a hurricane,
bringing devastation to the island. This unleashing of power and
fury is the act of the great mother herself, and "prayers go up in
Willow Springs to be spared from what could only be the work-
ings of Woman. And She has no name." (p. 251) Why now, just
as Cocoa has become ill with a mysterious fever from which she
is not recovering? The fever is caused by the evil magic of Miss
Ruby, jealous of Cocoa's flirtation with her young husband, Jun-
ior Lee. Braiding Cocoa's hair as she used to do when Cocoa was

a child, Ruby has poisoned her. And although Mama Day can cause lightning to strike Miss Ruby's house, she alone cannot save Cocoa from the madness and death that Ruby's magic portends. She needs George to help her. "How bad is it gonna be?" asks Abigail.

> "How bad is hate, Abigail? How strong is hate? It can destroy more people quicker than anything else."
> "But I believe there's a power greater than hate."
> "Yes, and that's what we gotta depend on—that and George."

But George will never believe this, Abigail says. He's from beyond the bridge, and they don't have his kind of words to explain. Miranda says they must wait for him to feel the need to come to them, that she will be waiting for him at the other place.

> "That boy'll never make it, Miranda."
> "Don't sell him too short too early. He'd do anything in the world for her."
> "I know that. But we ain't talking about this world, are we?"
> "No," Miranda says, "we ain't talking about this world at all." (pp. 267–68)

Love is the power that can overcome hate, but love is the most complicated force of all. In the final pages of the novel, both mother love and sexual/romantic love are examined and tested, by themselves and in their relationship to one another. If Cocoa's life is to be saved by love, then both her mother and her husband must be able to give her what is needed: each in her or his own right, and, more crucially, together: "So together they could be the bridge for Baby Girl to walk over." (p. 285)

Mama Day's visit to the other place gives her visions that take her deeper yet into the nature of her own identity and into the meaning of her family, for in order to save Cocoa, she needs to know even more. Miranda is led to the attic, to discover hidden there the very document that testifies to the beginnings of their family: Bascombe Wade's bill of sale for a Negress answering to the name of Sa——. The rest of the name is unreadable due to "water damage." Only a few other words are legible: "Law . . . knowledge . . . witness . . . inflicted . . . nurse . . . conditions . . . tender . . . kind." In seeking the name she does not know, Miranda calls it "the door to help Baby Girl." In a dream, Miranda opens door upon door, saying, "Tell me your name." And what she hears at last is not the great mother's name but a new name for herself: "daughter." For the first time in the book, and in her life, Miranda's identity shifts from mother to daughter. For Miranda has had to be "Mama" since her own mother went mad and drowned herself. Now she learns that need as well as strength is necessary, that the love that will save Cocoa is based in mutual need. To save her daughter, she must at last be mothered as well as mother.

Daughter. The word comes to cradle what has gone past weariness. She can't really hear it 'cause she's got no ears, or call out 'cause she's got no mouth. There's only the sense of being. Daughter. Flooding through like fine streams of hot, liquid sugar to fill the spaces where there never was no arms to hold her up, no shoulders for her to lay her head down and cry on, no body to ever turn to for answers. Miranda. Sister. Little Mama. Mama Day. Melting, melting away under the sweet flood of waters pouring down to lay bare a place she ain't known existed: Daughter. And she opens the mouth that ain't there to suckle at the full breasts, deep greedy swallows of a thickness like cream, seeping from the corners of her lips, spilling onto her chin. Full. Full and warm to rest between the

mounds of softness, to feel the beating of a calm and steady
heart. She sleeps within her sleep. (p. 283)

For me, reading as a mother who is a daughter, a daughter who
is a mother, this dream vision is the true center of the novel. It
acknowledges my own need—for my mother, yes, but also for
my daughters. We are never only one half of this bond. The
daughter helps to make the mother whole, even as the mother
does the same for her daughter. Because the mother never loses
the need for nurture—indeed, her maternal strength may depend
upon it. Miranda's joy as she is suckled by a ghost mother means
both that she has new strength with which to take care of Cocoa
and that she needs her daughter as much as her daughter needs
her. Cocoa's life, Cocoa's future are another way to care for Mama
Day. Miranda needs Cocoa, and they both need George.

Miranda recalls the will of the men who have loved Day women
to keep them alive. The first mother left by wind, Miranda's own
mother by water, for the lure of the mother who is death as well as
life has been the dark underside of their mother culture. "The losing
was the pain of her childhood, the losing was Candle Walk, and
looking past the losing was to feel for the man who had built this
house and the one who nailed this well shut. It was to feel the hope
in them that the work of their hands could wipe away all that had
gone before. These men *believed*—in the power of themselves, in
what they were feeling." (p. 285)

This is why Mama Day wants George to keep Cocoa
alive—to *connect* the part of Cocoa that belongs to the mother
with the part that belongs to the outside world. It is a matter of
the work of their hands. Mama Day needs George's hand in hers:
"his very hand—so that she can connect it up with all the believing that had gone before. A single moment was all she asked,
even a fingertip to touch hers at the other place. So together they
could be the bridge for Baby Girl to walk over." (p. 285)

Miranda knows that George believes in himself—" 'cause he ain't never had a choice. And he keeps it protected down in his center, but she needs that belief buried in George. Of his own accord he has to *hand* it over to her." (p. 285) And she is afraid, because—and this is the crux of the difference, upon which the entire novel has insisted—although she needs George, George does not need her. "The Days were all rooted to the other place, but that boy had his own place inside him." George, however, the orphan raised at the Wallace P. Andrews Shelter "to feel responsible for our present actions—and our actions alone" (p. 25) and to believe that "only the present has potential" (p. 35), embodies the most basic patriarchal principles for masculinity. Has his love for Cocoa truly modified his training? Has his experience of Willow Springs altered him? Mama Day sees that there's a way George could do it alone: "he has the will deep inside to bring Baby Girl peace all by himself—but no, she won't even think on that." She'll think of a way to get him to trust her: "by holding her hand she could guide him safely through that extra mile where the others had stumbled. But a mile was a lot to travel when even one step becomes too much on a road you ain't ready to take." (p. 285)

George wants to build a bridge all right, but he means it literally. He is spending all his energy in the days after the storm trying to repair the bridge to the mainland so that he can take Cocoa across it to seek medical help. Mama Day knows that a different kind of bridge is in order, one that is based in need and connection. It is Dr. Buzzard, who may be a bit of a charlatan but who nonetheless belongs to the island, who convinces George to go to Mama Day at the other place; who counters George's "We're going to be fine because I believe in myself" with: "That's where folks start, boy—not where they finish up. Yes, I said *boy*. 'Cause a man would have grown enough to know that really believing in himself means that he ain't gotta be afraid to admit there's some things he just can't do alone. Ain't nobody asking you to believe in what Ruby done to Cocoa—but can you, at least, believe that you ain't the only one who'd give their life to help her?" (p. 292)

To read these scenes is to hope, to pray, to try to give George the same push that Dr. Buzzard does. George is so stubborn, so sure of himself, and so damned logical—a lot like the young men in classes where I have taught *Mama Day*, who obstinately maintain that there is no "magic" in this story, that everything that happens has a "natural" cause. And yet, George loves her, and I have loved him just because he could give the heroine the unconditional and cherishing, the passionate love that makes him, in my book—in this book—the hero. "Come on, George," I urge, "get it!"

George does go to the other place, and his conversation there with Mama Day is a desperate Ping-Pong game, with lives at stake. Miranda tells him:

> "I can do more with these hands than most folks dream of—no less believe—but this time they ain't no good alone. I had to stay in this place and reach back to the beginning for us to find the chains to pull her out of this here trouble. Now, I got all that in this hand but it ain't gonna be complete unless I can reach out with the other hand and take yours . . ."
>
> (p. 294)

To George, all this seems like "a lot of metaphors"; but he'll try to be of use to her. "Metaphors," thinks Mama Day: "Like what they use in poetry and stuff. The stuff folks dreamed up when they was making a fantasy, while what she was talking about was *real*." (p. 294)

Her way (she tells him there is another) is for him to go back to her chicken coop, find the nest of the old red hen, take the old family ledger and her own magic cane in there with him; to search in the back of the nest and come back with whatever he finds.

George finds this "mumbo jumbo" crazy, but he goes. And there in the chicken coop, with the angry hen attacking him, sinking her claws into his wrist and tearing at his hand with her beak, he digs violently into the nest: "Nothing. There was nothing there—except for my gouged and bleeding hands. Bring me straight back whatever you find. But there was nothing to bring her. *Bring me straight back whatever you find.* Could it be that she wanted nothing but my hands?" (p. 300)

The idea is intolerable. The hen attacks George and, beside himself, he slashes at her with the walking cane and smashes in her skull. Like a madman, he goes through the coop, slamming the cane into feathery bodies and nests; when the cane breaks, he uses the book. A stitch in his side finally makes him stop his terrible rampage—and laugh.

> There was nothing that old woman could do with a pair of empty hands. I was sitting in a chicken coop, covered with feathers, straw, manure, and blood. And why? . . . I brought both palms up, the bruised finger clenched inward. All of this wasted effort when these were *my* hands, and there was no way I was going to let you go. (p. 301)

George heads for Cocoa's bedside, but on the way he has a heart attack. He reaches her and dies. Miranda knows. "He went and did it his way, so he ain't coming back. In the pantry she rolls up bundles of dried herbs into clean strips of cloth. Now that Baby Girl was going to live, she had to be nursed back to health." (p. 302)

George's death is so shocking not because it hasn't been prepared for (it has, all throughout the novel) but because its significance is so brutal. As George wreaks havoc on Mama Day's chickens, he incarnates all the mindless male violence of human history. And it's *George*—whom we have loved and desired and believed in. The maternal hero, the creation of our dearest and deepest fantasies. Not only has he turned into a savage male, but he has died. Both my dismay and my sense of loss are real, even though they appear to be contradictory.

And yet he has saved Cocoa. I have to understand that part. He has died so that she might live: died in the way of and on behalf of the patriarchy. His death returns her to the magic circle. Whereas Alcott insists that daughters must enter the patriarchy, offering the tenuous hope that the circle can enlarge to include it, Naylor tells us that the world beyond the bridge can never be joined with the magic island of mother love without radical change to its patriarchal nature, a change that seems impossible. The best the maternal hero can do for the heroine who inherits the great mother's mantle is to die for her. Only in this way does he get to become a part of her as she becomes in her turn the mother. Thus her own mother power is the result not of her developmental relationship with a maternal hero but of her legacy from the other mothers in her original family. The central difference between Alcott and Naylor is that for Naylor mother love, and all that comes with it, is understood to be stronger than the culture at large. It is the only power that will give true identity and validity. Alcott cannot downplay the strength of the white patriarchy, but Naylor, black as well as female, can. Perhaps because her position is one of such thorough marginalization, her belief in the resources of her alternative identity must be that much more forceful. If a white woman might try to hope for the best in the dominant culture, a black woman may well understand the utter foolishness of such a hope. George must go the way of all who would attempt to force masculine dominance upon the world of the mother.

Nonetheless, it's painful to read the pages that follow, as Cocoa regains her health but experiences the loss of her true love. Because although George as maternal hero is proved to be a fantasy, he remains the best one we have. My own desire for him, like Cocoa's, dies hard. Mama Day, watching Cocoa grieve, knows that George is gone but that he hasn't left her, much in the way that Beth March lives on in her sister Jo. I listen to Miranda for comfort and hope, and to understand from the mother's wisdom what this kind of not leaving means. "Naw, another one who broke his heart 'cause he couldn't let her go. So she's gotta get past the grieving for what she lost, to go on to the grieving for what was lost." (p. 308) From her individual life and identity to the life of the family, in which she comes fully into herself—that is the path she must take. Miranda speaks to the dead George of Cocoa's legacy and her mission. She speaks of Candle Walk:

> My daddy said that his daddy said when he was young, Candle Walk was different still. It weren't about no candles, was about a light that burned in a man's heart . . . He had freed 'em all but her, 'cause, see, she'd never been a slave. And what she gave of her own will, she took away. I can't tell you her name, 'cause it was never opened to me. That's a door for the child of Grace to walk through . . . And you'll help her, won't you? . . . One day she'll hear you, like you're hearing me. And there'll be another time—that I won't be here for—when she'll learn about the beginning of the Days. But she's gotta go away to come back to that kind of knowledge. And I came to tell you not to worry: whatever roads take her from here, they'll always lead her back to you. (p. 308)

As a ghost, George has shed the encumbrances of his masculinity. Now he can stay on in Willow Springs and in the life of its next mother. This "solution" is satisfying in its way, like the endings of

Tryst and *Wuthering Heights,* for Cocoa and George do get to be together always, in a space that is safe from the evils of the patriarchy (to which George no longer belongs). The ghost love story always suggests in its various ways that mother love and the culture are not compatible. Cocoa leaves New York and marries again—a nice man in Atlanta who is admittedly not the love of her life and consequently no threat to the magic circle. He provides her with affection and with two sons. She is thus free to come back, frequently, to Willow Springs, to sit by George's grave and listen, and speak without words, replaying their love and its resolution.

The words they speak without sound are the novel we are reading, brought into language by the collective maternal voice of Willow Springs. For Cocoa's story, the story of the daughter who becomes a mother, can only be told and only be heard within the maternal narration. This is how the novel ends, as that voice tells us of Mama Day's final days, in 1999. "When she's tied up the twentieth century, she'll take a little peek into the other side—for pure devilment and curiosity—and then leave for a rest she deserves." (p. 312) She can go, now that Cocoa can take her place.

It's Mama Day whom I love the best, Mama Day and the world of Willow Springs, which, although it changes, never *really* changes: "Some things stay the same . . . Some things change . . . And some things are yet to be," says the voice of Willow Springs. Because the novel is told not by a daughter but by the very spirit of maternal power, *Mama Day* is especially compelling in its insistence that there is a Willow Springs, that there has to be a Willow Springs, that it isn't on any map but that it won't go away and it won't be corrupted. The priorities of the mother voice are clear, persuasive, and reassuring—and they inform the place of the maternal hero in the daughter's evolution. Yes, he is, finally, a fantasy. But if there is always a Willow Springs, then maybe it doesn't matter so much.

The authority and the strength of Naylor's insistence upon the centrality of maternal power seem to me to come from a conjunction of the imperatives of blackness and those of femaleness, because the dominant white male culture would disempower both. Then where do I come into this myth, a white woman, mother and daughter? Despite my complicity in the world beyond the bridge, the novel has permitted me the reality of my feelings for Mama Day and Willow Springs. Black maternal power has helped me to confirm my own deep belief in the centrality of mother love, in this way affecting my grief over the "leaving" of Alexandra, Jennifer, and Antonia. The magic circle does *not* exist in my basement, after all. It is not *on* any map. It has to be inside us. All the changes that are occurring now between me and my daughters may mean not the breaking of our connection but a way of continuing it. I do know that our mutual love and need, which is one way to define the magic circle, really exist. Alex said so, last week, when we were having yet another fight. "You know this relationship isn't going to go *away,* Mom," she said. "Can't you stop riding it so hard right now?" Indeed. Reading Naylor's story helps me as a mother, now, as much as it nourishes me as a daughter, simply because of its undying belief in the good mother. Yes, it gives me a mother character right there on the page to love, but it also gives me faith in my own power to continue to love as a mother, to be loved as a mother, despite the loss of the shared past when we were all together at home.

5

Coming Out in
Lesbian Romance Fiction

ISABEL MILLER'S *PATIENCE AND SARAH*
AND VALERIE TAYLOR'S *PRISM*

The magic circle is a world of women. It is different from the "outside" world, in that it ignores or denies or defies the dominance of men that is the defining feature of the culture we call patriarchy. Patriarchy: rule of the father. In the magic circle, maternal modes are central. Thus the magic circle, as both *Little Women* and *Mama Day* show, exists uneasily in relation to the patriarchy, whether we understand its presence as before, within, or alongside the dominant culture.

That profound uneasiness is perhaps most clearly manifested in the central tenet of the female fantasy of true love that I have been describing throughout this book: the wave of the wand that turns a man into a mother. Put in its simplest form, the fantasy is to love a man who behaves like a woman. But why go through all the legerdemain required to imagine a man as a woman? Why not just love a woman? Isn't that the obvious solution? Not exactly. For there is a reason why not. Loving a man, you gain a place in the culture—you get a husband, a baby, and a house with a white picket fence. (Or something along those lines.) Heterosexual love, as Freud was not the first to notice, grants a woman admittance to the "real world." Thus the fact that the man in the story of true love is a man and not a woman is quite as important to the fantasy as the womanlike attributes allotted to him.

And yet—why *not* love a woman? The question must still be asked. For the other piece of the fantasy is that it is about desire for the kind of love a woman gives best, based in the original love between mother and daughter. Desire for a woman. Is this lesbian love? Not exactly, because lesbian love is not mother-infant love: it is love and sex between two adult women and therefore parallels rather than precedes heterosexual romance. Thus lesbian romance fiction, which is a well-developed genre, is as much a fantasy about true love as its heterosexual counterpart. It too imagines adult love that has an important relationship to the earliest mother-infant bond. Yet it is not simply a matter of substituting Ms. Darcy for Mr. Darcy and getting on with it. *Because* the lovers are both women, the fantasy itself changes—in its ideas about what constitutes female self-identity as well as about how relationships are best achieved. And because lesbian love is *not* culturally proscribed and is far from being culturally condoned, in direct contrast to heterosexual love, the perimeters and possibilities for having the romance change. What does a happy ending mean in lesbian romance fiction?

I have always read lesbian writing. However, my relationship to its fantasy of true love has been changing over the years. As a teenager I sobbed over Stephen Gordon in Radclyffe Hall's *The Well of Loneliness* (1928). There was no happy ending there, as social pressures—and a belief on the part of the author as well as the culture in the lovers' deviance—force them apart. I hated all that suffering. Much later, as a new feminist in the early seventies, I delighted in the joyous love of Patience and Sarah in Isabel

Miller's novel of the same name, written in 1969. I'm a fan of Jane Rule, Lisa Alther, Rita Mae Brown—not to mention the poets: Adrienne Rich, Olga Broumas, Audre Lorde, Marilyn Hacker. As a heterosexual woman, or so I believed, I had nonetheless always been drawn to depictions of women loving women.

When I first read *Patience and Sarah,* I read it as a woman who had love affairs with men but whose relationships to women in every other dimension of her life were primary. I had always been thus, and the feminist movement then sweeping the nation was giving me access to and an outlet for powerful needs and ideas all having to do with women—our roles, our situation, our identity in a patriarchal culture. I had a new Ph.D., no permanent position because I was a "faculty wife," and three small children. I had joined my first consciousness-raising group, sitting each week in a living room with eight other women, all but one of us faculty wives, all marginally employed at the university despite our impressive qualifications and talents. Issues around work drew us together. Eventually we wrote the first report on the status of women at that institution and ran a conference on women there. But what I remember always are the women themselves. I remember looking at them, telling them my secrets and my trivialities and listening to theirs. I remember loving them. There was a life in that room that I experienced nowhere else. I cherished it, as I changed wet beds and gave birthday parties and wrote my first book and tried to be what my husband expected in bed. I remember the first time I talked about *that* in the room, to discover that I wasn't the only one for whom the earth had never exactly moved. When I had to leave the group—when I finally did get a real job at another university far away—the loss was wrenching. But I was young and ambitious and eager for the life to which I thought I was entitled; I put those women resolutely behind me.

It was in that context that I read *Patience and Sarah.* Today,

I find its beauty undiminished. I think that it most eloquently and clearly develops a fantasy of true love that is frequently articulated in contemporary lesbian romance fiction. This fantasy is based squarely in the concept of mutual recognition as Jessica Benjamin describes it so clearly: "the necessity of recognizing as well as being recognized by the other." Here recognition becomes the constant companion of assertion. Benjamin writes: "The subject declares, 'I am, I do,' and then waits for the response, 'You are, you have done.'" Recognition is a two-way process, for "it includes not only the other's confirming response, but also how we find ourselves in that response." Consequently, the mother-infant bond remains the source and model for both identity and relationship, especially as it emphasizes both difference and sameness: something to curl up into; something to push against. Mutuality is the central and guiding principle for true love.

But when both lovers are women, mutuality has different resonances and consequences from what happens in heterosexual experience. From the start, the sameness of gender offers an arena for identification that is missing in heterosexuality. Looking for "like" in her love object, the heterosexual woman begins in a situation of difference. To establish the degree of sameness that she desires—what will make him her "soul mate"—she seeks out similar personality characteristics and qualities. (Gosh, we both love Thai food!) Darcy and Elizabeth discover that *both* of them are intelligent and lively, both are proud and prejudiced, even though one is a woman and the other is a man.

For the lesbian lover, on the other hand, the like that gender identity offers is seductive and powerful. It can, however, be extreme: too much connectedness can become a merging in which the sense of self gets lost. Difference is necessary; it can balance the pull toward merger. As Beverly Burch notes in *On Intimate Terms: The Psychology of Difference in Lesbian Relationships*, "a delicate tension between the interplay of sameness and difference occurs in lesbian relationships." Difference can be established in the area of characteristics and qualities. Personal qualities and characteristics can be flexible and varied, suited to the situation, to the particular two people and the relationship they are creating, rather than fixed or limited. It is in this give-and-take of attributes and competencies that mutuality is created, as power is most emphatically equal and shared.

Nonetheless, the romances insist that identity itself is not fluid or shifting, because it has an essential component, and that is being a woman. Female identity is formed by gender norms, sex, and sexuality, and although these factors combine in lesbians in significantly untraditional ways, their combination means womanhood. In particular, sexuality defines identity as much as it results from it. It is through and by means of a woman's love for another woman—and the kind of relationship that develops because both partners are women—that a strong female identity can result. "Lesbians, by necessity, are forced to confront and actively own the existence of their sexuality in a way that heterosexual women are not," writes Wendy Rosen in "On the Integration of Sexuality: Lesbians and Their Mothers." This is because in this culture heterosexuality is assumed; it "goes without saying." But if one must assertively recognize and define her sexuality, the very act of "saying" becomes a force that influences identity.

Rosen's essay explores the particular significance of the mother-daughter bond for lesbians. She points out how the heterosexual and sexist assumptions of the society are traditionally passed from mother to child. "That her daughter could become lesbian is simply not a culturally permissible image to which a mother can be openly receptive without threatening both the larger system and her own personal sense of order." Consequently, even as the mother becomes unable to serve as an empathetic resource for the daughter ("She will be, of necessity, selectively inattentive and . . . minimally attuned," says Rosen), so the daughter will need to disavow internal realities and be inauthentic in order to be in any kind of relationship with her mother. In other words, Rosen concludes, "this culture, by virtue of its sexist and heterosexist underpinnings, violates the relationship between the lesbian and her mother, and, in most cases, ensures the lack of mutual empathy between them."

The fantasy of true love in lesbian romance fiction both emphasizes the sought-after attributes of the mother-daughter relationship such as recognition and empathy and adds elements that would prevent the second romance from going astray. In these stories the sense of isolation and the ensuing pain associated with coming out as it affects both daughters and mothers are healed through an emphasis on mutual recognition and mutual empathy. Further, the idea of the lover as a new and better mother, who offers appreciation, nurture, security, and everlasting love without demanding the daughter's capitulation to the mother's (and the culture's) definitions for normative femaleness, deflates and renegotiates the mother's power. Because each lover can act as mother to the other, because there are as a matter of course two heroines rather than one, an idea about shared power can be created.

Coming out is the process, the metaphor, the image that defines the establishment of mature identity in lesbian fiction. It means recognizing one's sexual identity and then, rather than hiding from or disavowing it, saying out loud, "This is who I am: I am a lesbian." To the extent that the lovers come out to the world as well as to one another, which they regularly do in contemporary lesbian fiction, the happy ending is contingent upon a relationship between self-development and social responsibility that is similar to what we see in the heterosexual romance. After all, for women, heterosexual or lesbian, to claim identity and agency is an act that society disallows. Yet for lesbians, this act is at once more extreme, more conspicuous, and more dangerous. Coming out as a lesbian extends and revises the concept of womanness itself, as it challenges culturally constructed ideas about what is feminine, what is masculine, what is neither. As Beverly Burch writes:

> Thinking of the feminine as a double-faceted experience is how one comes to understand lesbianism as woman-to-woman love rather than as disguised heterosexual pursuit. Each lover seeks the woman in her partner, but perhaps a woman different from herself. She seeks the nurturing woman, the masterful woman, or some less clearly dichotomized femininity in her lover, and to know it in herself, in her own grasp of what it is to be female.

Consequently, coming out carves a space for woman-oriented values and processes—what I have been calling the maternal mode—that is particularly visible, particularly radical.

Reading lesbian romance fiction, I find myself participating in the same mutuality that the fantasy encourages between its heroines, precisely because there are two heroines. No matter that one may be the main character; each woman is capable of inspiring my empathy. To the extent that this happens, I experience the love between them as especially satisfying. I get to be on both sides of the interchange; I get to be all of it. The desire to enter the other, to be the other—that particular kind of union imagined by psychologists of romantic love, be they lesbian or heterosexual—is enhanced. As Ethel Spector Person writes in *Dreams of Love and Fateful Encounters: The Power of Romantic Passion:*

In idyllic love, the lovers achieve an oscillating balance between giving and receiving, active and passive roles, pleasing and being pleased, enacting the role now of the child, now of the parent. In moving back and forth between these two roles, the lover experiences the vital interests of the beloved as his own, and he values her pleasure and happiness as much as his own. His identification with her is so complete that she assumes an importance commensurate with his own.

But if we change the pronouns here to "*her* identification with her is so complete that she assumes an importance commensurate with *her* own," the possibility for identification seems that much more probable because the lovers share the affinities of gender, sex, and sexuality. And yet they are at the same time different people; they are *not* the same. Therefore, in the midst of the pleasure of identification I feel my sense of boundaries and of female potential—there are two different women—expanding.

When I read *Patience and Sarah* for the first time, the emphasis on a female identity reverberated in me, as it continues to do to this day. This focus makes sense when we place the novel in the context of seventies feminism in which it appeared. At that time lesbianism symbolized an escape route from the socially constructed gender roles imposed on women. Burch quotes Elizabeth Wilson's comment that "the role-playing falsity of gender was, according to this scenario, the mark of heterosexuality, while lesbianism by contrast became the arena for the flowering of real womanhood." This novel is still thought of today by many women of my generation as the quintessential lesbian romance. Because it has a happy ending, yes—and because this is a particular kind of happy ending, one that celebrates the resonance and strength of mutuality in female love and identity.

Inspired, as the title page tells us, "by the life of Mary Ann Willson, an American primitive painter of the early 1800s, who settled on a farm in Greene County, New York, with a devoted female companion," *Patience and Sarah* alternates the narratives of its two heroines, Patience White and Sarah Dowling, to tell the story of how they fell in love in Connecticut and how they got to that farm in Greene County, New York. In this novel coming out, for each of the lovers, is the achievement and assertion of female identity and power.

The novel begins with Patience, unloved and unwanted, living with her brother Edward and his wife, Martha. "Want"—i.e., desire, aspiration—is, in fact, the central word in the opening chapter and in the novel as a whole. If want signifies some kind of assertion—an expression of the self's needs—it is initially juxtaposed against the heroine's confusion about identity, occasioned and intensified by her aloneness. "One way Martha wanted me out of her kitchen, but another way she didn't want me burning wood to keep just myself warm," are the opening words of the novel. "Best would have been if I died," Patience continues. But she notes that this is unlikely: she's healthy, fairly young, unmarried. "Next best was to make me want to die, but I had enough spite in me to want to live, usually." (p. 8) Spite! Something to counteract Martha's wants. Patience goes on: "I couldn't say what I wanted. I could say what I didn't want, and maybe that's a start but no more than a start." Not to get married; so maybe to be a schoolmarm or an embroiderer? Not really. "All I wanted was to be a painter." (p. 9)

Patience is a likely romance heroine. She is smart, talented, funny, *different*. She's not a typical woman and not likely to be become one. Not, then, a woman? All the "what I didn't want"s ring out like Jo March's "manliness." Patience's father, who loved her and left her half of the house (plus legal arrangements to be carried out if Edward or his heirs ever refused her her due), had wished for her to be a boy; he had wondered "how someone with all that go could stand to be a woman. He said he'd half hoped naming me Patience would help a little." (p. 13) For Patience, the world into which she was born has closed, not opened, options in the related arenas of gender, identity, and desire—of wants. "It breaks my heart to think of childhood," comments Patience, "everybody bigger and whacking and shouting and teaching you not to reach for anything or look at anything, and not letting up on you till you get over wanting to." (p. 12)

Patience thinks that it was her father's care (he "never put his whole back behind breaking me") that made her as strong as she is: "If one of your folks will back you up, you don't get broken." But it is telling that her mother never did "back" her. It was her father who "spoiled" her by sending her to school, who even earlier on made her mother give her candles to read and draw by. "If he was late getting in, she'd never give me the candle." The love and support of a mother—a woman—was never there.

In Chapter 1 Patience discovers something that she does want. "I'd heard, too, about Sarah Dowling, and I wanted, after all these years as almost her neighbor, to get a look at her." (pp. 11–12) Sarah Dowling, who arrives to deliver half a cord of wood, is not wearing a dress. "Is it a woman or a boy?" asks Patience. Martha, "thoroughly scandalized," is not about to ask her in, as Sarah suggests they should. She won't have her children see Sarah, saying, "This is a Christian home." (p. 11) Martha is the well-socialized, culturally acceptable and accepting woman, standing behind her Christian "family values."

Thus, Patience's first "strong" act in the novel is to light a fire in her own kitchen and ask Sarah Dowling in to warm up, and to put her cattle in the barn. "The lady of the house didn't worry none about poor old Buck and Bright," says the girl in boots and breeches. "The house has two ladies," says Patience. (p. 15)

Patience meets Sarah. She sees Sarah's eyes (a clear bright hazel) and her smile: "a big smile, a little too big maybe . . . a smile like that could break a face in such weather." (p. 14) She sees her womanliness. "Her face is fine and sweet, crowned with a coiled braid. Her breeches didn't hide how soft she is below. Maybe they even brought it out. She is also soft above." (p. 16) She wants to cook for Sarah, offer "few small coddlings" that surely wouldn't spoil her or undermine her capable ways.

And Sarah? Sarah, who admits a want of her own—"I wanted to see your place inside . . . I never been in such a place before"— notices and understands Patience's paintings. " 'Look at that!' she'd say, and point to some little part I'd taken pains over. She laughed at all the little jokes I'd painted in." (p. 16)

This is mutual recognition, part and parcel of falling in love. When Sarah gets ready to leave, she notes, "I can't gab all afternoon, like womenfolk . . . I never wanted to till now." (p. 17) This focus on "wants" continues the questioning of gender identity that underlies the opening chapter. The talk turns to Sarah's role as "boy." How her father considered her a boy because she was biggest; how it seems natural now: "I'm twenty-one now. I like being outside. I couldn't've fetched the wood today if I wasn't a boy. I wouldn't be here with you." What does the boy Sarah want? "To take up land and make me a place . . . I want to live nice, and free, and snug." "Alone?" asks Patience. "I'm strong," says Sarah, and hardens her muscle. "I reached up and touched, just a touch. A strong arm, but not a man's." (p. 18)

Both heroines, like the heroines of heterosexual romance fiction, are not "feminine." Sarah, because she dresses like a boy and does masculine work, and also Patience, because she isn't interested in marriage, or even in spinsterly occupations; because she paints; because she possesses a generous portion of spite. But the stress of Miller's writing is on how womanly they both "really" are—a womanliness that exists despite or outside of cultural definitions. Their perceptions of one another bring out this female identity. We note this especially in Patience's response to Sarah, since she narrates; but Sarah's desire to stay and "gab" is equally telling. At the heart of their mutual recognition is the affirmation of womanhood. The love that grows between them will have the development of female identity at its center.

A wonderful thing about their love, and this novel, is the innocence around which the author constructs her plot. Society has no words for their feelings—this is the love that has no name—and so neither does either of the women. But their feelings, because they are natural, happen anyway. Acting on them is a way to create a reality that may be outside of cultural paradigms but is nonetheless true. As Patience and Sarah participate in this process of continual discovery of sexuality and identity, so do I. How could I say to them, "Girls aren't supposed to fall in love with girls," when they don't seem to know this, and go ahead and do it anyhow? Why would I want to say such a thing, when I delight in what is happening? It is so sensual, tender, and exciting.

> I felt her lips on my cheek, nibbling towards my mouth, and getting there, and staying; and I knew why she'd been afraid and wondered why I hadn't been, why I had lured this mighty mystery and astonishment into the room, into our lives. (p. 32)

"Was that a feeling I felt in you?" asks Sarah. Patience hesitates and then "told true": "Yes . . ." "She wouldn't look away. She wanted the corner of my mouth up too, and when I at last gave her that, she kissed me again. Oh, we were begun. There would be no way out except through." (p. 33)

They have no preconceived explanation for their feeling: "whatever this was I would live it." Rather, it happens—and then they try to understand it:

> So when I let my head fall back under Sarah's kiss, the frenzy I trembled at just wasn't there. Instead, comfort and joy

217

and simplicity and order and answers to questions I'd always
supposed unanswerable, such as, why was I born? why a
woman? why here? why now? (p. 33)

Yes, I say: yes. Nonetheless, the novel is not set in fairyland. No
lesbian romance can be, for there is always another side to the experience of lesbian love. This is homophobia. When Sarah in her
innocence tells her sister that she has found her "mate," society,
in the persons of the families of each girl, attempts to destroy
their relationship by separating them. Homophobia is both external and internalized. Whereas Sarah sets out each day for Patience's house, only to be whipped by her father and sent back,
Patience feels fear. "I seemed to hear all the neighbors, and all the
village, wondering and mocking and scandalized, and my life
made an example of. Outcast, I thought, and shut my teeth to
bite back a groan." (p. 41)

And so when Sarah leaves home to find her new life, she does
so alone. Patience, who has denied Sarah before their families,
is left to discover for herself the meaning of patriarchy and
homophobia.

The story of the Prodigal Son attracted and warned me. He
demanded his patrimony, as I had meant to demand mine. He
squandered it. I tried to imagine how one might squander—
what dissolute living might consist in. Searching my soul for
an answer, I found again my longing for Sarah's lips. But that
wasn't dissolute in a man. Men could have women's lips. And
I felt, I think for the first time, a rage against men. Not only
because they could say, "I'm going," and go. Not because they
could go to college and become lawyers or preachers while
women could be only drudge or ornament but nothing between. Not because they could be parents at no cost to their
bodies. But because when they love a woman they may be

with her, and all society will protect their possession of her.

(p. 51)

This is the conclusion of Patience's first narrative. Lesbian love cannot be condoned by society. To feel it, to express it, are acts of defiance that become integrally associated with what this love *is*. Likewise, repressing, hiding, and fearing it come to define the experience as well.

Part II is Sarah's narrative: the story of her journey away from and back to Patience. Sarah's adventures demonstrate that being a boy is impossible, even for a strong, independent, aggressive girl. To acknowledge her womanhood becomes an essential ingredient in the process of self-development that the enduring romance motif of the lovers' separation always promotes.

> My new name was Sam. Did learning to shoot cause that? I expect it could've. It made me feel I could take care of myself, and not be beholden, and love who my feeling went to. I suppose lots of girls loved Patience but never said. Maybe it was because I could shoot that I could say. No matter that Patience changed her mind and I had to cry and go alone. I was never for a minute sorry I'd said. (p. 57)

Patience has already noted the problems attached to Sarah's upbringing: "Time enough later to teach her that it's better to be a real woman than an imitation man, and that when someone chooses a woman to go away with it's because a woman is what's preferred." (p. 23) Later her reaction is even stronger: "It is a sin to raise a girl to be a man, believing in strength and courage and candor." (p. 47) A sin, because the culture will subsequently work to crush and kill those aspirations.

Thus Sarah must discover the power of the patriarchy. People think she's a runaway apprentice; one man imprisons her to get

219

a reward. "I began to see how boys aren't much better off than women. Men are the ones who get their way and run the world. I began to see that I could stop looking like a boy in ten or twenty more years without looking any more like a man, and that even if I could fight past all these people and get to Genesee, I still wouldn't be paid a man's wages or let to make my way." (p. 65)

Sarah's adventure takes a happier turn, however, when she meets an itinerant bookseller and defrocked parson, a musician and writer, who takes her on as his helper, begins to teach her to read and to think—but who also falls in love with her. Dan Peel is different from the majority of his gender—so good, so nice—because he is gay. As a consequence, when he finally confesses his love, Sarah has to reveal her gender. She learns that she really is a girl, and she learns as well that homosexuality exists in the world outside of her own personal love for another woman. And so she goes home—to her family and to Patience.

"I put my cheek against hers. It felt as good as a kiss. Oh what else is as soft and firm and downy smooth and cool as a woman's cheek? It made me proud that mine was the same and I could give it to her." (pp. 92–93) It is in this new understanding of her womanhood that Sarah discovers how to fulfill their sexuality: "I thought, I have to find a way to show you that I am yours and have no wishes apart from yours, and the thought caused my body to find a way, which later on we made a name for. We called it melting." (p. 95)

For Sarah, this is happiness. Good hard work all week, and wonderful Sunday afternoons with Patience. "I couldn't think of anything to want beyond what that day marked the start of . . . A person would have to be bolder than me to imagine something beyond perfect happiness and wish for it. But I already said, Patience is bolder." (pp. 93, 94)

Indeed, Patience and Isabel Miller have more in store for the lovers. Patience says, "I don't want to stop . . . I want to start." (p.94) Her idea of starting can be understood both politically and developmentally. Patience *wants* more. She wants a life together as adults in the real world. She wants as well a relationship that may be predicated on the lovers both being women but is not about merger, either—not about having no wishes other than one another's. Clearly, Patience's self-development has already progressed dramatically from her initial statement, "I couldn't say what I wanted. I could say what I didn't want." As her narrative resumes in Part III, now directly addressed to Sarah, the opening paragraph announces, "When I grumble at our half-loaf, you offer me a crumb. When I ask to launch our ship, you suggest we fish in the millpond with it. You do without, in everything, until you forget how to want. Luckily, I can be willful for two." (p. 102) I think that "doing without" refers not only to time spent together but to achieving full selfhood. Sarah, having identified herself as a woman, has given up being "manly." But this is not right either. "Who is this cautious unhoping young woman?" asks Patience. "Where is the hero who bore such batterings for love and stood up before witnesses to ask me to be a hero too? And I am a hero now. Can't you see? We can be an army of two . . . Let the world either kill us or grow accustomed to us; here we stand." (p. 103)

"Hero" and "woman" are not mutually exclusive terms. I always think of Adrienne Rich's lines here: "two women together is a work / nothing in civilization has made simple." To stand before the world as two women who are partners and lovers is a heroic act. But it is not an act based in typically masculine characteristics. "I'm not a man," argues Sarah. " 'No indeed,' " answers Patience, "smiling, I hope, wickedly." "I'm not even very much like a man," continues Sarah: "I haven't got everybody backing me up like a man, and I'm not strong enough by myself." Patience's answer is crucial: "You're not by yourself."

(p. 104) They will not be one, merged into sameness, but neither will they be independent, autonomous loners.

The remainder of the novel shows us what mutuality, difference, and relationship mean—and what this has to do with the heroism of coming out as lesbians. As Patience lays siege to Sarah's timidity by forcing them into regular social contact (she is teaching Sarah and her sisters to read) but keeping their love secret and occasional, she relies on difference, not sameness, to save them: "You are so much finer than I, noble, generous, devoted to freedom, unwilling to bully. But it is I, and the traits in which I differ from you, who will save us." (p. 112)

Critical to their coming out, however, is none other than Martha, the conventional heterosexual sister-in-law who seems to have been cast as Patience's strongest enemy. Yet early in the novel, when Patience allows herself to feel compassion for Martha's life of yearly pregnancies and servitude to her husband, she has a dream:

> In the dream, Martha's bosom was bare and I went, very afraid but full of longing, and put my mouth against it. I expected her to push me away, but instead I felt her hand on the back of my head, pressing me close, and she murmured, "Of course, of course." (p. 25)

Martha's association with Patience's own mother, who rejected her, is clear. The daughter needs a mother, even though, as wife of the father, she symbolizes patriarchy. Can there be another mother, one who would not repudiate her daughter? The complexities involved in this particular "want" are reflected in what happens when the lovers are discovered one afternoon by Martha. Edward may have suspected what Martha could not even imagine, but Patience, unlike Sarah, has never actually named out loud the nature of her relationship with Sarah. Nonetheless, she has left the door to her rooms unlocked. Later Patience, in answer to Sarah's question "Did you know Martha was going to come in?" says, "No. But I knew someday somebody would."

Of course Martha is shocked and horrified; of course she tells her husband. Of course she announces to Patience that she always knew something was wrong with her, but she also tells her how Edward has always defended his sister against his wife's criticism. And later she confesses to Patience, "It could've been so sweet, working and helping each other here. It was what I thought about. It was what I thought it would be. Edward and you and me together. And then you didn't like me anymore, and I forgot I liked you and I just lately remembered. Do you remember we used to like each other?" Martha continues: "I get so lonesome with just Edward. We don't kiss. There's something he does to me, but we don't kiss. We're not sweet together . . . So many times I wish I could sit by you of an evening, but I expect you wouldn't want that." (p. 120)

Martha's desire is the heterosexual woman's longing for intimacy with another woman, a need that is consistently thwarted because of her simultaneous commitment to heterosexual structures. Patience's reply underlines this fact: "How cruel and cold to leave her there, unhugged, unreceived. But she's too late. I am yours now, and my hugs are only yours." (p. 120) Yet it is Martha's revelation of Edward's love for her that makes Patience strong when, after two days of meditation and prayer, he confronts her with her evil. Edward's decision is not to separate the women, which is Martha's idea, for that would drive Patience mad ("It's a blot on the family, madness"), but to arrange a financial settlement for her property and to send the two women away, to Genesee. "The two of you alone can manage, if you'll go where land is cheap and the arts you know are wanted," says

Edward, and then, after a pause, "But what do you *do?*" "My maidenly blush calls forth in him a manly blush. He does not stay for an answer." (pp. 123–24)

Patience and Sarah set out together for their future. As the sleigh takes them to Stratford and to a boat that will carry them to New York City, Patience takes Sarah's hand.

> . . . in the open, under the sky, under the eyes of my brother, I reach for your hand inside the muff I gave you . . . We ride now palm to palm. I marry you. Embracing inside secret walls never married us. The open, the sky, the eyes of my brother marry us and the harness bells are our wedding hymn. There is no pleasure in it. Is there, usually, in a wedding? The object is a public declaration, and an earnest intent to build private joy again. (pp. 127–28)

Patience and Sarah have come out. The necessary connection between public declaration and private joy is underlined, recalling the seventies feminist slogan "The personal is political." And vice versa. When a wedge is driven between private life and the social world, the truth of identity is always fragile, always in question. Life in the closet does not, after all, ignore society; it makes society's power all too present *because* the lovers hide, protect, pretend.

Sarah speaks the next section, in which her own sense of selfhood is finally forged. This is possible only now, when they are not closeted but out—proclaiming their identity in and to the world. On their first night alone together in a rooming house, in their own room, Sarah discovers yet another aspect of their love.

> I listened to the wind and thought: I needn't walk in it. I can stay right here with a mother that will never drive me away

from her breasts and give them to some new child. All night I can be by her, and drink from her just by tipping by head. I can drink there whenever I can bear to pause from drinking the dear spit of her mouth, and without even leaving her mouth I can take them in my hands, all this heavy softness, and feel the ends pucker into little pebbles, little knots, little fingertips, little buds, little rose hips, pushing into the palms of my hands, all the nights of my life. (p. 148)

The need for the mother is satisfied there with the lover. Or so it feels to Sarah, and from the pride as well as the security of that moment her sense of adulthood emerges. "After last night I could know we felt the same, and I could keep my opinions and make my own mind up," is the paradoxical way in which she phrases it. "I just never felt so grown-up and worthwhile and able to manage in my whole life before, all because she'd wanted me so much and I'd had enough to give her and make her melt like that and then sleep like that, and wake up with her face full of light." (p. 150) Yet mutuality is not so much paradox as an interactive tension. Because we are similar enough, we can be different. Because she wants me, I can give to her; because she can give to me, I can be safe enough to care for her. Mutual recognition, mutual care are the source for maturity. And with maturity comes responsibility for one another. If difference is always present, then it must be negotiated over and over on behalf of relationship. "I couldn't, from now on, just say yes or no without finding out what she wanted too. It was kind of a hard lesson to get ahold of. I won't say I learned it once and for all right then. But I did get a start on it." (p. 159)

Indeed, responsibility proves complicated. Sarah discovers that land prices have skyrocketed in Genesee County, their destination. She concocts a plan to go to the less desirable Greene County but lies to Patience in order to get her to go there. She sees this gesture as a taking of responsibility, since she understands finances better than Patience does. But being Sarah— being, that is, raised to believe in "strength and courage and candor"—she can't go through with the lie. Her "manly" qualities now become her own: female. She confesses to her crime, fearfully certain that Patience will now leave her. However, "I saw something I needed more than love right then. I saw she wanted me, and I knew she couldn't unless the rest was settled. And it didn't matter that somewhere in the back of my mind I was still worried where we'd end up and how I'd take care of her. With my heart cleared of its lie, I could want her again too." (p. 167) "Want"—with its connotations of need, desire, and agency— now becomes a transitive verb, a relationship that can be fulfilled between subject and object.

For Patience, in return, this episode brings more than acceptance; it brings a recognition that she is angry! Patience doesn't have difficulty being devious (after all, she tricked Sarah by leaving the door of her bedroom unlocked, even as she fooled Edward by pretending to be hurt and frightened at his sending her away, so that he would in fact do just that), but covert action is a part of her feminine training, while overt expression is not. "But I am tender, I am only tender, always only tender," she tells herself. "You *are* angry," whispers Sarah. "No," denies Patience, "but I *want* [my emphasis] . . . to bite you." (p. 170) Thus she expresses her anger: "I wanted to delight you and you wouldn't be delighted. You made me afraid a whole day long that you'd stopped loving me!"

> And I caught her side in my teeth and clung there, hard. She
> stayed still and unresisting and stretched out like a sacrifice
> and let me learn what besides tenderness my love was made
> of . . . (p. 171)

Patience comes to experience her own aggression. This is a part of what happens as they learn to be together, to act together, as partners in the world. For Patience, the other side of this particular coin is to give up some of her control; for gentle and womanly or no, she has always had the upper hand. Even as she discovers upon selling her first painting for a dollar that she, too, can contribute to the practical upkeep of their relationship ("It . . . made me see there was more to be had from painting than the pleasure and relief of doing it. I gave Sarah shelter and food for half a week with that picture" [p. 179]), so she can accede to Sarah's knowledge of finance and farming. Sarah chooses the land upon which they will build their home: "One of us had to know, and it could not be I." (p. 175)

The farm is bought; the new life begins. "Ah, Sarah," says Patience, "in your eyes I see myself become what I always dreamed I could be." (p. 187) Thus the lesbian romance fantasy is fulfilled. Mutual recognition generates mutual empathy, which develops into a maturity of interactive strengths and qualities: "gender-free" as far as culture constructs gender; deeply womanly, as lesbian identity constructs the woman.

ᴬ

Patience and Sarah seemed to me, in the seventies, a model for true (feminist) womanhood. I responded to the sexuality that was at the heart of the heroine's enterprise with pleasure and delight, but I didn't think it was for me. I wasn't a lesbian, I thought. That was how it was. So I translated the fantasy into heterosexual terms. In seeking my own Sarah, who would, however, be Sam, I ignored the explicit instructions in this particular guidebook for true love that Sarah is never Sam. I was more Martha than I understood, longing for something that could never be mine in real life, as long as I subscribed to the other half of the fantasy: that a man was always necessary to a life in the real world. The yearning for intimacy with women is necessarily thwarted in heterosexual patriarchy.

For me, that yearning has found its most important and most consistent outlet in reading. In reading I have been able to experience the recognition, the intimacy, the nurture, that I associate with the mother-daughter bond. In reading, because it is an experience in the imagination, I have been able to find romantic fulfillment with the mother-lover in the heterosexual romance. But the "wants" in my life could never be entirely fulfilled by what is, after all, imaginary experience. Recently, I have sought nurture and self-development in another kind of facilitating environment, a therapy situation that has met my internal needs with profound psychoanalytic care. In this process I began to explore my sexual orientation.

As always, reading has served as the touchstone and repository for my emotional life. Naturally, I (re)discovered lesbian romance fiction. I read to be where I wanted to be; to understand, to live, to experience in the best way I know: in my mind. In the real world I was married to a man, more and more uncomfortably. More and more inadequately. Especially when I began to understand some of the lies I had told myself about my own sexuality in order to have romance, love, and yes, protection from a man. With my first husband I had replayed my relationship with my mother. With my second husband I think I replayed the other relationship—with my father. More and more avidly, I read lesbian romances.

But reading lesbian fiction had changed. The empathy and identification took on a new dimension, because I could identify not only with the gender of the heroine but also with her sexuality. Just as the novels don't separate these aspects of identity, neither, now, would I. In fact, I practiced not doing so by means of the reading. The sex scenes in the novels were particularly important, for they helped me to imagine what I wanted to experience. My feelings could coincide with the feelings of the heroines, even as their feelings helped me to have mine. The reading process, in other words, became a means for coming out.

I read Valerie Taylor's *Prism* (1981) in the summer of 1992. Valerie Taylor has written lesbian romances for years now. She is one of the mothers of the genre, but I didn't know that when a friend lent me her book. I knew only that I couldn't put it down. I read it in the course of a day. *Prism* is the story of a sixty-five-year-old woman, a lesbian all her life, who retires from her job in Chicago to live in a small town in upstate New York, where she meets and falls in love with a sixty-year-old widow who has always been heterosexual. Is there love after sixty (or in my case, fifty)? Is there the chance to discover one's sexual identity so *late?* Can maturity finally be achieved? Is there the possibility of a new life? It is no wonder that this particular novel caught my imagination at that particular time. In *Prism* the paradigm that I have outlined for *Patience and Sarah* is clearly present, although in a more simplified form. *Prism* is a true romance novel: focused entirely on the love story, less textually and psychologically complex. But when you're reading for recognition, as I certainly was that day, sometimes streamlining may be exactly what you want. To get caught up in it, to experience each truth and satisfaction straightaway. *Prism* buoyed me up: my own changes seemed possible.

In Chapter 1 Ann Bassani prepares to leave Chicago, meditating forlornly on the potential for any sort of new life. What is there to look forward to? "I am now a senior citizen," she informs herself. "Leaving a job you're not crazy about is like splitting up with a woman you don't love much any more." She has just accomplished both, having recently ended an affair with a part-time typist named Louise. "It wasn't much, but it was better than nothing, it was something to fill the time." Their relationship had been an "earnest striving to act like reasonable adults," even though they didn't actually like each other very much. "Maybe nobody ever grows up," she concludes. (pp. 3–4) Ann's hopelessness is understandable—and scary.

Yet as she sets off in the morning in her old VW bug, she is more optimistic: "Good little bug—Colorado last summer, and now it was carrying her into something less scenic but perhaps more meaningful: her own life." She reflects how the major changes in one's life are likely to come in prosaic ways. After all, Louise had been a fill-in typist. "Real Love, she supposed, might happen in some such way if it ever did happen. Ever had happened." (pp. 6–7)

Anne, at sixty-five, is intelligent; competent; independent. But the clues are all there. She isn't grown up, not yet, and (because) she's never really been in love. How could she be completely mature? And how could there be a novel here if she were driving into an old age that amounts to nothing? Still very much alive, she is driving into her own life. She is driving as well toward Real Love; I know that, too: toward the chance to come into her full identity.

Arriving in the little town, there is the excitement of a new place, of getting started. There is also, however, the loneliness and the futility: "She felt like crying. This was it, the end of everything she had known for the last forty years, a whole new way of life in a strange place." (p. 11) But then, in the market, she sees a woman: a small erect woman with a coil of gray-streaked red hair low on her neck, "an old-fashioned note among all these tinted and styled heads."

> She felt Ann's eyes on her and half turned. Her face was round and sprinkled with freckles, her grey-green eyes wide; she looked, Ann thought, like the Dutch and Flemish women who were painted in sixteenth-century kitchens . . . It was a

placid face, and interesting. Although she wore slacks and a pullover, Ann saw her in a white coif and full skirt, seated with a pan of apples on her lap, a cat at her feet. (pp. 16–17)

Ann's eyes kept returning to the woman, with her sturdy shoulders and smooth head. She looks gentle and strong, too. "Or was that just a stereotype from someone she had known a long time ago and forgotten, or read about, or seen in a picture?" Whatever the case, Ann's mood changes: "She felt brisk and lively, walking across the floor with her arms full of paper bags. I may be getting old, she thought, but I'm good for a long time yet, and it wouldn't surprise me if everything turned out different from what I've been expecting. It generally does." (p. 17)

The clues for mutual recognition are all here, the most important being that the narration surprisingly if convincingly gives us a brief shift of point of view: the woman feels Ann's eyes on her and turns. The gaze of the true lover is strong enough to elicit this response, and it's necessary that we feel the response of the object, who becomes subject through this narrative transaction. Ann is recognizing the stranger. We know this because she juxtaposes her "imaginary" images upon the unprepossessing presence of an ordinary woman. She "knows" her, as the references to a long-forgotten memory, or a book, or a painting are meant to suggest. It has begun.

I'm not surprised when in the very next chapter she overtakes the woman, who is walking down the road, in a rain shower. The lady accepts the lift, and Ann gets to drive her home. Eldora is a farmer—she raises cauliflower. Her son and his wife live with her. She comes from a long line of original Dutch settlers. " 'I'd like to write a book about it sometime.' 'Oh, you're a writer.' 'No.' Flatly. Ann followed her . . . feeling rebuffed, she wasn't sure just why." (p. 24)

Actually, Eldora is a poet, a secret poet. This is the key to her

231

true identity, but it's not time for that revelation. Not yet. The first revelation (or gift, or response to recognition) that Ann does get on this visit is Eldora's prism. The old-fashioned parlor has a whatnot shelf, and on it Ann discovers a tapered, many-faceted piece of glass. She asks Eldora what it is.

> "A prism. I don't know where my mother got it or why she kept it . . . When I was a little girl it was my favorite thing."
> "But why?"
> "Well, it's nothing unusual or valuable—here, let me show you."

She takes the prism to the window, holds it up, and the sunshine splinters into "bright streaks and lozenges of living color across Eldora's hand." Eldora says, in a small hushed voice, "See, it breaks up ordinary light and turns it into rainbows . . . I know it's childish. Maybe that's why I like it—it's one of the first things I can remember." (p. 26)

The transformation of ordinary light into rainbow beauty becomes the central symbol in the novel, emblematizing Ann's original intuition that the prosaic and the transcendent are inexorably linked. But I am struck more by the prism's connection to Eldora's childhood, to what she terms her childishness. The prism represents the part of her that still needs to grow. And Ann will surely be implicated in that growth. Ann returns home so vitalized that she feels "as if each cell of her body had a life of its own." Because Eldora likes her; Eldora has shown her the prism.

So they like each other. Fine. No, not fine. For Ann is a lesbian, and Eldora is straight—isn't she? In the next chapter Eldora, wearing white gloves, visits Ann in her apartment above the hardware store. Ann is struck with desire.

She was an upright little figure in the plain dress, with the great knot of hair on her sturdy neck; she held her shoulders erect. Her plump arms were a little freckled, her legs sleek in nylon. No makeup, no jewelry. When she turned there would be the rich curve of bosom, the curved hips that had been visible even under a loose shirt. A real solid woman. (p. 32)

Ann wonders what would happen "if she jumped up and threw her arms around Eldora, reached over her shoulders to cup those rounded breasts in hungry palms. Probably yell bloody murder and get out of here three steps at a time, she thought. And in fifteen minutes I'd be the local outcast." (p. 33)

This is a thrilling moment for me. Up to this point in the novel, I have been identifying with Ann, who is not only the heroine but the narrator. Although I am not sixty-five and have not been an out lesbian for forty years (nor an executive secretary, nor a resident of Chicago), I know her worry and fears over aging. Most important, I know her sense that although life has been full, something important and necessary has not occurred. I appreciate her energy, her inventiveness, her spirit. I understand, as well, her desire for Eldora. When it happens, I feel it too. I feel her yearning, her frustration and fear. How can she want a straight woman, in a tiny little narrow-minded town! "For the first time since her arrival in Abigail she realized how small the town was, how superficial any relationship she was likely to develop must be. It was a cramping situation." Suddenly she knows how much she wants sex. And this is hard. Because how, she thinks, did you meet people? Go to the city and cruise the bars? But sex wasn't a kind of therapy, like going to a Chinese or an Arabic restaurant when you were in the city.

God damn it, she thought, I don't want to meet somebody in a bar or even get involved with some nice young thing who's politically correct—not if that's all we have in common. If I ever make another relationship, which isn't likely, I want something that will stay with me for the rest of my life. Maybe that's stuffy, but it's the truth. (pp. 34–35)

When I read these passages, I feel how much I too want a woman. I want love and I want sex, and I know how hard it is to make it happen. But at the very same time, I begin to identify with Eldora. After all, I'm the one who had been a straight woman all my life. My erotic feelings about women had always been a secret, just like my difficulties with heterosexuality. I think, "Oh give her a chance; try. Try. You never know, Ann. She may have been waiting for *you* all her life." Now I am Eldora, and I am Ann, too, and I turn the pages eagerly. I know it's got to happen; this is a romance novel. But how? And when?

Ann is trying not to think about Eldora, but there's no help for it. Eldora finally shows up and invites her to Sunday dinner. It's a family affair, and Ann is yet more attracted, more frustrated. "The word was impasse—there was no way she could move— ahead, back or sideways." (p. 53) Until finally—time is clearly passing, and Ann is trying to occupy herself, but in terms of pages, it's only the next chapter—the opportunity presents itself. Eldora arrives. She has found a letter addressed to Ann in her rural post office box. (Apparently this kind of mistake happens regularly.) It's a typewritten letter from her old lover, Louise, and Eldora has read it. Ann tries to pass Louise off as a friendship, but Eldora will have none of it. "She loved you . . . Did you love her?"

This is an opportunity—for both of them, as it turns out. "I never liked going to bed with him," confesses Eldora in a rush: "what he did, not even after it stopped hurting. I never—had those feelings you read about, like an electric shock. I thought the books were just making it up . . . There were things he didn't

234

like about me, he wanted me to be someone else and I couldn't. There must be more than just— . . . I thought there was something wrong with me." (pp. 56–57) Utterly embarrassed, Eldora gets up to go. But then she turns back: "I have to tell you. I didn't want you to be in love with her."

Now that Eldora has comprehended not only her lifelong dissatisfaction with heterosexuality but also her attraction to Ann, the love affair can begin. She becomes as active in their relationship as Ann, in her imagination, has already been. Inevitably, now, their lovemaking commences. For me it has the same special pleasure I find in *Patience and Sarah,* in that at least one of the partners can say, "That never happened to me before." (p. 68) Yet there is also the satisfaction of the other side, of Ann's sigh of pure delight—"How long had it been?"—as she runs her tongue around one of Eldora's pink nipples, then gathers it into her lips and increases the pressure. I can read the sex scenes both ways—as the one who knows and the one who is surprised; as the one who is doing and the one who is receiving. And I do, for surely one of the important reasons for reading romances is to savor the lovemaking. The descriptions of Eldora's breasts, full and firm, is both exciting and particularly affirming because the women are both over sixty. Clearly, each finds the other's body beautiful. Good—there's still time for me.

Eldora takes to lesbian sex like the proverbial duck to the pond. Wonderful! What else does the novel need? Everything. To discover and affirm lesbian sexuality in these novels is to establish identity. But identity is only the beginning. Maturity—a full-blown self—will come from the interaction between the lovers, as we well know. Because maturity, despite their age and their general competence in the lives they have lived, depends on the development of a true love relationship. Therefore, there must be problems, the solutions of which will permit the necessary growth to occur, a process that will be equated with coming out.

The needs of each woman seem initially quite different, but they will intertwine and complement one another, until at last the solution to one will be the solution to the other.

Ann's need is for what was called at the start of the novel "Real Love," something she has never known in her life of impermanent affairs based primarily on sexual attraction. Real Love turns out to mean intimacy. The first night that Ann and Eldora make love at Eldora's house (Ann comes to help pick cauliflowers and sleeps over, and Eldora sneaks into her room in the night), Eldora can't have an orgasm. For Ann, though, suddenly, "it's still all right. There was a sweetness in being close without effort. Maybe when we get very old that will take the place of making love. Maybe it is a way of making love, one we could have oftener if we were together all the time." (p. 87) Ann begins to realize that she wants to live with Eldora, that an affair is not enough. She wants something like marriage, and she wants it for companionship, closeness. "She wasn't sure whether she was only concerned with Eldora or whether, possibly, she had begun to examine her new life and found it not enough." (p. 117) "I want us to have the rest of our lives together," say Eldora: "whatever's left. If I'm the one that stays behind, I'd like to have something to remember." Ann answers: "It's a strange thing, but right now I don't want to make love to you. I just want us to be close. Do you suppose old age is catching up with us?" Eldora's reply is, "I think that's what they call love." (p. 120)

What, then, is the problem? Eldora has a big beautiful country home; why can't Ann just move in? Because Eldora's son and daughter-in-law live there. "Restless, sharp-cornered Dot," the daughter-in-law, is a dissatisfied, self-centered woman who hates the farm but likes to live there so she can spend all her paycheck on herself. Living together with Dot in the house would mean sneaking around, just as they are doing now in Ann's little apartment. They are lesbians, after all—a fact that can never be forgotten. Their love is illicit from society's perspective, and Dot stands for society as much as does Ann's nosy neighbor, Mrs. Hammond. But Eldora won't kick her son and his wife out of her house. Eldora, after all, has never made a move on her own behalf in her life. "In all these years," thinks Ann, "Eldora has never done a single thing to change her life. She's been a wife and a mother and a farmer, she's written her poems in secret, she's kept her head down so nobody could shoot it off. Why should she change now?" (p. 112)

Poems? Yes indeed. Ann discovers that Eldora is a secret poet when Eldora writes her a poem after their affair has commenced, a poem titled, naturally, "Prism." She's a good poet, thinks Ann, but she has never shown her writing to anyone—not since she tried years ago with her husband, who laughed at her. Ann thinks the poem should be published. But Eldora is frightened; it would be like opening her life to strangers. "It's as though I've been asleep under a warm blanket all these years, and now you're asking me to wake up and come out into the cold. Does that make sense?" Ann replies, "It makes sense, all right. The question is, so do you want to stay asleep or do you want to live while you're alive?" Eldora answers: "I've got this far. If anyone had told me a year ago—I guess I can go one step further." (p. 101)

It's all a matter of coming out. To put oneself forward so that the world knows who one is. Being a lesbian makes this gesture quantitatively and qualitatively more problematic, and all the more necessary. Ann too has needed to take this step. Along different lines from Eldora, yes, but the novel juxtaposes the two kinds of coming out to make its point. Ann has gone to a meeting at a women's center in the nearest city, where she has met two older women, Liz and Nora, an out lesbian couple. She has written to them with her story and her problem. Later, she meets them at their home for dinner. It's the start of a friendship; it's as well the start of community. "It was good to be sitting here," thinks Ann: "the warmth and hospitality of the room were what she had been needing." (p. 111) Liz's advice is to give Eldora time. "You're walking around the periphery of a problem, trying to solve it by logic; she may have a flash of intuition and cut across it." (p. 112) Eldora is, after all, a poet.

The acceptance of the poem "Prism" is what sparks Eldora's initiative, as has, I think, Ann's earlier statement that what she wants most is closeness. As snow threatens in the final days of autumn, a moment of deep intimacy occurs between the lovers. The weather causes them to think about death, and at the same time about new life. Eldora evokes spring: "People used to think something like that happened to human beings when they died, an unknown blossoming." "You're a poet," says Ann.

> "I'm a farmer."
> "You and Robert Frost. George Herbert. Louis Bromfield."
> "Don't you know any women farmers?"
> "Patience and Sarah." (p. 120)

This reference is quiet but critical. By deliberately placing the novel we are reading in the tradition of lesbian romance, Valerie Taylor suggests that fiction itself plays a role in the coming-out process. The novel in which the lovers are invented and come out before their readers aids in the creation of identity for characters and readers alike.

Immediately afterwards Eldora, latter-day Patience, tells Ann, her own Sarah: "I'm going to mail some more poems. To the literary magazines this time. Then I'm going to find a way for you to move in, out here . . . Could you feel at home here?"

Yes, replies Ann, because this particular home takes her back to her own childhood, the farmhouse where she'd lived as a child. "It was really home for all of us, no matter where we lived or how often we moved—my grandparents' place." (p. 121) Now we understand why Eldora has been associated throughout the novel with the old-fashioned life. Eldora is a chance at security and growth; she is another mother. "Eldora seemed to her like a good loaf of homemade bread, solid and sustaining. Most of the women she had known were cake, sweet and quickly cloying . . . Living with Eldora might not always be exciting, although she now suspected that it would offer her enough surprises to keep her alert. But it would surely be nourishing." (p. 93)

How will Eldora give them their home? How will she be able to tell Dot to leave? The plot offers an opportunity for Eldora finally to make a gesture on behalf of her own needs. Tom, Eldora's son, is offered a good job as a dispatcher at a trucking firm, fifty miles away. This means that the couple would have to move from Eldora's house. But simultaneously, Dot accidentally becomes pregnant. Tom doesn't want to take the job, so that Dot can have the baby, live with Eldora, and have Eldora care for the child while Dot returns to work. (Ann suspects that the "accident" may have been more calculated than anyone knows; that Dot may have planned the pregnancy to ensure that the couple could live rent-free on the farm, with Eldora caring for the child, so that they could continue to have all their money at their own disposal.)

But Eldora thwarts the plan. She is able to say no. ("Hooray," I cheer.) "I intend to spend the rest of my life the way I want to. I told them so . . . I've only begun to find out what I'm good for." (pp. 122, 124) Promptly, Dot has an abortion. But it isn't until the publisher to whom Eldora has sent her poems invites her to publish a book that she can take the final step: she tells the young couple to leave. Suddenly, what had been difficult is simple. She tells them she knows they are staying on because they think she needs them. ("I hope God forgives liars, otherwise I'm going to hell for sure.") She assures them that they don't need to worry about her, because she has found someone to move in with her. And the deed is done.

Two scenes complete the novel, balanced against one another. The first is set in the warmth and safety of the new/old house. The feeling of the past is strong, and Ann's musings stress continuity—the idea that this new love extends and belongs to all the others that have been sheltered under this roof. The second and final scene takes place in the city, at the publishing house, where Eldora signs the contract for her book. The editor takes her and Ann to lunch afterwards. A woman editor, who says, "My lover and I are always talking about getting out of this damned town and buying a farm somewhere, like Patience and Sarah . . ." Well, well. Of course they're invited, anytime. "We could ask Liz and Nora over for dinner," Ann thinks, "and all get acquainted at the same time. It's a beginning. Start a little gay community right in Abigail." (p. 146) Private is juxtaposed against public. Each is needed, each feeds into the other. The novel ends with rainbow colors glowing from the glass that holds the martini Eldora has boldly ordered, even though she finds she can't drink it. Martini glass or Grandma's prism: both make rainbows.

The happy ending has been achieved. Ann and Eldora, each out to herself, to one another, to a wider community, will find true love and selfhood in their lives, as Patience and Sarah have done before them. The happy ending of lesbian romance fiction is a gesture of faith and hope even more idealistic—and courageous—than its counterpart in the heterosexual romance. In the teeth of homophobia and sexism, the reality of the social world, lesbian romances propose that an alternative way of being, living, and especially loving exists and can flourish, to have an effect on the world at large. The lesbian fantasy of true love is particularly insistent that gender matters: that being a woman, not a man, is central to self-identity as it operates privately and publicly. At the same time, it emphasizes that the ways in which gender is manifested—in looks, in acts, in qualities and attributes at every level of experience—can be very different from society's definitions and paradigms. The range is much wider, more variable, and much less restrictive. For the reader who is heterosexual, these ideas about women are both exciting and challenging. For the lesbian reader, the romance story is more. It lets you know you are real in a world that would hide you; it lets you know you are right in a world that calls you wrong. This is a form of maternal recognition, of course: nurture, support, and love. For the lesbian daughter, that interchange is all the more critical in a culture that makes coming out so frightening, dangerous, and necessary.

Epilogue

EVERYDAY READING AND TRUE LOVE

I sit and read in the blue chair, only now it's been moved to a tiny little sublet summer apartment. There's no space in the living room for a sofa, even—so the blue chair dominates the scene. I needed that chair here, whatever else had to stay behind until I move into my own new house at the end of July. I've just left my husband, my marriage. I'm on my own. Do I need novels? Is the Colorado summer sky bluer than blue?

Only I'm not doing so well. I can't seem to get into this novel, Penelope Lively's *Cleopatra's Sister* (1993). I don't exactly know why, because Lively is one of my favorite writers, and her new book received excellent reviews. I haven't talked much about this experience yet: about when it won't work. When you have a novel and you try and try, but you are locked out. Those people in the book seem to be having a life, all right, and the writer is clearly pleased as punch with what she's doing and how it's turning out. But I'm behind a glass wall as far as this book is concerned. I can't connect. It's just a novel that I'm reading: it's not a world I can enter.

Why not? The writing is smart enough. Penelope Lively is a novelist who knows her way around life. She's got a wry and trenchant way of laughing without condemning that amounts to something like wisdom. I like that. But in the process, the characters stay at a remove from her. She wants it that way. Yes, we know what they think (and why), but there's a precision to her narration: the edges are so clean. I mean, the writer and the character never spill into one another. There's no passion, you see, to catch the writer up in the character's struggles, to make her a little unsure of just how it might turn out. The author keeps her character at a distance, and me too. I'm supposed to feel the irony, the interesting tension between will and fate. And I get it, of course I do. I'm not stupid. But I don't particularly care, and that's the problem. I stay on the outside, when where I want to go is the inside. I want to be this character; I want to love her. Under other novelistic circumstances, I think I could. But not here.

I should add a few more things. That the novel is also careful about dividing its time between hero and heroine. And about him I couldn't care less. I wouldn't want to be him, and if I were the heroine, I wouldn't want to love him. I can appreciate his flawed but delicious humanity, but so what? As the heroine in her youth was unable to enjoy men, really, and so remained unattached, sort of by default, I admit that I kept thinking, "Well, maybe you'll fall in love with a woman." Which doesn't mean, however, that I can read *only* lesbian fiction now. I just finished Sue Miller's *For Love,* and I liked that romance. I understood why she loved that doctor; I understood why she didn't. I took part in her struggles and her process, and I was glad when she went back to him at the end. But in *Cleopatra's Sister,* no, I want something better for the heroine. I know that's the author's point: He's just a person. Men are just people. Except of course, they're not. They're privileged people, which is exactly what this book is not about. This book is about people in relationship to fate, all of them to a great extent powerless against that capricious force.

Then there are all the sections devoted to the history of Callimbia, a Middle Eastern country where the heroine and the hero are going to meet when their plane heading for Nairobi has to make a forced landing. "Really," I say. "Boring," I say. "Don't do this to me," I say. But Lively won't listen. She has her agenda.

Well, I just don't care. I'm going to finish it because it's intelligent and well written, and because Penelope Lively matters to me, and I read all her novels and wouldn't want to miss this one. All very good reasons for reading a book, but not the reason I've been discussing here. I read for intimacy, for identity—for recognition. Whether I am reading as a daughter or a mother or both, I try to enter a relationship with author and text that keeps me from being lonely. Maybe it's as simple as that, although I hope that I have demonstrated something about the complexity that generates the state I refer to as lonely. But not all novels, not all romances work in the way I have been describing here. Not every text is a facilitating environment; not every author is a mother. Entering the world of the book, you can find danger as well as safety; alienation as well as connection; boredom as well as life-enhancing energy.

For passionate reading is a day-to-day enterprise. It operates as a kind of support system in my life as well as an artistic pleasure and a mind-expanding intellectual experience. It interacts persistently and irrevocably with the rest of my life, even as the issues and concerns in my world beyond the book affect what I read and how I read it. I have, in other words, a relationship with reading that goes well beyond the peak moments of intensity—of pleasure and insight—that I have been describing. (This is true love, after all—not infatuation.)

For example, reading means a great deal more than sitting down with a book. Books have to be chosen, and this is an ongoing and complicated process. From poring over the reviews in the *New York Times Book Review* to filling out request cards at the Boulder Public Library; the long wait for the card to come back to me, in my mailbox, announcing that the book is there and waiting; streaking down to the library, hoping to find a parking space; claiming the book at the reserve desk—the order of my days includes a well-maintained system to ensure that books will be present on the shelf next to my bed, novels that have at least the potential to be right.

Remember that little girl and the Providence Public Library? Today the library is still central to the grid, or net, on which all of my other activities are suspended. After all, I can't *buy* all the novels I read in a month or a year. A new hardcover novel is twenty dollars. But the Boulder Public Library will order a new book if a user requests it, which works out fine for me. And even if I could shell out for every new novel that interests me, I don't think I'd do it. I prefer to own only books that I love and would like to read again and pass on to others, but I want to try many more. With the library, you can do this. You don't have to like the books you take out; you don't have to finish them. It's a great license. If I buy a book, I feel beholden to it. I still love the library.

Actually, I appreciate my system for its very randomness. It's always a surprise, the book that is meant for me just at that moment, or so it feels. It rises to the surface of my life from the long-submerged past of my requesting it, all the unseen library processes involved in my one day finding a white card in my mailbox—and then, there it is, waiting for me on the reserve shelf. I like to trust to that process and don't usually disarrange it, except for special occasions. If I know that one of *my* writers has a new book, the rule is: *I don't have to wait.* Otherwise, the books come to me when they come.

Of course, there are disadvantages. It can take months and months for books to arrive. If I keep the card flow active, then there is usually something in the hopper for me. But not always. Sometimes there are long gaps. And I need to have in my possession not just the book I am currently reading but many others in reserve. I can't run out, or, well, I'd die. And so I haunt the reserve desk, not waiting for my card to arrive in the mail as it's supposed to. They're sick of me. "Yuck," they think, "it's her again." But what can I do? I'm starving.

It's not that I'm not reading, of course. It's just that I'm not reading something really good. Something that takes me in and makes me its own. In the course of a month, most of what I read really doesn't play such an active role in my psyche. I read slight books that let me skate or glide right through them, just so I can be somewhere, be doing something. They don't ask much of me, I don't ask much of them, but our interaction isn't unpleasant. I read books I don't even finish because they're really bad or insulting—or just too boring. And I read many mystery novels—both lesbian and straight. Mysteries are a mainstay of women's fiction. Smart heroines (smart writers) and a plot that usually involves some self-development, some love, as much as it does crime solving. Their drawback is that they just don't last long enough. The authors try to get around the limitations of their genre by writing series, but it still doesn't quite work, because even when you get to see the character and her friends and lovers again and again, each particular book in which she appears is usually just too streamlined for real depth of thought and character. It can never become a world.

I think that during periods when I'm more or less at peace with myself, the intensity of the need for a wonderful book is less. The real world is clicking along and takes up a lot of the slack. But at other times, like now, like lately, when I'm in turmoil and in pain—and yes, when there's no other person who can share that with me, help me, encourage me, understand me, love me—then I turn to the book for comfort; for enlightenment; for relief; for pleasure and even joy; for feelings that are mine and others that are not mine; for a place to go where, when it's right, I belong.

When I can go to that place, curled up in the blue chair, when I know that place is there because the book I'm currently reading is a good one, and it's next to the bed, waiting for me, then the rest of my day is bolstered. I've been rattling around of late, trying one novel after another. Nothing has been working, and I hate it. I feel that I'm not tethered anywhere. That I'm on my own, floating free. Then, just when I thought that I was so weird, so anxious, so depressed that I was ruining all these perfectly well-meaning novels—that it wasn't the novels, it was *me*—I started one that worked. I could feel the warmth begin as I read the first page. It's a physical feeling, a glow that starts as a lilt of pleasure, from a phrase here, a comment there, turning swiftly into contentment, a settling in.

The book was Joanna Trollope's *The Men and the Girls* (1992). I'd picked it up off the New Books shelf because I've enjoyed her earlier ones. The dust jacket blurb didn't seem too exciting to me at the time, but I thought, "Why not? Bring it home; you never know." I left it on my shelf. I didn't choose it right away. I'd been trying others, to no avail. So I took it out and opened it and got a man not wearing his glasses driving along and knocking a person gently off her bicycle. I got, "He saw, with a shock of tenderness, that she was a true Oxford spinster, one of that dwindling band of elderly, dignified, clever women living out frugal lives in small flats and rooms, sustained by thinking." (p. 1). I got:

"Are you hurt? Have I hurt you?"

"Only my feelings," she said with emphasis.

"I forgot my glasses—"

"I'm not interested!" she cried, her voice sharp with shock. "Why should I care?" (p. 1)

The narrative consciousness here is that of a man, James Mallow. But the writer is a woman, and it is her attitude toward the characters, and toward me, that began to hold my interest. Especially her depiction of the other person in the scene, Beatrice Bachelor: "sustained by thinking"; "only my feelings." So I continued on.

To find myself in a world of interesting women, two of whom are married to much older men (hence the title). There is as well Joss, the fourteen-year-old daughter of one of the heroines; their Chinese cleaning woman, Mrs. Cheng; and of course, the tough, pragmatic, and wise Miss Bachelor. In this novel, as in *Cleopatra's Sister*, the narrative consciousness is shared by many of the characters, including the men, James and Hugh, but I don't seem to mind that here. This is because the author's voice and point of view support the whole. She is a mother-author. She is loving toward everyone but never uncritical. She makes me care about the characters, as they all struggle toward some kind of self-definition within and without their relationships. And she is helping them in their struggle. Her words about each one are the net in which they live—my touchstone as I persistently try to determine if and when they are misguided or on target. I trust her, all the way to the ending, where one older man goes back to the young woman from whom he has been estranged—and the other man does not, saying no to the woman who has originally left him and then wanted to come back. Is it a happy ending or not? There's a great deal to think about here, which I do as I put down the book and begin another activity. About love lasting and love changing. What does it take? What gets lost? Joanna Trollope has guided me, charmed me, given me an environment of care, intelligence, and humor. While I was in her book, I always had a place to go.

⁂

Everyday reading, then, is a story about need, sometimes satisfied, sometimes not. In reading, the need for the facilitating environment that replicates the mother-infant bond can be met by some books, some writers—or it can be thwarted. The actual dynamics of a reading week or month or year involve yearning, frustration, and the impetus to try again as much as pleasure and contentment. This is a lot like life: the life of relationships, of loves that help and those that hinder, of times without any love at all.

What this book about reading and loving relationships has revealed, I think, is the importance both of our need for true love and of the fantasies we create about getting it. The fantasy of a man who is a mother; the fantasy of a mother who is an equal; the fantasy of forever. The stories revolve around fantasies not because they are the opposite of life but because they are integral to life. There is no perfect mother-infant relationship, and the mother-infant relationship can never be experienced again. Yet our needs persist. For intimacy. Connection. Recognition. Those essential conditions for a real self to come into being and to be maintained. One way, if not the only way, to address the need is to imagine how it might be fulfilled. We may give shape to the fantasies with words and characters and plot. We may take part in the fantasy by reading these novels. Fiction can make these dreams of love and identity come true—for the characters; for the reader who is participating wholeheartedly in their story; for the author.

Because the mother-infant relationship is the prototypical situation of intimacy, connection, and recognition, it serves as a model for reading as well as for other kinds of relationships in which we seek to experience true love again.

In Edith Konecky's novel *A Place at the Table* (1989), the narrator tells of a writer who says that "part of her need to write is an insistence on being understood—properly, accurately known":

> 'I've been reading her work, and it's true; she has to restrain herself from overexplaining. Sometimes I see her as a child, black hair flying, stamping her foot, howling into the void, the void in which she doesn't want to be lost. This is what, this is why, this is how, and especially, this is who. But to whom, to what out there? Who cares? The world? The mother who died too early, whose absence was so much more intense than her presence might have been? It can only be to herself. When the mother is lost, the child of that mother is also lost. The one who knew me best knows me not at all; her knowing of me has died with her, leaving me perhaps forever insufficiently known. (p. 7)

"To be known" is Konecky's phrase for recognition. Initially unrecognized, the writer uses her words to help create her own identity, a process in which the presence of the recognizing mother is continually fantasized. It is now the reader who serves that purpose for her. That writer is a daughter-writer.

But as we have seen, the author can also be a mother, recognizing the daughter-reader in a process that involves both sameness and difference. Witness two mothers, characters in recent novels, thinking about their daughters:

> She *felt* Emily, almost as if she had never left her womb, were still attached to her by tendrils of tissue and interwoven muscle and reddened veins threaded through the flesh. Emily was an inexplicable emotion, a way of breathing in and out.

Epilogue

"Emily is, therefore I am," she had once said to herself, striving to understand the unfathomable wonder of her daughter's presence in her life.

It wasn't, of course, entirely true. Molly was because she was. But Emily's hold on her had a transcendental power that Emily did not seek and Molly could not penetrate. It gave her joy and made her suffer.

(Ethel Gorham, *Natural Light*, 1991, pp. 217–18)

Anna would come in from another room and see [Claire] seated on the floor. From the back, the great curve of her head with its brown-gold curls would taper into the hollow between the tendons of her neck, and somehow the tendons themselves would bespeak concentration. Although Anna loved Claire's . . . smiles and waves and kisses, loved, too, the stroke of a little hand on her breast while the child nursed, chancing upon this quiet business with a piece of cloth had touched her the most. It was so mysteriously inward when you hardly yet believed that the child had an inner life.

(Jane Smiley, *At Paradise Gate*, 1981, pp. 31–32)

The child, held in that gaze, feels the thrill of recognition. Reciprocally, the mother does too. This is the beginning of everything. And it can happen. The need can be met.

Yet countering these moments, which can occur in life as well as in reading, is a haunting passage from Ellen Gilchrist's *I Cannot Get You Close Enough: Three Novellas* (1990):

I cannot get you close enough, I said to him, pitiful as a child, and never can and never will. We cannot get from anyone else the things we need to fill the endless terrible need, not to be dissolved, not to sink back into sand, heat, broom, air, thin-

251

nest air. And so we revolve around each other and our dreams collide. It is embarrassing that it should be so hard. (p. 387)

Sometimes connection erases the loneliness; sometimes there is no connection. Not in life, not in literature. The mother can't always do it. For a thousand reasons, most of which she can't control, she is absent. The new love can't make up for the early, original loss. The novel, likewise, cannot always provide that nurture. It has a different aim. Or the writing can't sustain the author's purpose. There are so many reasons, so many ways in which need is thwarted. And so the longing remains, and so do the dreams: the fantasy. To write the fantasy, to take part in it as reader or writer—this is one resource we have as humans: the abilities of our minds. Yet the world of reading exists in a dynamic relationship with everyday life, each of them composed of yearning, disappointment, satisfaction. A yearning from everyday life may be disappointed or it may be satisfied in reading. A disappointment from reading may be subsequently satisfied in everyday life. The romance novel, as it tells the story of true love to its characters, its readers, its writer, evolves out of a dance of desire in which need and fantasy are irrevocably linked. Reading, we participate in the story—as nurturing, enabling, and incomplete as it may be.

Appendix

WOMEN'S DEVELOPMENT,

OBJECT-RELATIONS THEORY, AND READING

In *Reading from the Heart* I propose that my experience of reading women's romance fiction is informed by needs and desires that stem from the earliest relationship between mother and infant. I describe how both the fantasy of true love as many women writers render it in romance fiction and my own experience of reading these novels arise from and attempt to replicate the facilitating environment of the mother-infant bond. This appendix provides more detail about the psychoanalytic theories that have helped me to arrive at these conclusions and to write *Reading from the Heart*.

I. A MODEL FOR SELF-DEVELOPMENT

The Self-in-Relation
I have used D. W. Winnicott's ideas about maternal nurture and infant self-development as the basis for my thinking about how a heroine would need to grow in the textual environment of her novel and what it would mean for her to arrive at self-identity for her happy ending. Object-relations theory in general is particularly important for such an

253

enterprise. Its concentration on the mother, and on the earliest months of the child's life, shows us not symbiosis and merger of baby and mother but a formative, dynamic, and complex period of interactive growth. Right from the start. Consequently, the mother-infant matrix is neither extraneous nor previous to a woman's self-development but crucial to it, because self-identity emerges through connection with another.

Daniel Stern's recent work is even more emphatic about this matter. In *The Interpersonal World of the Infant* he challenges the notion of a state of fusion or undifferentiation from which the infant gradually separates and individuates to arrive at a sense of self and other. Recent findings drawn from experimental observation adjust these generally accepted timetables and sequences.

> These new findings support the view that the infant's first order of business, in creating an interpersonal world, is to form the sense of a core self and core others. The evidence also supports the notion that this task is largely accomplished during the period between two and seven months. Further, it suggests that the capacity to have merger- or fusion-like experiences as described in psychoanalysis is secondary to and dependent upon an already existing sense of self and other. (p. 70)

Stern notes that the British object-relations school (along with Harry Stack Sullivan, the American parallel) was "unique among clinical theorists in believing that human social relatedness is present from birth, that it exists for its own sake, is of a definable nature, and does not lean upon psychological need states." (p. 44)

It is true that early object-relations theory defined the developmental process in more linear terms, but in stressing the ongoing alternation and interaction in the psyche between dependence and separation, Winnicott too, I believe, described the same relation between individuation and connection that I find so compelling. As Stern points out, although object-relations theorists assume an initial period of undifferentiation, which they imbue with subjective feelings of security and belongingness, they nonetheless "see separateness and relatedness as concomitant and equal developmental lines." (p. 242)

What is most important to me about Winnicott's picture of the mother-infant matrix is its intimation of reciprocity, mutual empathy, and an ongoing dynamic between what he called "dependence" and "separation"; what contemporary feminist psychologists Judith Jordan and Janet Surrey would prefer to see as "relationship-differentiation." "This new model," they write, "emphasizes that the direction of growth is *not* towards greater degrees of autonomy or individuation or the breaking of early emotional ties. Rather, development is a dynamic process of growth within the relationship, in which all people involved are challenged to maintain connection and to foster, allow, or adapt to the growth of the other." ("The Self-in-Relation: Empathy and the Mother-Daughter Relationship," p. 96.)

Winnicott and other object-relations theorists emphasized the primacy of relationship itself in self-identity and questioned the proposition that the self could ever be truly or totally autonomous. Indeed, Winnicott predicates the capacity to be alone, "so nearly synonymous with emotional maturity" (*The Maturational Processes and the Facilitating Environment*, p. 31), upon the original two-body relationship, as the mother, and the ego-support she represents, is introjected into the developing ego. The one experience basic to the capacity to be alone is *"that of being alone, as an infant and a small child, in the presence of mother."* (*MP*, p. 30) In Nancy Chodorow's words, the "true self" or "central self" emerges "through an internal sense of relationship with another." ("Gender, Relation, and Difference," p. 10.) Thus, for Winnicott and his heirs, "being alone" means something more like authenticity than alienation.

Three Aspects of the Maturational Process
At one point in his essays Winnicott outlines the developmental process, from the point of view of the infant's psyche, as follows:

When I look I am seen, so I exist.
I can now afford to look and see.

I now look creatively and what I apperceive I also perceive.
In fact I take care not to see what is not there to be seen
(unless I am tired). (*Playing and Reality*, p. 114)

I use this paradigm as a shorthand way of describing three necessary aspects of the maturational process: the formation of the facilitating environment, transitional object relating, and the entry into the social world. There are other ways and terms to describe similar dynamics. Stern's discussion, for example, of the sense of a core self, a subjective self, and a verbal self is another compelling description of early development. However, I have found Winnicott's model to be especially useful for explaining the fictional evolution of the heroine in women's romance novels, because its outlines are broad enough that they can be applied to situations other than the ones they literally describe, and because its surface simplicity is actually elastic enough to contain a myriad of complexities and complications.

The Facilitating Environment
"When I look I am seen, so I exist." The developmental process "depends on being seen." (p. 114) It depends on the mother's recognition of the infant as someone who is there: "The mother is looking at the baby and what she looks like is related to what she sees there." (*P & R*, p. 112) The "good-enough mother" empathizes with the baby, even as the baby with her or his primitive ego organization, empathizes with the mother. This is primary identification, and it is a condition of mutuality.

Stern's notion of core-relatedness helps to explain how this mutual recognition transpires. He describes a period, from two to six months old, of maternal "responsivity and regulation" (p. 210). "Baby talk" and "baby faces," for example, are instances of adult behavior that are elicited in response to an infant's social presence, because they are best suited to an infant's innate perceptual biases; for example, infants prefer sounds of higher pitch. "The result is that the adult's behavior is maximally attended by the infant." (pp. 72–73) In such mutually regulatory social behavior the infant can discover the basic invariants that specify a core self and a core other. Sense of self, as Stern points out, "is not a cognitive construct. It is an experiential integration." (p. 71)

Such maternal recognition is at the root of Winnicott's all-essential "holding environment," in which the presence and care of the mother supports the developing infant self. Winnicott insists on the element of dependence here, necessary because it establishes a security of being that is requisite for any further development. Without it, there is, for the infant, the fear of annihilation itself.

Winnicott's best-known idea, that there is no such thing as an infant—there is, rather, an infant-mother—is based on the premise that the self can come into being only in the maternal "environment." "The infant and the maternal care together form a unit." (*MP*, p. 39) Proper establishment of a facilitating environment is the beginning of having a self.

> With "the care that it receives from its mother" each infant is able to have a personal existence, and so begins to build up what might be called a *continuity of being*. On the basis of this continuity of being the inherited potential gradually develops into an individual. If maternal care is not good enough then an infant does not really come into existence, since there is no continuity of being; instead the personality becomes built on the basis of reactions to environmental impingement. (*MP*, p. 54)

This process, decisive for the earliest months of the infant's life, is as well a template for what will come later. "Most of the processes that start up in early infancy," says Winnicott, "are never fully established, and continue to be strengthened by the growth that continues in later childhood, and indeed in adult life, even in old age." (*MP*, pp. 73–74) There is thus room in life for other facilitating environments, such as romance, such as reading.

Transitional Object Relating
"I can now afford to look and see." In the safety net of the facilitating environment, of the mother's ego in support of the baby's, the baby can

explore beyond this place. "I now look creatively and what I apperceive I also perceive." The mother has another function for the baby: she is "object-mother" as well as "environment-mother." This means that she represents not only internality but externality, the "not-me" as well as the "me."

> It is useful then, to think of a third area of human living, one neither inside the individual nor outside the world of shared reality. This intermediate living can be thought of as occupying a potential space, negating the very idea of space and separation between the baby and the mother, and all developments derive from this phenomenon. (*P & R*, p. 110)

This "transitional space" is still a part of the mother-infant matrix. It is, however, confidence in this kind of interaction that permits the baby eventually to engage effectively with the world beyond the two of them.

Winnicott's developmental theory attempts to explain how mother and baby negotiate the space between them. This space is filled with what he calls "transitional objects," "symbols that stand at one and the same time for external world phenomena and for phenomena of the individual person" (*P & R*, p. 109), the "products of the baby's own creative imagination" (*P & R*, p. 102), all that "eventually adds up to a cultural life." (*P & R*, p. 109)

Now the mother's breast, or the mother herself, or some other object that the baby relates to the mother, like a piece of blanket, is experienced as both a part of or inside the baby (the baby "creates" it) and, at the same time, outside of the baby (it obeys rules of existence over which the baby has no control). The baby's initial sense of "omnipotence" must be frustrated (by the mother) so that the baby will try to destroy the object—and fail. It will not be destroyed, since it is actually outside of the baby's dominion. Thus, "at the point of development that is under survey the subject is creating the object in the sense of finding externality itself, and it has to be added that this experience depends on the object's capacity to survive." (*P & R*, p. 91)

It is the mother, of course, who survives in this way. She does not "go away" because the baby has tried to destroy her, and in this way she fosters the infant's ability to believe in external reality. The key point, here and throughout, is the steady reliability of the mother, from the first stage of "holding" through the establishment of object use. The infant's confidence to give up the idea of omnipotence, to admit that boundaries exist, to investigate a world beyond the self, is established by the never-going-away of the mother, ultimately internalized into the self as a core part of its structure.

It is useful to associate Winnicott's concept of the transitional object with Stern's development of a subjective self, although Stern focuses more on the infant's discovery of the externality of the other's mind than on the objects that mediate between the minds. "Only when infants can sense that others distinct from themselves can hold or entertain a mental state that is similar to one they sense themselves to be holding is the sharing of subjective experience or intersubjectivity possible." (p. 124)

Stern's extensive observations of "affect attunement"—his version of the classic psychoanalytic "mirroring"—seem like another way of describing what transpires in that transitional space where mother and infant experience both profound connection and the necessity of self-boundaries, before the infant must deal with the world beyond the mother-infant matrix. For affect attunement is more than simple imitation: it is "the performance of behaviors that express the quality of feeling of a shared affective state without imitating the exact behavioral expression of the inner state." (*The Interpersonal World of the Infant,* p. 142) Whereas imitation does not permit the partners to refer to the internal state, "attunement behaviors . . . recast the event and shift the focus of attention to what is behind the behavior, to the quality of feeling that is being shared." (p. 142)

In romance novels, we remember, the lover can function as such an object-mother, thus replicating the period of transitional object-relating, so important for self-development.

Entry into the Social World

"In fact I take care not to see what is not there to be seen (unless I am tired)." The completed maturational process allows for both a self and an external world, a society. "Maturity of the human being," writes Winnicott, "is a term that implies not only personal growth but socialization." He continues:

> Let us say that in health, which is almost synonymous with maturity, the adult is able to identify with society without too great a sacrifice of personal spontaneity; or, the other way around, the adult is able to attend to his or her personal needs without being antisocial, and indeed, without a failure to take some responsibility for the maintenance or for the modification of society as it is found. We get left with certain social conditions, and this is a legacy we have to accept, and if necessary, alter; it is this that we eventually hand down to those who come after us. (*MP*, p. 83)

Winnicott's ideas about the adult self in relation to society are essentially an expansion of his picture of the child's relationship to the mother. If that relationship develops properly,

> . . . the child is able gradually to meet the world and all its complexities, because of seeing there more and more of what is already present in his or her own self. In ever-widening circles of social life the child is identified with society, because local society is a sample of the self's personal world as well as being a sample of truly external phenomena. (*MP*, p. 91)

Recognizing the existence of a world beyond the self is essential to self-identity. The completed maturation process allows for both a self and an external world, as well as a transitional space between them—the world of the imagination, or culture—where interaction and interplay occur between boundaries that are real but nonetheless negotiable. In this theory, then, culture is not initiated by Freud's Oedipal moment, which splits the child from the mother with the presence of the father, who represents and enacts the power of a patriarchal culture—a power based on radical separation, with desire as an organizing energy fueled by its essential unsatisfiability. Rather, with the mother-infant matrix as source and model, culture itself is imagined as a relational, affiliative dynamic: "local society is a sample of the self's personal world as well as being a sample of truly external phenomena." Thus novels by women about female maturation, having brought their heroines through something close to the process described above, conclude with concerns that address the responsibility of the mature woman toward society—that legacy we have to accept or, as Winnicott warns, alter. Personal agency and authenticity demand reciprocity between care for the self and for the world beyond the self.

For Stern, this third stage corresponds with the sense of a verbal self. And even as Winnicott's developmental theory expands the maternal mode into society, rather than postulating a sudden break into a paternal system (Freud's Oedipal crisis, Lacan's symbolic order), so Stern's ideas about language and language acquisition challenge the neo-Freudian notion that entry into language is precisely the point where the maternally identified subject is split, fragmented, and brought into the social order. Stern points to the double function of language: On the one hand, it is true, language can cause a split in the experience of self, driving a wedge "between two simultaneous forms of interpersonal experience: as it is lived and as it is verbally represented . . . And to the extent that events in the domain of verbal relatedness are held to be what has really happened, experiences in these other domains suffer an alienation." (pp. 162–63) On the other hand, however, the possible ways of "being-with" another increase enormously. Language "makes parts of our known experience more shareable with others. In addition, it permits two people to create mutual experiences of meaning that had been unknown before and could never have existed until fashioned by words." (p. 162)

Stern notes that although "the acquisition of language has traditionally been seen as a major step in the achievement of separation and individuation, next only to acquiring locomotion, [the] present view asserts that the opposite is equally true, that the acquisition of language is potent in the service of union and togetherness." (p. 172) Like Winnicott, he suggests that the being-with that defines the mother-infant matrix can be expanded to include social experience, rather than being cut off to attain it:

> With each word, children solidify their mental commonality with the parent and later with the other members of the language culture, when they discover that their personal experiential knowledge is part of a larger experience of knowledge, that they are unified with others in a common culture base. (p. 172)

Consequently, the maternal mode of self-in-relation has the potential, which the romances portray, to influence and sustain the individual's participation in the social order, the wide world that encompasses the self.

Gender and the Social Order

Both Winnicott and Stern see the social order as potentially developing out of the maternal order; however, we do not see much evidence for this phenomenon in the culture as it presently exists. There seems to me to be a correlation between this idealism and the fact that neither writer directly introduces issues of gender into his analysis, nor do either of them directly account for the powerful effects on the original maternal mode of the father and the social order organized around patriarchal values. And yet gender arrangements influence the process of self-development, particularly in the ways that the process diverges for females and males. For boys, especially because of their vested interest in identifying with the father rather than the mother, the attraction of the power and authority to be gained from autonomy, separation, and distance as a model for self-development starts to prevail. Society teaches girls, on the other hand, to support male dominance, not to share it; but embracing culturally sanctioned femininity means devaluing the interactive and mutually supportive activity of the maternal mode. At the same time, its normative structures linger. As recent feminist theorists have shown, notably Nancy Chodorow in *The Reproduc-*

tion of Mothering, girls do retain their strong connection with their mothers even when they establish a heterosexual attachment to their fathers. Thus they often live with a deep conflict between the two paradigms that are represented by the preoedipal and the Oedipal, which is probably what Freud was noticing when he said that women had trouble making the transition from the mother to the father and so ended up in a murky place of unrealized feminine identity.

Indirectly, however, in their accounts of inadequacies and distortions in early parenting, both Winnicott and Stern reveal how frequently the ideal pattern they describe does not work. Indeed, Winnicott's clinical practice, upon which he amply reports, was populated with people experiencing difficulties initiated in the infant-mother matrix, and there he attempted clinical reparation of the developmental processes. Both psychologists imply causes for these psychodynamic difficulties that to me suggest societal gender arrangements at work. Winnicott acknowledges the fact that some mothers are not "good-enough," although he doesn't suggest that their problems with mothering stem from their own upbringing as daughters in the culture. He notes that "there are certainly many women who are good mothers in every other way and who are capable of a rich and fruitful life but who are not able to achieve this 'normal illness' which enables them to adapt delicately and sensitively to the infant's needs at the very beginning; or they achieve it with one child but not with another." (*Collected Papers: Through Paediatrics to Psycho-Analysis*, p. 302)

Stern's descriptions of a caretaker's non-attunements, mis-attunements, selective and inauthentic attunements describe how these distortions come into being. When a mother's affect is consistently lower (or higher) than her child's, for example, or lower (or higher) in selected instances—or if it is inauthentic, again in selected instances—what results is far from trivial. "With Molly," for example, a baby whose mother very much valued and sometimes appeared to overvalue "enthusiasm" in her, "one could begin to see a certain phoniness creep into her use of enthusiasm. The center of gravity was shifting from inside to outside, and the beginning of a particular aspect of 'false self' formation could be detected. Her natural assets had joined forces with parental selective attunement, probably to her later disadvantage." (p. 209) Winnicott's notion of the "false self" has been central to my discussion of romance heroines. Stern notes how misalignments in attunement behaviors can be the first step in that process, since they represent "the exclusion from intersubjective sharing of certain experiences." The remaining, equally legitimate portions of inner experience may be relegated out of consciousness altogether, or remain a private but devalued aspect of the self. "In essence," explains Stern,

> attunement permits the parents to convey to the infant what is shareable, that is, what subjective experiences are within and which are beyond the pale of mutual consideration and acceptance. Through the selective use of attunement, the parents' intersubjective responsivity acts as a template to shape and create corresponding intrapsychic experiences in the child. It is in this way that the parents' desires, fears, prohibitions, and fantasies contour the psychic experiences of the child. (p. 208)

Like the novelists discussed in this book, I am especially concerned with the distortion of the early experiences that leaves daughters with few resources for achieving selfhood, which is the condition of all the heroines when their stories begin. "What the infant needs," says Winnicott, "is just what he usually gets, the care and attention of someone *who is going on being herself.*" (*MP*, p. 88, my emphasis) But what if the mother for her part lacks that sense of self? A particularly vicious cycle is perpetuated when the mother, lacking authenticity herself because of her own gender socialization, uses her daughter as the self she never had; never recognizing, therefore, the infant's own reality, which is a prerequisite for the entire process that Winnicott describes.

The work of psychoanalyst Alice Miller is relevant here. In studies such as *The Drama of the Gifted Child*, she explores the ramifications of parental narcissism, describing inappropriate attunement behaviors from a psychoanalytic perspective. "What happens," she asks, "if the mother not only is unable to take over the narcissistic functions for the child but also, as very often happens, is herself in need of narcissistic supplies?"

> Quite unconsciously, and despite her own good intentions, the mother then tries to assuage her own narcissistic needs through her child, that is, she cathects him narcissistically. This does not rule out strong affection. On the contrary, the mother often loves her child as her self-object, passionately, but not in the way he needs to be loved. Therefore, the continuity and constancy that would be so important for the child are missing, among other things, from this love. Yet what is missing above all is the framework within which the child could experience his feelings and his emotions. Instead, he develops something the mother needs, and this certainly saves his life (the mother's or the father's love) at the time, but it nevertheless may prevent him throughout his life, from being himself. (pp. 34–35)

Again we encounter the idea of a false self, developed so that the child can receive whatever version of love the parent has to offer, while the true self goes into hiding. Whereas the false self complies with environmental demands, the true self is not involved in the reacting. In this way the true self can preserve a continuity of being: however, it "suffers an impoverishment . . . that results from lack of experience." The false self, on the other hand, "may achieve a deceptive false integrity," but "it cannot, however, experience life, and feel real." (Winnicott, "On Transference," p. 387) Central to the enterprise of reclaiming and activating the true self, which is in essence the project of women's romance fiction, is a reexperiencing of the facilitating environment with a "mother" who can recognize and attune helpfully and lovingly.

The Problem of Domination
The psychologists whose work I have been describing are especially perceptive about these patterns of early development, both when they succeed and when they don't. However, their neglect of gender prevents them from seeing how a mother's difficulties may have much to

do with her own gender socialization and how in turn her daughter can easily fall prey to these same obstacles to developing an authentic self. In *The Bonds of Love: Psychoanalysis, Feminism, and the Problem of Domination*, Jessica Benjamin focuses on gender issues in a theory of intersubjective relationship that is premised on Stern's and Winnicott's work. However, she discusses the power of the father as well as the love of the mother, identifying the sexual politics of psychoanalytic theory as follows:

> The oedipal model takes for granted the necessity of the boy's break with his early maternal identification. It ratifies that repudiation on the grounds that the maternal object is inextricably associated with the initial state of oneness, of primary narcissism. In this view, femininity and narcissism are twin sirens calling us back to undifferentiated infantile bliss. Communion with others is understood as dangerous and seductive—as regression. The elevation of the paternal ideal of separation is a kind of Trojan horse within which is hidden the belief that we actually long to return to oceanic oneness with mother, that we would all sink back into "limitless narcissism" were it not for the paternal imposition of difference. The equation *oneness=mother=narcissism* is implicit in the oedipal model. (pp. 147–48)

This theory of gender difference, as Benjamin notes, rests on the notion that agency and authority go only with the father, with masculinity, while the mother embodies all regressive states of infantilism. ("To the extent that until recently 'man' and 'individual' were synonymous, the male experience of differentiation has stamped the image of individuality." [p. 78]) A boy develops gender and identity by establishing discontinuity and difference from the person to whom he has been most attached. Domination can be seen as a "casualty of this characteristically male form of establishing separation," because "the need to sever the identification with the mother in order to be confirmed both as a separate person and as a male person—and for the boy these are hard to distinguish—often prevents the boy from recognizing his mother." (p. 76) Rather than existing as another person, a subject, she is seen as other, as object.

> In breaking the identification with and dependency on mother, the boy is in danger of losing his capacity for mutual recognition altogether. The emotional attunement and bodily harmony that characterized his infantile exchange with mother now threaten his identity. He is, of course, able cognitively to accept the principle that the other is separate, but without the experience of empathy and shared feeling that can unite separate subjectivities. Instead, the other, especially the female other, is related to as object.
>
> (p. 76)

The corollary to the male refusal to recognize the other is woman's own acceptance of her role as object, "her willingness to offer recognition without expecting it in return." (p. 78) She recognizes him so that the self she valorizes will reflect back and create her, in turn. Benjamin calls this "ideal love, the wish for a vicarious substitute for one's own agency. It takes the passive form of accepting the other's will and desires as one's own; from there it is just a step to surrender to the other's will. Thus we see in ideal love a 'perversion' of identification, a deformation of identificatory love into submission." (p. 122)

This perversity must be recognized. If a woman is object, not subject, to the man to whom she submits, or if she presents him with a false self that will satisfy his expectations for love, and this kind of interaction is representative of her emotional and sexual alliances, then how can she, as a mother or a daughter, be capable in her turn of nurturing or being nurtured into a person, a woman, with a true self capable of agency and authenticity? Present gender arrangements all too often undermine the reciprocity of recognition and intersubjectivity—both in adult relationships and in the earliest relationship between mother and child.

II. EMPATHY, MUTUAL RECOGNITION, AND READING

Empathy, as a crucial aspect of the ideal facilitating environment, becomes central as well to the kind of reading experience that can replicate and help to mend the original site of recognition and care. The ideas of Winnicott, Stern, and Judith Jordan about empathy have helped me to understand how empathetic reading becomes a way to enter an environment of mutual recognition. Winnicott talks about maternal empathy—what fuels the mother's ability to recognize the baby: "There is an overlap between what the mother supplies and what the child might conceive of"; and Stern goes on to connect empathy to intersubjectivity, a process that seems equivalent to Benjamin's mutual recognition. Two selves, two minds, involved in dynamic interaction. The sharing of subjective experience is "a working notion that says something like, what is going on in my mind may be similar enough to what is going on in your mind that we can somehow communicate this (without words) and thereby experience intersubjectivity." (*The Interpersonal World of the Infant*, p. 124)

At this stage the caregiver's empathy becomes a different experience. "It is one thing for a younger infant to respond to the overt behavior that reflects a mother's empathy, such as a soothing behavior at the right moment . . . It is quite another thing for the infant to sense that an empathetic process bridging the two minds has been created." (pp. 125–26) Thus empathy comes to mark not merger experiences but a more developed stage: "Paradoxically, it is only with the advent of intersubjectivity that anything like the joining of subjective psychic experience can actually occur . . . both separation/individuation and new forms of experiencing union (or being-with) emerge equally out of the same experience of intersubjectivity." (p. 127)

Empathetic Attunement

Judith Jordan is one of the feminist psychologists associated with the Stone Center for Developmental Services and Studies at Wellesley College. As a group, the Stone Center psychologists have stressed "women's growth in connection," a concept that associates relational development specifically with gender issues. In her writing on empathy Jordan underlines the ways in which empathy demands both similarity and difference between two minds or selves, and she points to how empathy facilitates both development and a deep pleasure.

In order to empathize, one must have a well-differentiated sense of self in addition to an appreciation of and sensitivity to the differences as well as sameness of the other. Jordan combats the prevailing notion of empathy as "regressive merging" and notes the "error in the sense of seeing the self as either distinct and autonomous or merged and embedded. Is it not possible to experience a sense of feeling connected and affectively joined and at the same time cognitively appreciate one's separateness?" (p. 72) Empathy "involves temporary identification with the other's state, during which one is aware that the source of the affect is in the other. In the final resolution period, the affect subsides and one's self feels more separate." ("Empathy and Self-Boundaries," p. 69)

Jordan points to gender differences in the ability to empathize (and I would add, to enjoy it): "males and females tend to be equally able to recognize and label the affective experiences of another person (cognitive awareness), but . . . females demonstrate generally more vicarious affective responsiveness to another's affect." (p. 71) For example, women tend to imagine themselves in the other's place more—which does not mean they don't know that that place is the other's and not their own.

In a second paper, "The Meaning of Mutuality," which extends her investigation into a study of mutual intersubjectivity, Jordan observes that "when empathy and concern flow both ways, there is an intense affirmation of the self, and, paradoxically, a transcendence of the self, a sense of the self as a part of a larger relational unit." Jordan calls this process empathetic attunement, "a process during which one's self-boundaries undergo momentary alteration, which in itself allows the possibility for change in the self. Empathy in this sense, then, always contains the opportunity for mutual growth and impact." (p. 82)

Empathetic Reading

Thinking about empathy in the reading process, I begin with Stern's descriptions of attunement. The way in which this behavior occurs in different modalities is a clue to what happens during reading—why it can become a facilitating environment. The book takes place in words—one modality; I respond to and engage with it in another modality: thoughts, feelings, imagination. If the book is mother and I am child, our interaction is reciprocal. I need to read the book, but the book needs me to read it. From the very start the situation displays the hallmarks of interdependence that make me feel that I am participating intensely in an activity with another.

Empathy is my means of entering into the world of the book. As I read about the heroine, I identify with her state: I can feel her feelings, think her thoughts. At the same time, I am always aware that I am not her—there may be genuine overlap between us and there may not. The ways in which she is like me and the ways in which she is not are both important here. In pretending to be her—or in empathizing with her or identifying with her—my own ego boundaries stretch to encompass experiences that may support or gratify what I have known before, enhancing and enriching, or even challenging my previous experience.

I empathize with the author as well as with her characters. I can experience her presence as it comes alive in the book by means of her words. Her personality is expressed not only when she is speaking as the narrator (if there is such a presence in the novel) but also when she brings the characters alive—or in fact does anything. These are her words—her way of writing, her kind of sentences and images; these are her thoughts, observations, questions, and conclusions. Reading, I engage in a dialogue with her mind. And if she is an author-mother, I feel her care and love informing all that transpires, I experience her ongoing reliability, both as she supports and as she challenges. Whom or what is she supporting or challenging? Her heroine, yes, but also me. Her words about the heroine reveal her concern, understanding, and appreciation, but they also contain critique, judgment, discipline, and knowledge drawn from a wider experience. There needs to be what Winnicott calls "frustration"—obstruction and externality. The heroine is not perfect; she must be helped to grow. The heroine is nurtured by her author-mother, and I am, too. When Austen asks me to participate in Elizabeth's rejection of Darcy, calling up my deepest fears of loss and abandonment, and then brings him back in the very next chapter, she has shown me both that I can trust her and that I must experience challenges to my present psychodynamic condition.

To foster such a response, she has to be empathizing with me, too. She is aware of me—of what I want and what I need, or so it feels. This is the reason I get so attached to an author as well as to a particular book of hers. She is more than the story, but the only way I can be with her is through the story. This is why I try to read everything she has written, why I prefer that her books be long ones. Each time I read her, we can be together.

Writing as Maternal Recognition

Thinking about empathy and the facilitating environment provides insight into the writing as well as the reading of romance fiction. I believe that both writer and reader share the same need for mother love and nurture, and that writing can aid the author in her own growth and development. Benjamin's idea of mutual recognition is instrumental here. " 'I recognize you as my baby who recognizes me,' " is how she describes the mother's response to her newborn child, noting the mutuality that persists in spite of the tremendous inequality of the parent-child relationship. (p. 15) Both the inequality and the mutuality are important in textual mothering. The author-mother initiates the process. She creates the words; she gives them to the reader. She expresses design and purpose. Consequently, she is "in charge." But of course the reader must interpret those words. Thus the text is a transitional object. When the daughter-reader recognizes the author-mother as she is manifested in her words and in her story, she verifies the author's identity, even as in the other half of the transaction the mother-author recognizes the reader-daughter. As Benjamin writes: "Recognition is . . . reflexive; it includes not only the other's confirming response, but also how we find ourselves in that response." (p. 21) Writing may participate in this process. For when the author writes aspects of her own selfhood into a character or a plot, its existence outside of her in the words she has written can confirm her own identity.

Reading, Need, and Joy

Empathizing with heroines in fiction, I appreciate the tension between like and different, as long as we are within a certain ballpark of like. What disturbs me is going inside of minds that are too different, too alien, especially when that difference undermines my own values or needs. For this reason I don't read much fiction by men; and there are certain women novelists, like Anne Tyler, or Joyce Carol Oates, or Barbara Pym, whose characters often frighten me. I don't want to be in their heads. Of course, if I would distance myself and read more "objectively," I could see that this is good writing. But why should I, when an essential pleasure—and need—is not going to be addressed?

As a scholar and professor, I know full well that the mode of empathetic reading I have just been describing is frowned upon in the academy. "Identification," writes Marilyn Yalom, "has gone out of style; indeed, in a play upon the traditional terms 'minor' and 'major' writers, Nabokov is reputed to have called those who still identify with characters 'minor readers.' " ("Postmodern Autobiography," p. 114) Consequently, a gap opens up between "personal" and "serious" reading with which I take issue. Especially because I know that gender differences operate in reading styles as much as they do in psychological styles (the two are of course entirely related). Men frequently *prefer* to read from a distance, as indicated in some new studies of gender and reading, like David Bleich's "Gender Interests in Reading and Language," which proposes that many men are more instinctively distant from the book, while many women have a tendency to enter its "world." I know that the choice of literary canons and scholarly modes is neither arbitrary nor neutral nor God-given. Traditionally, it has been white middle-class men who have established these norms and procedures, codifying a masculine mode that in its dominance discriminates against the inclinations and practices of many women. Surely one of the reasons why my private reading life is so deeply important to me is that, although I became a literary scholar because I love books and reading, my professional work is not supposed to have much to do with either the passion or the need that I feel for fiction.

And yet need is the source, passion the expression, of my attachment to the world of fiction. My engagement with stories and with their authors is the occasion of growth, I believe, as well as a deep and abiding pleasure. Judith Jordan notes the pleasure that empathetic experience brings, and she associates it with the original mother-infant relationship.

> I would like to suggest that in addition there is intrinsic pleasure in mutuality in relationships. This pleasure may grow from the early spontaneity and joy that exists in the mother-child interactions characterized by cuddling, hugging, babbling, smiling, "oohs" and "aahs." Both participants in these early exchanges often seek to extend these engagements, and there is true pleasure and growth for both people in the back-and-forth interplay.
>
> (p. 87)

Reading and writing are experiences that extend the mother-child relationship, kindling self-development and, often, joy.

Notes

CHAPTER 2

page 69. "Winnicott tells us . . . cannot develop." "The Capacity to be Alone" (1958).

page 72. "When Freud thought . . . 'civilization of Greece.' " "Female Sexuality" (1931).

page 84. "Through a window . . . bourgeois culture." Many years ago Dorothy Van Ghent first called our attention to the function of windows in Brontë's text (in *The English Novel: Form and Function* [1953]). In a story so insistent on boundaries, windows consistently serve as ambiguous symbols, both permitting and refusing intercourse.

page 87. "Catherine's struggle . . . of marriageable age." Gilbert and Gubar make this point in *The Madwoman in the Attic: The Woman Writer and the Nineteenth-Century Literary Imagination* (1979).

CHAPTER 3

page 120. " 'driven in . . . the cold.' " Winifred Gerin, *Charlotte Brontë: The Evolution of Genius,* p. 4.

275

page 120. " 'did not require . . . his daily life.' " Elizabeth Cleghorn Gaskell, *The Life of Charlotte Brontë*, p. 33.

page 120. " 'Patrick Brontë stood . . . her father's side.' " Irene Taylor, *Holy Ghosts: The Male Muses of Emily and Charlotte Brontë*, pp. 110, 113.

page 125. " 'a shadowy image . . . the single occasion' "; "the 'terrifying sense . . . their mother.' " Gerin, p. 4.

page 132. " 'It darted . . . but herself!' " Jane Austen, *Emma*, p. 398.

page 136–37. "The myth . . . both of them." Jessica Benjamin, *The Bonds of Love: Psychoanalysis, Feminism, and the Problem of Domination*, p. 136.

page 137–38. " '. . . Or, it may internalize . . . its negative aspect.' " Nancy Chodorow, *The Reproduction of Mothering*, p. 70.

CHAPTER 4

page 158. "As she cradles . . . Yes, you do.' " Benjamin, p. 13.

page 161. " 'frightfully wet little novels.' " Rosamund Pilcher, quoted in a *New York Times Book Review* interview (1988).

page 171–72. " 'but our queer plays . . . I doubt it.' " Quoted in Edna D. Cheney, *Louisa May Alcott: Her Life, Letters, and Journals*, p. 199.

page 172. " 'The second series . . . the stock market.' " Cheney, p. 191.

page 172. " 'they wept aloud . . . grief and excitement.' " Cheney, p. 191.

page 172. " 'Girls write . . . to please anyone.' " Cheney, p. 201.

page 172. "As I can launch . . . more play." Cheney, p. 201.

CHAPTER 5

page 209. " 'the necessity . . . by the other.' " Benjamin, p. 23.

page 209. " 'The subject declares . . . you have done.' " Benjamin, p. 21.

page 209. " 'it includes . . . in that response.' " Benjamin, p. 21.

page 209–10. " 'a delicate tension . . . in lesbian relationships.' " Burch, p. 98.

Notes

page 210. " 'Lesbians, by necessity . . . heterosexual women are not.' " Rosen, p. 7.

page 210. " 'That her daughter . . . personal sense of order.' " Rosen, p. 6.

page 211. " 'She will be . . . minimally attuned' "; " 'this culture . . . empathy between them.' " Rosen, p. 6.

page 212. " . . . She seeks . . . to be female." Burch, p. 120.

page 213. "His identification . . . with his own." Person, p. 122.

page 213. " 'the role-playing falsity . . . real womanhood.' " Quoted in Burch, p. 216.

page 221. " 'two women together . . . made simple.' " Poem XIX, *Twenty-One Love Poems,* in *The Dream of a Common Language,* p. 35.

Bibliography

Alcott, Louisa May. *Little Women*. New York: Modern Library, 1983.

Alther, Lisa. *Other Women*. New York: Random House, 1984.

Austen, Jane. *Emma*. New York: Penguin Books, 1966.

———. *Pride and Prejudice*. New York: Penguin Books, 1983.

Balderston, John Lloyd. *Berkeley Square*. New York: Macmillan, 1929.

Benjamin, Jessica. *The Bonds of Love: Psychoanalysis, Feminism, and the Problem of Domination*. New York: Pantheon Books, 1988.

Bleich, David. "Gender Interests in Reading and Language." In Elizabeth A. Flynn and Patrocinio P. Schweickart, eds. *Gender and Reading: Essays on Readers, Texts, and Contexts*. Baltimore: John Hopkins University Press, 1986, pp. 234–66.

Brontë, Charlotte. *Jane Eyre*. New York: Penguin Books, 1976.

Brontë, Emily. *Wuthering Heights*. New York: Penguin Books, 1971.

Broumas, Olga. *Beginning with O*. New Haven: Yale University Press, 1977.

Brown, Rita Mae. *Rubyfruit Jungle*. New York: Bantam Books, 1977.

Brownstein, Rachel. *Becoming a Heroine: Reading about Women in Novels*. New York: Viking Press, 1982.

Burch, Beverly. *On Intimate Terms: The Psychology of Difference in Lesbian Relationships.* Urbana and Chicago: University of Illinois Press, 1993.

Burnett, Frances Hodgson. *The Secret Garden.* New York: Bantam Books, 1987.

Cheney, Edna D. *Louisa May Alcott: Her Life, Letters, and Journals.* Boston: Roberts Brothers, 1890.

Chodorow, Nancy. *The Reproduction of Mothering: Psychoanalysis and the Sociology of Gender.* Berkeley: University of California Press, 1978.

———. "Gender, Relation, and Difference in a Psychoanalytic Perspective." In Hester Eisenstein and Alice Jardine, eds. *The Future of Difference.* New Brunswick, N.J.: Rutgers University Press, 1985.

Chopin, Kate. *The Awakening.* New York: Capricorn Books, 1964.

Coward, Noël. *Private Lives.* New York: Samuel French, 1947.

Denham, Alice. *The Ghost and Mrs. Muir.* Mattituck, N.Y.: Amereon, 1968.

Dickinson, Emily. *The Poems of Emily Dickinson.* 3 vols. Ed. Thomas H. Johnson. Cambridge, Mass.: Harvard University Press, 1955.

Donald, Annabel. *Hannah at Thirty-Five.* London: Hodder & Stoughton, 1984.

Eliot, George. *The Mill on the Floss.* New York: Oxford University Press, 1980.

Fallon, Eileen. *Words of Love: A Complete Guide to Romance Fiction.* New York: Garland Publishing, 1984.

Freud, Sigmund. "Female Sexuality," *Standard Edition of the Complete Psychological Works,* Vol. 21. London: Hogarth Press, 1953–74, pp. 223–43.

———. "Femininity," *New Introductory Lectures on Psychoanalysis, SE,* Vol. 22, pp. 3–182.

Gaskell, Elizabeth Cleghorn. *The Life of Charlotte Brontë.* London: J. M. Dent & Sons; New York: E. P. Dutton, 1908.

Gerin, Winifred. *Charlotte Brontë: The Evolution of Genius.* London: Oxford University Press, 1968.

Gilbert, Sandra, and Susan Gubar. *The Madwoman in the Attic: The*

Woman Writer and the Nineteenth-Century Literary Imagination. New Haven: Yale University Press, 1979.

Gilchrist, Ellen. *I Cannot Get You Close Enough: Three Novellas.* Boston: Little, Brown and Co., 1990.

Gorham, Ethel. *Natural Light.* Cambridge, Mass: Zoland Books, 1991.

Hacker, Marilyn. *Going Back to the River.* New York: Random House, 1990.

Hall, Radclyffe. *The Well of Loneliness.* Garden City, N.Y.: Sun Dial Press, 1928.

Hirsch, Marianne. *The Mother/Daughter Plot: Narrative, Psychoanalysis, Feminism.* Bloomington: Indiana University Press, 1989.

Jewett, Sarah Orne. *The Country of the Pointed Firs.* New York: W. W. Norton, 1968.

Jordan, Judith. "Empathy and Self-Boundaries," in Judith Jordan, Alexandra Kaplan et al, eds. *Women's Growth in Connection: Writings from the Stone Center.* New York: The Guilford Press, 1991, pp. 67–80.

———. "The Meaning of Mutuality," in *Women's Growth in Connection,* pp. 81–96.

Jordan, Judith, and Janet Surrey. "The Self-in-Relation: Empathy and the Mother-Daughter Relationship." In Toni Bernay and Dorothy W. Cantor, eds. *The Psychology of Today's Woman.* Hillsdale, N.J.: Analytic Press, 1986.

Konecky, Edith. *A Place at the Table.* New York: Random House, 1989.

Lively, Penelope. *Cleopatra's Sister.* New York: HarperCollins, 1993.

Lorde, Audre. *Undersong: Chosen Poems, Old and New.* New York: W. W. Norton, 1992.

Miller, Alice. *The Drama of the Gifted Child.* New York: Basic Books, 1981.

Miller, Isabel. *Patience and Sarah.* New York: Ballantine Books, 1990.

Miller, Sue. *For Love.* New York: HarperCollins, 1993.

Modleski, Tania. *Loving with a Vengeance: Mass-Produced Fantasies about Women.* New York: Methuen, 1982.

Montgomery, L. M. *Anne of Green Gables.* New York: Crown, 1986.

Nathan, Robert. *Portrait of Jenny.* New York: Knopf, 1982.

Naylor, Gloria. *Mama Day.* New York: Ticknor & Fields, 1988.

Ogden, Thomas, "The Mother, the Infant, and the Matrix: Interpretations of Aspects of the Work of Donald Winnicott," *Contemporary Psychoanalysis,* Vol. 21, No. 3 (July 1985), pp. 346–71.

Person, Ethel Spector. *Dreams of Love and Fateful Encounters: The Power of Romantic Passion.* New York: Penguin Books, 1988.

Pilcher, Rosamund. *The Shell Seekers.* New York: St. Martin's Press, 1987.

Quindlen, Anna. "Feeling at Home in a Favorite Book," *Chicago Tribune,* 15 (October 1986), Sec. 5, p. 1.

Radway, Janice. *Reading the Romance: Women, Patriarchy, and Popular Literature.* Chapel Hill: University of North Carolina Press, 1984.

Rich, Adrienne. *The Dream of a Common Language.* New York: W. W. Norton, 1978.

Rosen, Wendy. "On the Integration of Sexuality: Lesbians and Their Mothers," *Working Papers.* Wellesley, Mass.: Stone Center for Developmental Services and Studies, 1992.

Rule, Jane. *Desert of the Heart.* Tallahassee, Fla.: Naiad Press, 1992.

Shakespeare, William. *Much Ado About Nothing.* Baltimore: Penguin Books, 1958.

Smiley, Jane. *At Paradise Gate.* New York: Pocket Books, 1981.

Stern, Daniel. *The Interpersonal World of the Infant: A View from Psychoanalysis and Developmental Psychology.* New York: Basic Books, 1985.

Taylor, Irene. *Holy Ghosts: The Male Muses of Emily and Charlotte Brontë.* New York: Columbia University Press, 1990.

Taylor, Valerie. *Prism.* Tallahassee, Fla.: Naiad Press, 1981.

Thane, Elswyth. *Tryst.* Mattituck, N.Y.: Amereon, 1974.

Thurston, Carol. *The Romance Revolution: Erotic Novels for Women and the Quest for a New Sexual Identity.* Urbana and Chicago: University of Illinois Press, 1987.

Trollope, Joanna. *The Men and the Girls.* New York: Random House, 1993.

Van Ghent, Dorothy. *The English Novel: Form and Function.* New York: Rinehart, 1953.

Webster, Jean. *Daddy Long Legs.* New York: Bantam Books, 1982.

Woolf, Virginia. *To the Lighthouse.* New York: Harcourt Brace, 1955.

Winnicott, D. W. "On Transference." *Journal of the American Psychoanalytic Association,* Vol. 2 (1954), pp. 386–88.

———. *Collected Papers: Through Paediatrics to Psychoanalysis.* London: Tavistock Publications, 1958.

———. *The Maturational Process and the Facilitating Environment.* New York: International Universities Press, 1965.

———. *Playing and Reality.* London and New York: Tavistock Publications, 1971.

Yalom, Marilyn. "Postmodern Autobiography." In Shirley Geok-lin Lim, ed. *Approaches to Teaching Kingston's* The Woman Warrior. New York: Modern Language Association of America, 1991, pp. 108–15.

Index

Index

289